Simply

Shakespeare

Simply
Shakespeare

Toby Widdicombe
University of Alaska

New York San Francisco Boston
London Toronto Sydney Tokyo Singapore Madrid
Mexico City Munich Paris Cape Town Hong Kong Montreal

Editor-in-Chief: Joseph Terry
Acquisitions Editor: Erika Berg
Marketing Manager: Melanie Craig
Production Manager: Denise Phillip
Project Coordination, Text Design, and Electronic Page Makeup: WestWords, Inc.
Cover Design Manager: John Callahan
Cover Designer: Laura Shaw
Cover Image: Courtesy of Bridgeman Art Library
Manufacturing Buyer: Lucy Hebard
Printer and Binder: Courier-Westford
Cover Printer: Phoenix Color

For permission to use copyrighted material, grateful acknowledgment is made to the copyright holders on p. 227, which are hereby made part of this copyright page.

Library of Congress Cataloging-in-Publication Data
Widdicombe, Toby, 1955–
    Simply Shakespeare / Toby Widdicombe.
        p. cm.
    Includes bibliographical references (p.) and index.
    ISBN 0-321-07704-0
    1. Shakespeare, William, 1564–1616—Criticism and interpretation—Handbooks
manuals, etc. 2. Shakespeare, William, 1564–1616—Criticism and
interpretation—Problems, exercises, etc. I. Title.

PR2976 .W52 2001
822.3'3—dc21   2001029545

Please visit our website at http://www.ablongman.com

ISBN 0-321-07704-0

5 6 7 8 9 10—CRW—04 03

To Mr. W. S.
The only begetter of this ensuing book

Contents

Part 2
Staging *113*

Chapter 5
Shakespeare's Genres *114*

Chapter 6
Shakespeare's Stagecraft *150*

Appendix

Illustrations

Preface

By any measure, Shakespeare has always been a popular and highly regarded playwright. The view of his fellow dramatist Ben Jonson in the 1623 Folio that Shakespeare "was not of an age, but for all time" has proved unerringly prophetic. Even the writers of the Neoclassical period (Johnson, Dryden, and Pope among others), whose literary theories ran counter to the practice of Shakespeare's art, praised him. Recognition of his achievement has crossed the boundary of the English language, for his work has been translated into scores of languages and is appreciated throughout Europe and, indeed, much of the world. Shakespeare's achievement has in every sense stood the test of time.

Yet, quite remarkably, his popularity seems to have *increased* with the passing of the years. There are no less than five major scholarly journals or newsletters devoted to discussing his work; there is even a journal (*Hamlet Studies*) devoted to the investigation of just one play. There are Shakespeare festivals around the world dedicated to staging his plays, and innumerable sites on the Internet focused on his achievements as poet and dramatist. Even Hollywood has discovered that Shakespeare is big business. There have been three cinematic versions of *Hamlet* in the last decade alone (those starring Mel Gibson, Kenneth Branagh, and Ethan Hawke). There have been modernizations such as Baz Luhrmann's trendy *Romeo + Juliet*. And then there was *Shakespeare in Love*, which won no less than seven Academy Awards in 1999 and grossed more than $100,000,000.

It's not hard, I think, to explain why Shakespeare is the symbol of all that is great and good in Western literature, why his work is the single greatest achievement in Western literature. The beauty of his language, the subtlety of his characterizations, the inclusiveness of his point of view, and the sensationalism of his stories are part of the explanation. Part of it, too, derives from Shakespeare's simultaneous appeal to the head and to the heart, to the intellect and to the emotions. More than that, however, his work compels recognition, for it is saying something of universal value to which everyone responds. In essence, Shakespeare tells us more about the paradox of the human condition into which each of us is born than any other writer, for the people he created so long ago seem sometimes more alive and real than even our friends and family.

Because of Shakespeare's popularity and importance there is a need for books which help those who want to understand Shakespeare's genius better. That is the purpose of this book—to provide that help. Shakespeare is difficult, in places very difficult. Nonetheless, the pleasure and understanding (in fact, the pleasure *of* understanding his works) can be greatly increased if those who read and watch his plays aren't simply thrown in the deep end and told to swim. *Simply Shakespeare* is designed principally for use in courses that introduce Shakespeare's works whether in the context of general education courses, upper- or lower-division courses in renaissance literature, or a single-author Shakespeare course.

To achieve its purpose of helping students to understand Shakespeare's genius better, *Simply Shakespeare* has four main goals:

1. To show students how to read Shakespeare for understanding *and* enjoyment.
2. To show students how to be receptive to Shakespeare's persistent appeals to their imagination.
3. To show students how to understand and appreciate Shakespeare's dense language.
4. To show students how to appreciate the intricate way in which Shakespeare constructs his plays.

Flexible Organization

To accomplish *Simply Shakespeare*'s goals, I have organized the chapters flexibly so that they can be read in any sequence depending on the particular needs of the course in which the book is being used. *Simply Shakespeare* consists of six sections:

◆ An Introduction outlining the strategies students can adopt to make Shakespeare easier to understand.
◆ Four chapters (Part I of the book) focusing on the single greatest hurdle to student enjoyment of Shakespeare: language. The first deals with the most obvious difficulties they will encounter with Shakespeare's words. The second looks at imagery (both literal and figurative). The third covers rhetoric. The fourth discusses Shakespeare's humor.
◆ Three chapters (Part II of the book) covering Shakespeare's work as a dramatist. The first looks at genre. The second discusses stagecraft. The third examines the transformation of Shakespeare's plays for stage and screen. The emphasis here is on spurring students to imagine how the words on the page become living drama.
◆ A Resources section (in the Appendix) providing an annotated list of Shakespeare material: websites, books, and journals. The emphasis here is on the best websites and the latest scholarship.
◆ A comprehensive index listing (among other things) all the technical words used in the text as well as the plays that are discussed.

◇ Front and back inside covers featuring a chronology of Shakespeare's life and times, a glossary of the most misunderstood words in Shakespeare's works, and a simplified family tree (for the Wars of the Roses) of the Houses of York and Lancaster. The purpose of the endpapers is briefly to provide readers with the essential context that will make their experience of Shakespeare more worthwhile and pleasurable.

Additional Key Features

Simply Shakespeare also offers other key features, all of which are directed at achieving the book's goals:

◇ **It is written in an accessible style.** *Simply Shakespeare* neither talks down to students nor talks above their heads. It shows rather than tells by providing an extensive discussion of passages from Shakespeare's plays as well as detailed explanations of Shakespeare's dramatic and poetic techniques. Chapter 3, for example, is organized around the rhetorical terms (from *adage* to *stichomythia*) that Shakespeare uses most extensively in his plays as well as around three recurring Shakespearean strategies: pattern, repetition, and variation. Chapter 4 examines and explains with concrete examples the sharpness and complexity of Shakespeare's humor.

◇ **It emphasizes the major ideas visually.** *Simply Shakespeare* uses boxes and other devices to highlight the major points in any topic being discussed. Each chapter, for example, begins with a brief overview set off from the rest of the text. Chapter 5 features boxes devoted to outlining the major characteristics of the four traditional genres: comedy, history, tragedy, and romance. Chapter 6 includes a box outlining the major devices Shakespeare uses in his stagecraft.

◇ **It analyzes key passages in depth.** *Simply Shakespeare* uses test cases to pull together the ideas presented in a particular chapter. Chapter 2, for example, highlights the famous "barge at Cydnus" speech from *Antony and Cleopatra* to show students how effectively Shakespeare uses imagery. Chapter 3 uses Portia's speech in *The Merchant of Venice* about justice to illustrate for students how skillfully Shakespeare uses rhetoric to move the audience both emotionally and intellectually.

◇ **It lists key information clearly.** *Simply Shakespeare* uses bulleted lists frequently. Doing so breaks up the sameness of prose paragraphs as well as enabling students to zero in on particularly important material. Chapter 1, for instance, provides a bulleted list of the major sentence structures Shakespeare uses because students are often put off from appreciating his poetry by the peculiar word order he often uses. Chapter 4 presents bulleted lists analyzing some of the cultural humor Shakespeare dwells on in his plays.

◇ **It helps students with Shakespeare's vocabulary.** *Simply Shakespeare* includes a glossary in the inside back cover of the most troublesome Shakespearean words. Students can become confused in particular by common words that mean something different today from what they meant four hundred years ago. *Modern,* for example, means *up-to-date* now; in Shakespeare's time, it meant *ordinary. Sensible* means *level-headed* now; in Shakespeare's time, it far more often meant *sensitive.*

Acknowledgments

In writing *Simply Shakespeare* I was helped a great deal by many academic reviewers: Scott Douglass of Chattanooga State Technical Community College, Maurice Hunt of Baylor University, Frank Kelly of SUNY Farmingdale, Jay Ludwig of Michigan State University, Frank Madden of SUNY Westchester Community College, Rick McDonald of Utah Valley State University, Michael Mullin of the University of Illinois, Urbana Champaign, Francesca Royster of De Paul University, Bill Smith of Western Washington University, Lolly Smith of Everett Community College, and Andy Solomon of the University of Tampa. Their advice was always thoughtful and helpful; the book is much improved as a result.

I would also like to thank my many Shakespeare students for their feedback on the book as it developed. Shehla Anjum, Laura Cunningham, Matt Fox, Jessi Maus, Jo Ann Miller, Pam Wheaton, and Priscilla Wilson stand out particularly in this regard. They were tremendously helpful in getting a sense of whether the book's "voice" worked.

I owe a debt of gratitude to Erika Berg at Longman Publishers, who first encouraged me to write this book after hearing my complaint that there was no Shakespeare book out there that did what I felt needed to be done to teach Shakespeare well. Her constructive suggestions for change at various points in the history of this book have made it a much better work. She's the editor that every writer should be lucky enough to have.

Finally, I would like to acknowledge my father's contribution to this book. He read almost every chapter in draft form, and made many pointed suggestions for change. He is that rare being: a scientist who is also a polymath. And then, most importantly, there's my wife's role. A Shakespeare scholar herself, she listened patiently and thoughtfully to so many different ideas in this book as they gelled. She was always there to give me the best advice.

Toby Widdicombe
University of Alaska

Can you not read it? Is it not fair writ?

King John *4.1.37*

Introduction
How to Read Shakespeare

Chapter Overview

◇ Concentration: using seven sure-fire strategies to get the most out of Shakespeare's plays.
◇ Imagination: putting yourself in Shakespeare's world.
◇ Flexibility: understanding how Shakespeare varies his sentences.
◇ Subtext: listening for the emotion behind the words *and* supplying it.

Your reaction when faced with having to read a Shakespeare play is more likely than not apprehension. The man's reputation precedes him; his language is odd; the shape of his sentences peculiar. I don't mean to diminish the genuine challenge that reading Shakespeare represents; however, I know from my own experience when I first had to study Shakespeare that it's too easy to fall prey to a self-fulfilling prophecy: Shakespeare will be beyond me, so it is. Soon you fall into a habit of assuming that if what Shakespeare has written remains obscure, it's either because you're simply not up to the task or because Shakespeare's no good at what he does. Frustration and annoyance replace the pleasure that should come from engaging yourself in understanding his work. The truth is, reading Shakespeare—and in particular reading Shakespeare *aloud*—can be a profoundly enjoyable and enriching experience. It doesn't matter whether you're an English major or a student studying Shakespeare for a general education requirement or someone simply interested in cultural enrichment; you only need to make an effort, to use your imagination, to stay flexible in your thinking, and—perhaps above all—to listen to what

Shakespeare is saying. If you do all of these, you can have the magical experience of being caught up in some of the best plays ever written.

Making an Effort

We merely glance at much of what we read today: newspapers, magazines, popular fiction, television shows, "edutainment" of all sorts. The pace of our lives is such that there is a premium on being quick. Shakespeare is altogether a different proposition: his language is dense; his ideas complex; his plots multilayered. If you rush at the task of reading his lines, then, much of what is there will remain invisible to you. At this point, you may be thinking, "Yeah, but if I spend too long looking up words and trying to understand everything he's saying, I'll get bogged down." There's some validity to that point, but there are ways of mitigating the problem. One or more of the following strategies may help:

1. Concentrate really hard as you read and eliminate distractions as far as possible. Read the play twice. Read it quickly the first time to get a general sense of what's happening. On the second time through, focus on those passages that you had problems with and on those parts you liked.
2. Make a note in the margin of the text of places or passages that really mystify you; you'll need to focus on them when you go through the play again. If you take notes, remember to cite act, scene, line, and page numbers so you can talk specifically with your instructor or fellow students about these difficult places in the play.
3. Keep a photocopy of the cast list (or dramatis personae) handy; some of Shakespeare's plays—particularly his histories—seem to have a cast of thousands, and it can get irritating to have to flip back and forth to remember who's who. Even better, write the cast list down by hand and draw lines among the characters to indicate relationships. In that way, you become actively engaged in the creation of meaning.
4. Read one or two passages aloud (especially the soliloquies) and with as much feeling as you can muster. One of Shakespeare's greatest qualities as a playwright is the beauty of the sound of his words. That's lost if all readers ever do is read lines silently to themselves.
5. Watch a video version of the play or better still, if you can, see a live performance. It really helps to see the play acted.
6. Summarize your sense of what happened in the play. It will probably be easiest to do so after you've read each act rather than waiting until you've finished the entire play.
7. Write down questions about those parts of the play that you didn't get. There's not a lot of point, after all, in an instructor dwelling on what the class understands; he or she will need to know what wasn't understood.

Let's see how you can apply these suggestions to the beginning of *Hamlet*: from the time the play opens to the entrance of the ghost. Forty-three lines in all. (Incidentally, throughout this book I'll be using the Bevington edition of Shakespeare for my quotations.)

1.1 Enter Bernardo and Francisco, two sentinels, [meeting]

BERNARDO	Who's there?	
FRANCISCO	Nay, answer me. Stand and unfold yourself.	
BERNARDO	Long live the King!	
FRANCISCO	Bernardo?	
BERNARDO	He.	5
FRANCISCO	You come most carefully upon your hour.	
BERNARDO	'Tis now struck twelve. Get thee to bed, Francisco.	
FRANCISCO	For this relief much thanks. 'Tis bitter cold,	
	And I am sick at heart.	
BERNARDO	Have you had quiet guard?	10
FRANCISCO	Not a mouse stirring.	
BERNARDO	Well, good night.	
	If you do meet Horatio and Marcellus,	
	The rivals of my watch, bid them make haste.	

Enter Horatio and Marcellus

FRANCISCO	I think I hear them.—Stand, ho! Who is there?	15
HORATIO	Friends to this ground.	
MARCELLUS	And liegemen to the Dane.	
FRANCISCO	Give you good night.	
MARCELLUS	O, farewell, honest soldier. Who hath relieved you?	
FRANCISCO	Bernardo hath my place. Give you good night.	20

Exit Francisco

MARCELLUS	Holla! Bernardo!	
BERNARDO	Say, what, is Horatio there?	
HORATIO	A piece of him.	
BERNARDO	Welcome, Horatio. Welcome, good Marcellus.	
HORATIO	What, has this thing appeared again tonight?	25
BERNARDO	I have seen nothing.	
MARCELLUS	Horatio says 'tis but our fantasy,	
	And will not let belief take hold of him	
	Touching this dreaded sight twice seen of us.	
	Therefore I have entreated him along	30
	With us to watch the minutes of this night,	
	That if again this apparition come	
	He may approve our eyes and speak to it.	
HORATIO	Tush, tush, 'twill not appear.	

```
BERNARDO                              Sit down awhile,
          And let us once again assail your ears,              35
          That are so fortified against our story,
          What we have two nights seen.
HORATIO                              Well, sit we down,
          And let us hear Bernardo speak of this.
BERNARDO  Last night of all,
          When yond same star that's westward from the pole    40
          Had made his course t' illumine that part of heaven
          Where now it burns, Marcellus and myself,
          The bell then beating one—
```

Strategy #1: *Reading the play twice.* When you read this passage quickly for the first time, you get the sense that one group of guards is replacing another, and that they all seem scared of something: "this thing" (25) and "this dreaded sight" (29). On the second reading, you are likely to focus on some of the difficult parts, for instance Bernardo's comment about "yond same star that's westward from the pole," which "Had made its course t' illume that part of heaven/Where now it burns" (41–42) or Horatio's odd remark about "Friends to this ground" (16).

Strategy #2: *Taking notes.* Just the act of writing things down sometimes helps to clarify thinking. As you note your puzzlement over Bernardo's comment, you may suddenly realize that "yond" sounds like "yonder" and "illume" like "illuminate." So, Bernardo seems to be telling time by the stars.

As you note down Horatio's remark, you may see that he's saying something different from Marcellus one line below. Marcellus seems to be saying that he is loyal to the new king; Horatio swears loyalty to Denmark. These two statements are not the same at all.

⚡ **Strategy #3:** *Keeping a cast list handy.* If you've done this, then figuring out what's going on is much easier. You know that Bernardo, Francisco, and Marcellus are guards, and that Horatio is the odd man out and probably more important than the rest because he's listed as "Hamlet's friend."

Strategy #4: *Reading the play aloud.* Some people like doing this; some people think it's slightly (or really) nerdy. If you belong to the second group, find somewhere private to read the passage aloud. It's worth it because when you do you'll see that the lines have a definite rhythm and that the repetition of certain sounds means that the words trip off the tongue. There are, for example, the t and s sounds in line 29: "Touching this dreaded sight twice seen of us" and the w and s sounds in line 40: "When yond same star that's westward from the pole." Shakespeare wants you to hear the beauty of the language.

Strategy #5: *Watching a video version.* By the time you've finished reading the scene twice, you will have some mental image of what is going on, but there are likely to be some gaps in your understanding. A video version will fill in those gaps and probably help you to see why you missed some things that went on. It can be difficult, for example, to appreciate the fact that the anxiety that Bernardo and Francisco feel at the very beginning of the play comes in part from the cold and dark that surround them. The ability of film to make those elements real may help to remind you of the importance of the setting for the scene.

Strategy #6: *Summarizing the action.* You could summarize its content simply as "One guard goes off duty, some other guards and Horatio take his place. They discuss the earlier appearance of something (a ghost?) that frightened them." What the summary allows you to do is to see how well you've understood what has happened, and to remember the details of the story once it's over. Shakespeare never spends time on unimportant material; everything has some purpose in his plays.

Strategy #7: *Asking Questions.* There are many questions even in a short passage such as this one that any reader might have about what goes on. Here are just a few examples:

◇ Why is Francisco not only cold but also "sick at heart"? (Because of his sense of foreboding?)

◇ Why is Bernardo so concerned that the other guards join him on watch given that Francisco's watch was so quiet that "Not a mouse stirr[ed]"? (Because of his fear of the "apparition"?)

◇ Why does Horatio reply "A piece of him" when Bernardo greets him? (Because as an intellectual, he's making a distinction between his body and his soul?)

◇ Why doesn't Marcellus call Francisco by name instead of calling him simply "honest soldier")? (Because Shakespeare has already named him at line 7?)

◇ Why does Horatio agree to listen to Bernardo talk about the ghost when we already know from lines 27–29 that he's heard the story before? (Because Shakespeare needs to tell the reader/audience the story, too?)

The key point is to get used to asking questions of the play, to get drawn in to the world that the play depicts. Asking questions always puts you on the road toward understanding.

Using Your Imagination

Shakespeare's plays are now four hundred years old. Fifteen or 16 generations have lived on this earth since Shakespeare first began his extraordinary career. The world is an utterly different place now from what it was then. Human nature has changed little, but how we live has radically altered. In order fully to appreciate Shakespeare's plays, you must put yourself in his landscape. This requires using your imagination in two particular ways: to imagine what Elizabethan England was like; and to imagine what Shakespeare's staging involved. You need to see with your mind's eye the world in which Shakespeare lived, and the theatre for which he wrote.

Imagining the World

Shakespeare's plays talk to us so directly and so immediately that it is hard sometimes to remember they were written long ago and that the playwright was definitely a child of his time. Just as people in Western Europe and the United States today make certain assumptions about life (for example, that the majority of us will lead healthy lives into our 70s and that democracy is the best form of government), so Shakespeare took certain political, social, and economic realities for granted.

◇ Capitalism was an idea whose time had not yet come. Feudalism (the ownership of the poor by the rich) was still the means by which society and the economy were organized.

◇ The English did not live in a democracy, but were ruled by a monarch with considerable powers. There was a parliament whose power was mainly financial. Universal suffrage was unknown. The vote was only given to those with money (merchants) or land (gentry).

◇ Great Britain did not exist (indeed it would not exist as a political entity until the very early nineteenth century). Instead, England, Scotland, Ireland, and Wales were independent nations, two of which (Ireland and Scotland) repeatedly caused England considerable grief.

◇ The British Empire was an utterly foreign concept. At the time Shakespeare was living, England was repeatedly under threat of foreign invasion. Indeed, one of the greatest achievements of Queen Elizabeth's long reign (1558–1603) was to ensure England's independence.

◇ The New World was still there to be explored and developed by Europeans. The first English settlement (at Jamestown in Virginia) dates from only nine years before Shakespeare's death.

◇ Modern medicine was unknown; the discovery of anesthetics was more than two hundred years in the future; even something as basic as the circulation of the blood was not yet understood. The state of the art in medicine at that time was to see the body as a battleground among four "humours" which corresponded to the four elements of the physical world: earth, air, fire, and water. Physiology and psychology were understood in terms of the proper balance of these four humours.

◇ Sanitation was primitive in the extreme. A central uncovered sewer ran down the middle of a street, and plumbing was very basic: pit toilets called "privies" or "jakes."

◇ Life expectancy was half what it is today. Outbreaks of the plague were common; the disease was untreatable.

◇ Marriage was essentially for life because divorce could only be granted by Act of Parliament. Women became the property of their husbands.

◇ Privacy was a rare luxury; living was often communal; sharing beds was common.

◇ Religion was not a matter of choice; people died for their beliefs, sometimes by being tortured and then burned at the stake. Hell and Heaven were not just ideas (as they are for many today) but realities that you faced after death.

◇ The English language was not yet regularized (the first English dictionary dates from 1604), and so experimentation was very much the norm.

◇ London had a population of only about 100,000 people, but was the major commercial city in Western Europe.

This act of imagining Shakespeare's world is important to understanding the themes of the plays. Shakespeare's world was hierarchical; it was a hierarchy of which Shakespeare seems generally to have approved. Again and again in the plays, the action ends with the restoration of order. Such a restoration (whether political, marital, or social) means that life can go on. In his famous political treatise, *Leviathan* (1651), Thomas Hobbes describes the life of man in a state of nature as "solitary, poore, nasty, brutish, and short" (89). Life as experienced by the great majority of Shakespeare's contemporaries was all of these with the exception of the first.

Imagining the Stage

In these days of breathtaking special effects that trick the eye, it is hard sometimes to remember that Shakespeare wrote his plays to be performed on an almost bare stage. "Discovery" scenes such as the one that occurs at the end of *Othello* (when Desdemona's body is revealed) or sounds from the ghost beneath the stage in *Hamlet* constitute the state of the art at the time. *This distinction between his age and ours is crucial, for your imagination is required to provide the effects that are missing.* Initially, it may feel rather strange to become self-conscious about the cues that tell you what the scene looks like. None of us is used to dwelling on how our senses (sight, touch, taste, hearing, and smell) are stimulated by words alone, yet the effect produced on us by our imaginations at work is, I think, more satisfying by far than the passive, unengaged acceptance of images from, say, the latest *Star Wars* prequel.

The opening of *Hamlet* (1.1.1–43) excerpted above is a useful example of what I'm talking about. Here, Shakespeare gives you everything through his language and his treatment of the action that you need in order to create an entire scene in your own mind. What's more, that scene is a unique creation of your own (unlike cinematic special effects, which are essentially identical for every viewer). In a quick and sure way, Shakespeare tells us everything we need to know, and you can get at it with some simple questions:

"Where does the action take place?" Bernardo and Francisco are called "sentinels" in the stage direction at the beginning of the scene, and Bernardo refers to their being on "watch" (14), so it looks as if the action takes place in a guardhouse, right? You can get this far without even having to glance down at the footnotes where (in my edition at least) there's a note that says that the location is "Elsinore castle. A guard platform."

"What time of day is it?" Bernardo says "'Tis now struck twelve" (7) and comments at line 40 that the stars are out. Marcellus refers to "the minutes of this night" (31). It's also hard to see, for Bernardo isn't sure that he recognizes Horatio when he first sees him (22). So, it must be past midnight, right?

"Why are the guards afraid?" It's not made clear at this point, but it seems as if an apparition of some sort has appeared a couple of times before, and now Bernardo and Marcellus want Horatio to be with them to observe the sight. Safety in numbers? Then, as long as you're reading carefully and imagining the scene, you can sense that it must be lonely and it certainly is cold (Francisco complains "'Tis bitter cold" [8] and at least one of them, Bernardo, is wearing a cloak [2]).

"How are the characters different?" Well, it looks as if the three guards (Bernardo, Francisco, and Marcellus) are similar although Marcellus may not know Francisco well at all because he simply calls him "honest soldier" (19). Horatio seems skeptical about it all unlike the rest, for (as Marcellus says) he "will not let belief take hold of him/Touching this dreaded sight" (28–29). Yet, the guards seem to defer to Horatio, for Marcellus really wanted him to come and observe what happens. Indeed, he wants Horatio to be the one to speak to it. As Marcellus remarks to Bernardo about Horatio:

> Therefore I have entreated him along
> With us to watch the minutes of this night,
> That if again this apparition come
> He may approve our eyes and speak to it (30–33).

Then, by glancing at the cast list you have conveniently at your elbow you can see that Horatio is a friend of Hamlet's. Later on in the play, you discover that he is, like Hamlet, a student. Perhaps, the guards hope that

Horatio with all his learning will be able to explain what happens to them. Perhaps, he will even be able to explain it away?

Shakespeare's concern, then, is to stimulate through language the imagination of the audience or reader into providing what is missing on the bare stage. As we've seen, the opening to *Hamlet* is a good example of this concern in action. However, it's in the Prologue to *Henry V* (a play written in about 1599, a year or two before *Hamlet*) that Shakespeare's call to the reader's imagination is most beautifully and most powerfully made. A summary of the first 31 lines of the Chorus's speech might go something like this: *I wish I could get Henry V to play himself, but I can't and the stage I'm working with anyway is pretty inadequate, so you'll just have to imagine what England and France at war might be like, in particular the soldiers, the horses, and the two kings. I've also condensed things a bit, for which I apologize.*

Now, here's the speech itself. As you read it, instead of analyzing what Shakespeare's saying or disagreeing with his point of view, simply allow yourself to conjure up out of your own mind what he's *explicitly* asking you to envision as the Chorus talks of Henry V ("Harry" in the speech) and his desire to conquer France:

CHORUS

> O, for a Muse of fire, that would ascend
> The brightest heaven of invention!
> A kingdom for a stage, princes to act,
> And monarchs to behold the swelling scene!
> Then should the warlike Harry, like himself,   5
> Assume the port of Mars; and at his heels,
> Leashed in like hounds, should famine, sword, and fire
> Crouch for employment. But pardon, gentles all,
> The flat unraisèd spirits that hath dared
> On this unworthy scaffold to bring forth   10
> So great an object. Can this cockpit hold
> The vasty fields of France? Or may we cram
> Within this wooden O the very casques
> That did affright the air at Agincourt?
> O, pardon! Since a crooked figure may   15
> Attest in little place a million;
> And let us, ciphers to this great account,
> On your imaginary forces work.
> Suppose within the girdle of these walls
> Are now confined two mighty monarchies,   20
> Whose high uprearèd and abutting fronts
> The perilous narrow ocean parts asunder.

> Piece out our imperfections with your thoughts:
> Into a thousand parts divide one man,
> And make imaginary puissance.   25
> Think, when we talk of horses, that you can see them
> Printing their proud hoofs i' the receiving earth.
> For 'tis your thoughts that now must deck our kings,
> Carry them, here and there, jumping o'er times,
> Turning th' accomplishment of many years   30
> Into an hourglass . . .

◇ Aren't there some wonderful pictures in these lines?
◇ Wasn't it a rather easy job, not to say an enjoyable one, to create them?
◇ Don't the images have an intensity and permanence that abstract descriptions do not?
◇ Can't you see the two coastlines (of France and England) separated only by a narrow but dangerous stretch of water, the English Channel?
◇ Can't you multiply the forces you see on stage by a thousand?
◇ Can't you see the horses, massive chargers, galloping across the soft ground of Agincourt (the "receiving earth")?
◇ Can't you imagine what kings look like?
◇ Can't you ignore the fact that Shakespeare (as he says at lines 28–31) condenses historical fact and frequently changes the settings for his scenes?

If, for a moment, you were also to analyze how Shakespeare structures this speech, you could show how in the first eleven lines he says (through the Chorus) that he would love to be able to depict reality by having Henry V play himself in his historical account of the famous English defeat of the French. However, the inadequacy of the stage means he couldn't do that even if King Harry were still alive, so the audience or, in this case, you the reader and your "imaginary forces" must do the job. In fact, you've probably noticed, Shakespeare asks you *twice* to use your creativity (once at line 18 and once more at line 28). All it needs is some effort and imagination. More importantly, you *need* to use your imaginative powers if you are to get the most from what Shakespeare has to offer.

Staying Flexible

So, Shakespeare places a premium on your paying attention to his words and on using your imagination. He also asks you to focus on the *order* of those words so that what he says will be remembered. So, when you read his plays you need to suspend your expectation that what his characters say will follow the usual grammatical sequence of subject—verb—object (as in a sentence such as "He hit the ball," for example). If you don't suspend your expectation, then confusion will often result. Shakespeare frequently does the unexpected with his sequence of words. He does so in order to grab the reader's or audience's attention and to reinforce the meaning of the play. His doing so isn't random or pointless or mere flourish. So, it's crucial that you stay mentally flexible as you read his plays.

To understand the significance of Shakespeare's word order—and the importance of staying mentally flexible—let's look at the most famous soliloquy in a play noteworthy for so many wonderful speeches, *Macbeth*. The soliloquy, which is spoken by Macbeth as his enemies are closing in on him and just after he receives word that his wife has died, goes as follows:

> Tomorrow, and tomorrow, and tomorrow
> Creeps in this petty pace from day to day   20
> To the last syllable of recorded time,
> And all our yesterdays have lighted fools
> The way to dusty death. Out, out, brief candle!
> Life's but a walking shadow, a poor player
> That struts and frets his hour upon the stage   25
> And then is heard no more. It is a tale
> Told by an idiot, full of sound and fury,
> Signifying nothing (5.5.19–28).

Much of this speech looks routine, but two parts of it draw attention to themselves. First, there is the change in normal word order at lines 19–21; then, there is the long description modifying the word *life* at lines 24–26. The change in word order draws attention to how pointless and boring life has become for Macbeth because it strings out the opening phrase "Tomorrow, and tomorrow, and tomorrow" along one entire line and then switches the expected sequence of subject ("this petty pace") and verb ("creeps in"). So, the reader's or watcher's focus is thrown onto the slowness of his life—and by implication, all our lives. Imagine how weak, for example, the poetry would be if Shakespeare had in fact done the expected and had written something like:

> This petty pace creeps in from day to day
> To the last syllable of recorded time:
> Tomorrow, and tomorrow, and tomorrow.

The description (lines 24–26), which defines what life has become for Macbeth, works wonderfully because it throws attention through ambiguity and detail on Shakespeare's dual vision. First, Macbeth as an actor on stage uses a **metaphor** to describe the experience of living. That is, his life has been like that of an actor who is forgotten after he leaves the stage.

Second, Macbeth as that actor on stage is the representative of all humanity in our transitoriness.

Sometimes, the sentence structure is played around with not in order for Shakespeare to emphasize particular themes (the slowness of life or the way in which all of us assume roles) but to indicate something important about the personality of the speaker. In *Hamlet*, for instance, the beginning of Claudius's first speech before the assembled court since he murdered his brother and became king in his place (1.2.1–16) is remarkable for its awkwardness. He begins with two subordinate clauses:

> Though yet of Hamlet our dear brother's death
> The memory be green, and that it us befitted
> To bear our hearts in grief and our whole kingdom
> To be contracted in one brow of woe . . .

The first subordinate clause (or part of the sentence that cannot stand on its own as a complete idea) is peculiar in itself because some of it is redundant (the word "Hamlet" is unnecessary in the sentence) and because, just as in Macbeth's soliloquy that we looked at earlier, the subject-verb combination is delayed—this time to the second line. The second subordinate clause delays the appearance of the main clause ("Yet so far hath discretion fought with nature") until line 5. The main clause is then followed by a third subordinate clause that is twice as long as the main clause:

> That we with wisest sorrow think on him
> Together with remembrance of ourselves.

Figuratively speaking, Claudius is trying to bury the battle within himself between self-preservation ("discretion") and supposed brotherly love ("nature") either in hopes that those listening won't notice it or because he himself can't or won't articulate the idea clearly.

Claudius's unsuccessful effort to appear calm continues into the lines immediately following the sentence we just looked at (with its three subordinate clauses and its buried main clause). Now, Claudius comes up with a breathtakingly twisted sentence where the subject and the crucial part of the verb are separated by four separate phrases:

> Therefore our sometime sister, now our queen,
> Th' imperial jointress to this warlike state,
> Have we, as 'twere with a defeated joy—
> With an auspicious and a dropping eye,
> With mirth in funeral and with dirge in marriage,
> In equal scale weighing delight and dole—
> Taken to wife.

10

So, as far as staying flexible when reading Shakespeare is concerned, my point is this: don't assume that Shakespeare's lines will follow the customary sequence of subject—verb—object. Try to untangle those lines that seem strangely constructed. If necessary, **paraphrase** one or two of them (that is, rewrite the lines in your own words in order to bring out their full meaning). Try, also, to see why the word sequence in particular places should be so unexpected. After a time, you will get used to the natural rhythm and structure of Shakespeare's lines.

Listening for the Subtext

Subtext may be an unfamiliar term to you. It has been broadly defined by Konstantin Stanislavsky, the well-known Russian actor, producer, and teacher, as "the manifest, the inwardly felt expression of a human being in a past which flows uninterruptedly beneath the words of the text, giving them life and a basis for existing . . . (quoted in Jorgens 11). In narrower and simpler terms, it means the emotions and body language that accompany the actor's delivery of a speech in character.

Recall that Shakespeare's plays were written for an extraordinarily simple stage. They were also published with very few stage directions to indicate what the subtext might be. In this regard, his plays are very different from, for example, those of other playwrights such as George Bernard Shaw or Henrik Ibsen, men whose plays go to great lengths to specify setting and subtext. It's very likely, of course, that in manuscript and at rehearsal Shakespeare was far more forthcoming about how he wanted certain lines to be read, and how he wanted particular scenes performed. That, however, doesn't do *us* any good. We have only the plays themselves, and since they were written to be performed rather than published, Shakespeare's particular ideas for subtext rarely made it into the published version of a play. So, in addition to using your imagination to have Shakespeare's language come alive, you need to listen carefully to how the lines should be spoken and supply the gestures that would go with the emotion. This may sound hard. In fact, it's simple because even though Shakespeare puts his characters in extreme situations, whether funny or sad, and sometimes deals with historical events of which we have little or no knowledge, he deals with issues with which all of us are surely very familiar. Haven't we all loved and hated, been jealous and kind, used and abused power and been used and abused by it? Haven't we all wondered what happens to us after we die and why good people can commit terrible acts?

Shakespeare has universal appeal precisely because he speaks directly to each and every one of us. All you as a reader have to do is to put yourself in the character's situation to know what emotion or vocal tone a particular speech might have, and what body language would accompany the words. The task of bringing the subtext to light is, then, simple. And there's more good news, too: there is no one correct "reading" of the subtext for a particular speech or scene. If you've ever watched several versions of one of Shakespeare's plays, you'll notice that even though the lines stay pretty much the same, the interpretation varies quite markedly because each actor's sense of the subtext differs. Laurence Olivier, Nicol Williamson, Derek Jacoby, Mel Gibson, and Kenneth Branagh have all performed the role of Hamlet. Their interpretations are available on video (and in Chapter 7, "Shakespeare in Performance: Stage and Screen," we will look at how they interpreted a particular scene). For now, it's enough to point out that each interpretation is markedly different from the others. That's not to say, however, that *any* reading of a line will work, for the interpretation needs to be consistent and to fit in with the context and with the character's previous and future actions. So, for example, it wouldn't be a reasonable interpretation of Othello's dying speech (5.2.348–66) to deliver it humorously or to present him as happy. Similarly, Cordelia's response to her father about the nature of her love for him—"So young, my lord, and true" (*King Lear* 1.1.107)—can only be read as earnest.

Let's return to the opening scene of *Hamlet* as a way of underlining the importance of being sensitive to the subtext of the play. It is reproduced here in exactly the same form as earlier in the chapter, with the exception of subtext readings that have been added. These appear in boldface and within square brackets.

BERNARDO	Who's there? **[loudly and taking hold of his spear or sword]**
FRANCISCO	Nay, answer me. Stand and unfold yourself. **[assertively]**
BERNARDO	Long live the King! **[confidently and pulling back the hood of his cloak]**
FRANCISCO	Bernardo? **[uncertainly because of the darkness]**
BERNARDO	He. 5
FRANCISCO	You come most carefully upon your hour. **[gratefully; they shake hands or embrace]**
BERNARDO	'Tis now struck twelve. Get thee to bed, Francisco. **[solicitously]**
FRANCISCO	For this relief much thanks. 'Tis bitter cold, **[shivering]** And I am sick at heart. **[despondently]**
BERNARDO	Have you had quiet guard? **[with an edge in his voice]** 10
FRANCISCO	Not a mouse stirring. **[gratefully]**
BERNARDO	Well, good night. If you do meet Horatio and Marcellus, The rivals of my watch, bid them make haste **[seriously]** *Enter Horatio and Marcellus*
FRANCISCO	I think I hear them.—Stand, ho! Who is there? **[loudly]** 15
HORATIO	Friends to this ground. **[he points downwards]**

MARCELLUS	And liegemen to the Dane. [assertively]
FRANCISCO	Give you good night.
MARCELLUS	O, farewell, honest soldier. Who hath relieved you?
FRANCISCO	Bernardo hath my place. Give you good night. 20

Exit Francisco

MARCELLUS	Holla! Bernardo! [happily]
BERNARDO	Say, what, is Horatio there? [quizzically]
HORATIO	A piece of him. [humorously or sententiously]
BERNARDO	Welcome, Horatio. Welcome, good Marcellus. [they shake hands or embrace]
HORATIO	What, has this thing [emphasized] appeared again tonight? 25
BERNARDO	I [emphasized] have seen nothing.
MARCELLUS	Horatio says 'tis but our fantasy,
	And will not let belief take hold of him
	Touching this dreaded sight twice seen of us. [dismissively]
	Therefore I have entreated him along 30
	With us to watch the minutes of this night,
	That if again this apparition come
	He may approve our eyes and speak to it.
HORATIO	Tush, tush, 'twill not appear. [chidingly]
BERNARDO	Sit down awhile, [gestures towards a bench]
	And let us once again assail your ears, 35
	That are so fortified against our story,
	What we have two nights seen.
HORATIO	Well, sit we down, [grudgingly]
	And let us hear Bernardo speak of this.
BERNARDO	Last night of all,
	When yond same star that's westward from the pole [he points] 40
	Had made his course t' illumine that part of heaven
	Where now it burns [he makes a sweeping gesture], Marcellus and myself,
	The bell then beating one—

These subtext additions are *not*, it needs to be stressed, the only ones that might work. What matters, however, in the reading process is that you add the emotion that isn't marked in stage directions on the page, and that you imagine how the characters would act in real life. If you don't, then the words fail to live and the characters can never come across as real.

The example from *Hamlet* is fairly straightforward; even if you misinterpret some of the subtext an understanding of the play won't elude you. What happens, however, if subtext is absolutely crucial to the meaning of a play? The answer is that you need to think through the range of possible readings very carefully and decide which one best fits your overall interpretation of the meaning of the play. By way of illustration, let's look at a very particular series of speeches from Act 3 Scene 13 of *Antony and Cleopatra*. At this point in the play, Antony's fortunes are in rapid decline. His and Cleopatra's forces have just been defeated at sea near Actium because Cleopatra's fleet fled from the battle. It looks as if Octavius Caesar, Antony's military rival, may permanently defeat him. So the issue of what Antony's lover, Cleopatra, will now do becomes crucial to the play. In this particular scene (3.13), Cleopatra gives an audience to Thidias, Octavius Caesar's messenger. The question any reader has to decide is: Does Cleopatra intend to betray Antony? Clearly Enorbarbus, Antony's trusty friend, believes so ("Thy dearest quit thee," he says [65]), but Cleopatra does defend herself towards the end of the scene by swearing on the lives of herself, her child (Caesarion), and all Egyptians that she won't betray Antony. Then, she enigmatically asks Antony, "Not know me yet?" Readers have to decide on the basis of subtext whether they do know Cleopatra, and what such knowledge means.

Let's pick up the action from Thidias's entrance:

CLEOPATRA		Caesar's will?
THIDIAS	Hear it apart	
CLEOPATRA	None but friends. Say boldly.	
THIDIAS	So haply are they friends to Antony.	
ENOBARBUS	He needs as many, sir, as Caesar has,	
	Or needs not us. If Caesar please, our master	50
	Will leap to be his friend. For us, you know	
	Whose he is we are, and that is Caesar's.	
THIDIAS	So.	
	Thus then, thou most renowned: Caesar entreats	
	Not to consider in what case thou stand'st	
	Further than he is Caesar.	
CLEOPATRA	Go on: right royal.	55
THIDIAS	He knows that you embrace not Antony	
	As you did love, but as you feared him.	
CLEOPATRA	O!	
THIDIAS	The scars upon your honor therefore he	
	Does pity as constrainèd blemishes,	
	Not as deserved.	
CLEOPATRA	He is a god and knows	60
	What is most right. Mine honor was not yielded,	
	But conquered merely.	

Is Cleopatra being obsequious here or sarcastic? The tone of voice and even the gestures would be similar in either case although sarcasm would likely be more exaggerated. A decision about the subtext of, for example a single one-letter word "O!" is tremendously difficult to make. Is she shocked, amused, annoyed, or angry when she says the word? Ultimately, your reading of the subtext depends on your assessment of the entire play up to that point. At its starkest, are Antony and Cleopatra unlucky lovers, or is Antony being made a fool of by a self-interested and opportunistic queen? Shakespeare doesn't tell us; we have to decide on the basis—in large measure—of subtext.

The intent here is to introduce rather than to exhaust the range of ways in which Shakespeare uses subtext, but the discussion will conclude by mentioning a couple of other types of subtext so that you will be able to listen sensitively for what Shakespeare puts between the lines of his plays. How do you decide on a gesture when that choice depends on another character's words? How do you assess body language in the absence of words?

The first question comes up most memorably at the end of *King Lear*. The stage direction that marks Lear's entrance at 5.3.261 reads: "*Enter Lear, with Cordelia in his arms; [Captain].*" His dying words as he looks at the apparently dead Cordelia are, "Do you see this? Look on her, look, her lips,/Look there, look there!" (5.3.316–17). Is the reader to assume that Lear is deluded, or has he actually seen something? Is there hope rather than limitless despair? Is the subtext that Cordelia is alive and actually moves her lips?

The second question—how to interpret silence—becomes crucial at the end of one of Shakespeare's best-known "problem" plays, *Measure for Measure*. The Duke proposes marriage to the play's pivotal character, Isabella: "for your lovely sake," he says to her, "Give me your hand and say you will be mine" (5.1.502–03). To this proposal, Isabella says nothing. The play, however, has 46 lines left. Almost at the very end of those lines, the Duke again repeats his offer:

> Dear Isabel,
> I have a motion much imports your good,
> Whereto if you'll a willing ear incline,
> What's mine is yours, and what is yours is mine.—
> (5.1.545–48).

Again, Isabella says nothing. So, how does she react in either instance? How is the reader to assess her silence? Does she acknowledge agreement by giving the Duke her hand? Does she shake her head in refusal? We don't know, but she clearly has to respond in some way. Indeed, in this case, doing nothing is tantamount in itself to an act. The only advice I can offer here is to think of the situation in which Shakespeare has put you:

you have to listen in your memory to all that has gone before; you have to assess—as Stanislavsky put it in his definition of subtext—the characters' past history. Throughout, the Duke has been a hidden, masterful manipulator of the lives of others. On the one hand, he has saved Isabella's brother, Claudio, from execution. On the other hand, Claudio would not have found himself in such a situation if the Duke hadn't put the viciously corrupt Angelo in charge of the state, a man about whom the Duke has his doubts from the very beginning of the play.

Writing and Discussion Assignments

1. Choose one speech from a Shakespeare play that you find important *and* confusing. First, describe the experience of reading the speech silently, then of reading it aloud. What *specifically* did you gain, if anything, from sounding the words out? Edmund's soliloquy in *King Lear* 1.2.1–22 may work well for this assignment.
2. Choose one significant speech from a Shakespeare play. Paraphrase it. What *specifically* is lost in your version? Antony's speech in *Antony and Cleopatra* 1.1.35–42 may work well for this assignment.
3. Look carefully at one substantial speech from a Shakespeare play. List all the images that Shakespeare creates through his appeal to your imagination. Do you see these images as forming a pattern? Do you see these images as contributing to an understanding of the speaker? *Richard III* 1.1.1–41 may work well here.
4. Imagine that you are a director of a production of Shakespeare's *Hamlet*. What advice would you have for the actors playing Polonius, Laertes, and Ophelia in *Hamlet* 1.3 with regard to the subtext of their roles in the scene? What emotions should their speeches convey, and how should their body language reinforce the emotional content of what they say? Along with the advice, you need to explain briefly the reasons behind any subtext choices that are not self-evident.

Further Reading

Dawson, Anthony B. *Indirections—Shakespeare's and the Art of Illusion*. Toronto: U of Toronto P, 1978.

Homan, Sidney, ed. *Shakespeare's "More Than Words Can Witness": Essays on Visual and Nonverbal Enactment in the Plays*. Lewisburg, PA: Bucknell UP, 1980.

Linklater, Kristin. *Freeing Shakespeare's Voice: The Actor's Guide to Talking the Text*. New York: Theatre Communications Group, 1992.

McDonald, Russ, ed. *Shakespeare Reread: The Texts in New Contexts*. Ithaca, NY: Cornell UP, 1994.

Thompson, Marvin and Ruth, eds. *Shakespeare and the Sense of Performance*. Newark: U of Delaware P, 1989.

Wallis, Mick, and Simon Shepherd. *Studying Plays*. London: Arnold, 1998.

Part

Language

Chapter 1

Shakespeare's Dramatic Language

Chapter Overview

◇ Understanding the peculiarities of Shakespeare's language.
◇ Appreciating the sophistication of Shakespeare's sentence structures.
◇ Distinguishing among rhymed poetry, unrhymed poetry, and prose.

Words are to Shakespeare what music is to Mozart: the element he lived in. It is what he is most famous for; it is his greatest gift to Western culture. Yet, it is clear to me that *for many students, Shakespeare's words constitute the single greatest obstacle to enjoying his plays.* For many, the meaning of individual words, the structure of the sentences, and the formal aspects of his poetry and prose get in the way of, rather than enhance, the enjoyment of Shakespeare's plays.

Tackling these issues will be the goal of the next four chapters. In this chapter, we'll look at Shakespeare's dramatic language. In the next, we'll look at one feature which is fundamental to Shakespeare's use of language: **imagery** (or the literal and non-literal appeals Shakespeare makes to the senses and the imagination). In Chapter Three, we'll look at Shakespeare's use of **rhetoric** (or the arts of persuasion); and in the chapter after that, we'll finish our examination of Shakespeare's language with an analysis of his humor. My focus is on Shakespeare's language because the key point is this: if you can see the pattern of what Shakespeare is doing—the remarkable variety of ways he uses language—then when you come to read individual plays his meaning will be so much easier to understand. Instead of seeing chaos and hearing sound, you'll see order and hear the words lining up neatly into the clear and memorable expression of profound ideas.

Some Preliminary Suggestions

1. Remember the general advice from the Introduction on how to read Shakespeare:
   - ◇ Make an effort
   - ◇ Use your imagination
   - ◇ Stay flexible
   - ◇ Listen or read for the subtext.
2. Remember these three points about appreciating what Shakespeare has to offer. They will help to reduce any stress level you feel when encountering his work:
   - ◇ One of the major reasons Shakespeare seems difficult is that Western culture has elevated him to such a high status. You assume he's going to be difficult, so he becomes so for you.
   - ◇ You can't expect to get everything Shakespeare has to offer from a first or even a second reading. *It's not essential that you do.* There is so much to appreciate about what he's doing that one of the true joys of his work is that every time you reread him you find something new. If you try to get everything first time through, only frustration will result.
   - ◇ Everyone in the audience at a Shakespeare play—from neophytes to experts—is initially overwhelmed by the words that come so thick and fast. The curtain comes up; the characters come on stage; the words pour forth. That feeling of being overwhelmed disappears, however, once the spectator can make sense of what's being said. And the secret to making sense of what's being said? To see that Shakespeare's characters speak in several different types of language, each with its own distinct characteristics.
3. Remember these four peculiarities of Shakespearean English:
   - ◇ Shakespeare's vocabulary is vast, much bigger—at 25,000 words— than any other writer's and considerably larger than the normal working vocabulary of about 5,000 words. One of the reasons, then, that Shakespeare seems difficult is that he does use words which will be initially unfamiliar to you—indeed, some would have been unfamiliar even to an audience in his own era, too.
   - ◇ The English language was in flux in Shakespeare's age. The first English dictionary, Robert Cawdrey's *A Table Alphabeticall*, dates from 1604 (only a dozen years, that is, before Shakespeare's death), and, as you might expect, the absence of formal rules of spelling and usage meant that there was a delight in experimentation. Shakespeare is famous for using verbs as nouns and nouns as verbs as well as for inventing neologisms (or new words) when he needed to.

◇ Shakespeare was tremendously aware at all times of his audience. His many responses to that awareness materially affect the language of his plays. For example, the language of his plays written to be performed at the Globe, an outdoor venue, is markedly different from the language of those plays—broadly the late romances—designed for a smaller indoor theatre, Blackfriars. In *Hamlet*, you can see Shakespeare's awareness of the importance of audience expressed in a conversation between the hero and the First Player of the traveling group of actors that is visiting the royal castle at Elsinore. Hamlet comments explicitly on a speech he once heard the First Player give:

> ...the play, I remember, pleased not the million; 'twas caviar to the general. But it was—as I received it, and others, whose judgments in such matters cried in the top of mine—an excellent play, well digested in the scenes, set down with as much modesty as cunning. I remember one said there were no sallets in the lines to make the matter savory, nor no matter in the phrase that might indict the author of affectation, but called it an honest method, as wholesome as sweet, and by very much more handsome than fine (2.2.435–45).

Encouraged by Hamlet's praise for his performance, the actor launches into a speech of 29 lines. It is *not* a success, however, because both Polonius and Hamlet consider it too long and too dull. The latter remarks: "It shall to the barber's" (i.e. it will have to be cut) and wishes it included something entertaining, "a jig or a tale of bawdy" (499, 500). In its present shape, Shakespeare has his characters suggest, the speech would fail because it would fail with the audience.

◇ Remember above all that Shakespeare wrote to be understood. You need to reject outright the elitist notion that Shakespeare is so complex in his language that he is best discussed by experts for the betterment of other scholars. If that were the case, the playwright then and now would have seen his works played before empty houses. It is true that the more you know the more you appreciate Shakespeare's talent, but Shakespeare was and always has been quite accessible. One need only think, for example, of the simplicity of Othello's appeal at the end of the play to be remembered for who he really was:

> Soft you; a word or two before you go.
> I have done the state some service, and they know't.

No more of that. I pray you, in your letters,
When you shall these unlucky deeds relate,
Speak of me as I am; nothing extenuate,
Nor set down aught in malice (5.2.348–53).

Test Case #1: Hamlet's Famous Soliloquy

Before looking at particular instances of Shakespeare's several languages, we will analyze the most famous speech in all of Shakespeare (Hamlet's "To be, or not to be" soliloquy) with two goals in mind:

1. To show you the range of language devices Shakespeare uses *in less than 35 lines.*
2. To show you that Shakespeare is simply not that hard as long as you concentrate on the task at hand.

This justly famous speech appears in 3.1.57–91 and goes as follows:

HAMLET

To be, or not to be, that is the question:
Whether 'tis nobler in the mind to suffer
The slings and arrows of outrageous fortune,
Or to take arms against a sea of troubles   60
And by opposing end them. To die, to sleep—
No more—and by a sleep to say we end
The heartache and the thousand natural shocks
That flesh is heir to. 'Tis a consummation
Devoutly to be wished. To die, to sleep;   65
To sleep, perchance to dream. Ay, there's the rub,
For in that sleep of death what dreams may come,
When we have shuffled off this mortal coil,
Must give us pause. There's the respect
That makes calamity of so long life.   70
For who would bear the whips and scorns of time,
Th' oppressor's wrong, the proud man's contumely,
The pangs of disprized love, the law's delay,
The insolence of office, and the spurns
That patient merit of the unworthy takes,   75
When he himself might his quietus make
With a bare bodkin? Who would fardels bear,
To grunt and sweat under a weary life,
But that the dread of something after death,

The undiscovered country from whose bourn 80
No traveler returns, puzzles the will,
And makes us rather bear those ills we have
Than fly to others that we know not of?
Thus conscience does make cowards of us all;
And thus the native hue of resolution 85
Is sicklied o'er with the pale cast of thought,
And enterprises of great pitch and moment
With this regard their currents turn awry
And lose the name of action.—Soft you now,
The fair Ophelia. Nymph, in thy orisons 90
Be all my sins remembered.

Initial Reactions

The first thing you'll probably notice is all the unfamiliar words, but the list is actually a short one: *slings* (missiles); *rub* (an obstacle in the game of bowls); *coil* (turmoil); *contumely* (insolence); *quietus* (a technical term meaning settlement); *bodkin* (dagger); *fardels* (burdens); *bourn* (boundary); *orisons* (prayers). Of these, only four are not in use today. How can you quickly master Shakespeare's vocabulary? By keeping an alphabetized list of uncommon words in your notebook, and by falling in love with the *sounds* of the words themselves. Sometimes, Shakespeare rated more highly the criterion of sound than almost any other. If you do these two things, pretty soon the unfamiliar becomes well known.

The second characteristic you *should* notice is that Hamlet begins very simply and gets more complex as the speech goes on. It's hard to imagine an easier opening than "To be, or not to be, that is the question." The sentences at the beginning and at the end are fairly short; the three questions that form the core of the speech (58–61, 71–77, and 77–83) are noticeably longer and more complex.

The third noteworthy aspect of this famous speech (and it's something that most of Shakespeare's speeches share) is that the speaker is arguing about something, and that his argument (with himself in this case) is organized into parts. In the first section (57–61), Hamlet presents the issue: should he kill himself or fight against those who mean him harm (principally, Claudius). In the second section (61–69), Hamlet embraces the idea of death, but hesitates to do the deed because he's unsure about the hereafter. In the third section (69–83), Hamlet lists all the awful things that happen to people in life. Yet they do not commit suicide. Why not? Because they don't know what will happen to them after death. In the fourth section (84–89), Hamlet comes back to his present problem and shows how this fear of the unknown after death has made him hesitate to act to avenge his father. In the final section (89-91), Shakespeare ties the soliloquy to Hamlet's meeting with Ophelia through two-and-a-half lines of transition.

The fourth feature of this soliloquy (and this feature is again typical of Shakespeare's poetry) is that **figurative language** (or nonliteral imagery) is everywhere. (We'll be looking in detail at this aspect of Shakespeare's language in the next chapter.) Much of the density of Shakespeare's language derives from his characters' habit of always seeing the literal in terms of the nonliteral. They are always using metaphors and **similes** and **personifications**. We do it ourselves all the time almost without thinking; Shakespeare simply emphasizes it. So, we say, for example, that we are "dog tired." Why dogs particularly should be tired, beats me. Have you ever seen an easier life than a pampered pet's? We say that we are "thrilled to bits" about something. Would you really like to disintegrate as a sign of pleasure? So, Hamlet sees those who wish to harm him in terms of missiles ("slings and arrows") and his "troubles" as a "sea" against which he could fight (or "take [up] arms"). The fact that Shakespeare here uses a mixed metaphor (how can taking up arms against a sea result in anything other than a severe case of rust?) need not worry us. After all, Hamlet *is* distraught. And so, too, Hamlet sees humanity as "heir" to the pains of life, but this cannot be considered a literal statement since we can only be heir to the worldly goods of those who name us in their wills.

So much for metaphors. There are also examples of other types of figurative language. There's **synecdoche** where something is represented by a part or stands for a larger whole. Again, we use this device all the time almost without thinking. We talk of farm or ranch "hands" when we really mean the whole person. When police officers say they are "the law," they don't mean it literally. They are only representatives of a large organization. And so, in this soliloquy Shakespeare refers to humanity by only one part, its "flesh"(64). There's **metonymy**, too, where something (often an abstract idea) is represented by something with which it is emotionally associated. So we talk of justice as "blind" because statues of the figure of justice are blindfolded, and so we talk of "the crown" when we mean the monarchy because we associate an object with a role. And so Shakespeare, when he writes of "the insolence of office" (74), refers to bureaucrats in terms of a quality that many associate with them: rudeness.

The final characteristic of the soliloquy is its poetry, the rhythm and structure of the lines. You've no doubt noticed that some of the words are abbreviated: "'tis" or "'Tis" (for "it is" and "It is"); "Th'" (for "The"). I know it's distracting, but don't worry about it: it's simply Shakespeare trying to save syllables in order to make his poetry run more smoothly. There's a distracting dash toward the end of line 89. Again, it's not that important. It simply marks the end of the soliloquy and the transition to Hamlet's dialogue with Ophelia.

The soliloquy is written in what is called **blank verse** or unrhymed **iambic pentameter**. This term is simply jargon (in this case a useful abbreviation) for lines with a capital letter at the beginning, ten syllables each, a rhythm of alternating unstressed and stressed syllables, and no rhyming words at the ends of the lines. You can hear the iambic rhythm in a line such as this one from Hamlet's soliloquy: "Fŏr ín | thăt sléep | of déath | whăt dréams | măy cóme" (67), where I've marked off the pairs of syllables with a |; the unstressed syllables with a ˘; and the stressed syllables with a ´. Not every line in this soliloquy is regular (that is, consists exactly of this alternating rhythm) and not every line has only ten syllables (indeed, the first five lines each have eleven syllables). This apparent irregularity need not surprise you, however, for one of Shakespeare's great strengths is how he varies the basic model. He knew that regularity would bore, and variety captivate. Nonetheless, whether you read this soliloquy, listen to it, or watch it performed you will be aware, perhaps unconsciously, of an underlying pattern of sound. It's that sound that is in itself melodic and beautiful.

As to the structure of the lines, there is frequently a pause in the middle of each so that one line becomes two half lines. Often that pause (which is called a **caesura**) is emphasized by punctuation, as in "That flesh is heir to. 'Tis a consummation" (64). Sometimes the pause is emphasized by the effect of both parts of the line being cumulative, as in "Th' oppressor's wrong, the proud man's contumely" (72). Shakespeare also achieves variety by mixing lines which finish with punctuation (termed **end-stopped** lines) and those which run over onto the next line without pause and are punctuated somewhere in the middle of the next or later lines. This technique is called **enjambment**. So, the first line is end-stopped: "To be, or not to be, that is the question:" (57); lines four and five are "enjambed": "Or to take arms against a sea of troubles/And by opposing end them" (60–61).

Summary

What does this famous **soliloquy** reveal about Shakespeare's language?

1. The words are not as difficult as they are often thought to be. Only as a last resort, look at the footnotes. Begin by asking yourself what word in modern English Shakespeare's word sounds like. This practice can sometimes mislead you, but doesn't "bourn" at line 80 look a lot like "boundary" and sound a little like it too? Regardless of how you come to understand Shakespeare's vocabulary, keep a list of the difficult words. Writing the words down again and, if necessary, again is the quickest way to remember them for good.
2. Shakespeare's speeches have a structure to them and often move from simple ideas to more complex ones. Finding the structure in his plays' speeches helps in understanding Shakespeare's meaning.

3. Shakespeare uses all types of figurative language repeatedly. It's what sparks the imagination so that Shakespeare's words live on in the minds of audience and readers alike.
4. Shakespeare's language is like music and can be appreciated *solely* in an aesthetic way. Listen to the sounds of the words and the rhythm of the lines. It's hard to resist the attraction they have for the human ear.
5. Shakespeare operates on several levels at once. Don't get discouraged if you don't see every level the first or second time through. Understanding Shakespeare comes more and more easily with practice, and that practice is worthwhile because of the profundity of his insights.

Shakespeare's Peculiar Language

"You" and "Thou"

The first word usage that you're likely to trip up over in Shakespeare is his use of *you/ye/your* and *thou/thee/thy*. The basic rule is that *you* is formal and used with acquaintances or with those higher in rank while *thou* or *thee* is affectionate and used with friends and relatives or with those of lower social rank. So, Hamlet constantly refers to Claudius as "you" (Claudius may be his uncle and step-father, but Hamlet has no desire to get to know him well) and to his great friend, Horatio, as "thou." By contrast, Horatio uses "you" when addressing Hamlet (who is, after all, a prince). "Thou" is also used, in a way that may surprise you: to show contempt. If you think of *Twelfth Night* and the wonderfully funny scene in which Sir Toby Belch coaches Sir Andrew Aguecheek to challenge Viola/Cesario to a duel, then you may recall one of Sir Toby's instructions: "Taunt him with the license of ink. If/thou 'thou'-est him some thrice, it shall not be amiss" (3.2.43–44).

If you think too of Edgar's battle with Oswald in *King Lear* 4.6, the pair of them insult each other using "thou." Oswald shouts angrily at him, "Slave, thou hast slain me" (249); Edgar gives as good as he gets: "I know thee well: a serviceable villain" (255). He doesn't do so, however, *until* Oswald has died because he is playing a role—that of a poor man from the country—which makes him Oswald's inferior. So, since Oswald, Goneril's steward, is *apparently* his superior, Edgar uses the terms "ye," "your," and "you" when referring to him earlier in the exchange (243–45).

Such a range of distinctions does not, however, tell the whole story, for Shakespeare uses the difference among the forms of address with great subtlety. In *King Lear*, for example, the scene between Gloucester and his disguised son, Edgar, is remarkable for the value that the "you/thou" distinction adds to the drama (4.6.1–80 and 204–90).

You probably need a little context. The blinded Gloucester is being lead towards Dover by Edgar who, he has been told, is a "[m]adman and beggar too" (4.1.30). Gloucester wishes to throw himself off the Dover cliffs; Edgar wants to fool him into thinking he has thrown himself off and miraculously survived. Gloucester begins by addressing Edgar as "thou" (7). Why, when you would expect him to say "you" since he believes Edgar is his social inferior and poor and mad, too? Because, as Gloucester himself puts it, Edgar sounds more cultivated than he did earlier: "Methinks thy voice is altered, and thou speak'st/In better phrase and matter than thou didst" (7–8).

In truth, Edgar's disguise is slipping; he's not too swift with accents. However, Edgar persuades Gloucester that he is mistaken ("You're much deceived. In nothing am I changed/But in my garments" [9–10]). What does Gloucester do in response? He changes to "you" even though he still holds with his original view that Edgar's language and accent have changed: "Methinks you're better spoken," he says (10). At line 30 Gloucester suddenly changes back and starts referring to Edgar as "thee." Why? Because Gloucester now, at—he supposes—the end of his life, thinks of Edgar as his friend. He explicitly calls him this at line 28. And even though he still considers him his social inferior (note the term "fellow" at line 41), their friendship matters more. This time, Gloucester doesn't change his form of address to Edgar until he believes he has jumped from the cliffs but somehow miraculously survived. Since he believes that he is speaking to someone for the first time, he uses the formal "you": "That thing you speak of,/I took it for a man" (77–78). He doesn't change back until he needs Edgar's aid in fighting Oswald, at line 233. Here he asks Edgar for "thy friendly hand" (233). These are his last words directed to Edgar in the scene.

Edgar is even more subtle in his use of "you" and "thee." He begins by addressing Gloucester as "you." This is exactly what one would expect, for Gloucester is—from Edgar's assumed perspective of poor mad Tom—his social superior. He even briefly continues to say "you" to Gloucester after he assumes the role of the unnamed man who finds Gloucester at what Gloucester supposes is the bottom of the cliff. And he does so even though he terms Gloucester "Friend" (46). Why? Well, they haven't been introduced, right? As far as Edgar is concerned, he just happened to be at the right place at the right time to help this unknown man. He can call him "Friend" because he's a fellow mortal in pain, but he also calls him "sir" (46) because he supposedly doesn't know him. Three lines later, however, Gloucester becomes "thou" and "Thy." He is called such no less than five times in seven lines. Again the reasonable question has to be asked: Why? Well, this time there's a change because Edgar is ministering to someone who thinks he is near death and still contemplates suicide. ("Away, and let me die" [48], Gloucester says to him when they first meet.) Edgar, of course, must show affection for the awful suffering of a fellow human being. Once it becomes clear to Gloucester himself that he is alive and unharmed, Edgar switches back to "you": "Feel you your legs? You stand"

(65). He continues in this vein until, overcome with emotion at seeing the suffering of old, blind Gloucester, his father, he comes close to revealing who he is. He calls Gloucester "thou happy father" (72) when he thanks the gods for his preservation. He is, of course, using the term to mean blood relation; Gloucester, who suspects nothing, thinks he uses the term generically to mean any old man.

Then Lear enters at line 80, so that the conversation between Edgar and Gloucester is interrupted until line 222 where the son returns to calling his father "you" because he has mastered his emotions and is still that unknown helper at the base of the cliff. Afraid that Gloucester may think he sounds too much like the role he played earlier, that of poor Tom, he adopts an exaggerated rural accent when he encounters Oswald and kills him (240–45). He remains consistent, however, in calling Gloucester "you." He remains so even though he calls Gloucester "father" (in the sense of old man) thrice more (at lines 222, 259, and 290).

So, what's the total effect? Ten changes among two people in about 160 lines of dialogue. And what should you as reader make of it? Well, first of all, that something which seems superficially distracting is actually quite fascinating. That which begins as looking quaint can become itself a source of study in order to understand better the full range of Shakespeare's meaning. Second, that modern English has lost some wonderful subtlety by giving up "thou," "thee," and "thy."

"Hath" and "Doth"

Another feature of Shakespeare's plays that—like *you* and *thou*—draws attention to itself is their use of old-fashioned verb forms, *forms which were a little out of date even in Shakespeare's time.* Students frequently ask about their meaning because they look strange. Why did Shakespeare, the question goes, write *hath* when *has* was available to him, or *doth* when *does* was around, or—for that matter—*durst* when *dares* is fine?

The easiest way to explain the use of such verb forms is to look at one particular scene, *King Lear* 1.1. In this justly famous scene, the king divides his kingdom between two of his daughters, Goneril and Regan, and in the process disinherits his third daughter, Cordelia. The one word to describe the tone of the scene is *elevated.* Lear is being a king with power for the last time, and everyone knows it. So, all the characters are aware of the appropriately grave behavior they should display. The result as far as language is concerned? The old-fashioned verbs sprout up like corn in the summer sun. Lear begins with the key question: "Which of you shall we say *doth* love us most,/That we our largest bounty may extend/Where nature *doth* with merit challenge?" (51–53; emphasis mine here and subsequently). Goneril and Regan pass the test with flying colors; Cordelia fails miserably. In response, Kent jumps to Cordelia's aid, and incurs Lear's grave anger.

Hast, durst (172), and *do allot* (176)—old-fashioned verbs, all—rain down on Kent. And how does Kent react? Not to be outdone, he responds with a *sith* (for "since"), a *think'st* (for "think"), and another *hast* before he accepts banishment (183; 186).

Next, Lear moves on to the question of who will marry Cordelia: the Duke of Burgundy, the King of France, or no one? Another serious matter, so the old-fashioned, faintly grandiloquent language reappears. Lear opens with a *hath* (194); Burgundy responds in kind (197). Cordelia has her part in the discussion, and asks her father, King Lear, to admit that she has not been disinherited because of a "vicious blot, murder, or foulness" (231), but rather because her inability or unwillingness to flatter him "*Hath* lost me in your liking" (237). Lear answers the challenge with a *hadst* (238). Despite Cordelia's request for a clarification from Lear, Burgundy declines to marry Cordelia, but France accepts the implicit challenge and offers to marry Cordelia, doing so with an unusual form of the verb "to be": *art* (254) for *are*. He concludes in a like vein with an unusual form of the verb "to lose": *losest* (265). Finally, the scene closes with Goneril and Regan reflecting on Lear's earth-shattering decisions to disinherit Cordelia and banish Kent. Regan sums up Lear's faults: "[H]e *hath* ever/but slenderly known himself" (296–97). Goneril chimes in with something similar: "The best and soundest of his time *hath* been/but rash" (298–99).

This is <u>not</u> to suggest that Shakespeare never uses old-fashioned, elevated language elsewhere. In fact, Edmund uses some of the same verb forms in his soliloquy at the beginning of the next scene. But, that's the point precisely. Soliloquies are elevated pronouncements made by characters alone on stage. Lear and his court are similarly aware in 1.1 that something extraordinary is happening, and their language (or, rather, *Shakespeare's* language) reflects that understanding. It's something that an audience, listening to the words instead of reading them, would have understood very well.

Some Other Shakespearean Oddities

In addition to the oddness of the "thou/you" and "hath/has" and "doth/does" distinctions, there are many ways in which Shakespeare's words challenge the reader. Here, I'll just mention a few:

◇ *Archaisms.* This term includes words which were old even when Shakespeare used them: *certes* (certainly), *clepe* and its past tense *ycleped* (a verb meaning "to call" or "to name"), *eager* (acrid), *egregious* (very great), *eke* (moreover), *iwis* (indeed), *wight* (man), and *would* (in the sense of "wish").

◇ *Colloquialisms.* This term includes words which are informal but not as loose as slang. S.S. Hussey, in *The Literary Language of Shakespeare*, mentions *brabble* (meaning "a brawl") and *sneck up* (meaning "get lost"). My personal favorite, however, is "bully" (meaning "a fine fellow," as in Pistol's calling Henry V a "lovely bully" [4.1.49]).

◇ *Compound words.* This phrase covers that tendency in Shakespeare (especially early in his career) to yoke together two words either as a playful experiment or as a means to maintain audience and reader involvement. In *I Henry IV* (which dates from 1596–1597), Falstaff insults a group of travelers whom he robs as "whoreson caterpillars, bacon-fed knaves" (2.2.84). Shakespeare's liking for such a device doesn't entirely disappear from his later work, however. In *King Lear* (which dates from 1605–1606), Kent insults Oswald, Goneril's servant, in a remarkable speech that consists of one sentence of 11 lines (2.2.14–24). That speech includes six double compounds ("three-suited," "hundred-pound," "worsted-stocking," "lily-livered," "action-taking," "glass-gazing") and one triple compound ("one-trunk-inheriting"). All the compounds are directed at showing precisely what kind of a "knave" Goneril's servant is. Kent wins hands down over Falstaff.

◇ *Dialect words.* This phrase covers words which were used in that part of England, the Midlands, where Shakespeare grew up, but which were largely unknown to the mainstream, London, dialect. The list (primarily from C. T. Onions's *Shakespeare Glossary*) includes *ballow* (a club or cudgel), *batlet* (a bat used for washing clothes), *bawd* (a hare), *blood-bolter'd* (which means "matted with blood"), *bum-baily* (a sheriff's officer), *elder-gun* (a harmless gun because made out of wood), *gallow* (to frighten), *geck* (a fool), *grow to* (to be united with), *handsaw* (meaning *hernshaw* or a heron), *honey-stalks* (clover flowers), *mobled* (muffled), *pash* (the head), *potch* (to thrust at), *tarre* (to incite), *tun-dish* (a funnel), and *vails* (perks).

◇ *Jargon.* This term covers words which belong to particular professions. This list includes *gad* (a term from horseback riding), *lampass* (a disease of horses, a medical term), *on* or *upon the hip* (a wrestling term), *poniards* (daggers, a term from fencing), and *quiddities* (fine distinctions in scholastic argument).

◇ *Lower-class words.* This list according to Hussey includes *bawcock* (meaning "a fine fellow") and *chuck* (a term of endearment).

◇ *Misleading words.* This phrase covers words which still mean something today but meant something different to Shakespeare. This list includes *conscience* (where in *Hamlet* 3.1.84 the word means "consciousness" rather than "sense of guilt"), *constant* (where in *King Lear* 1.1.42 it means "firm" rather than "uninterrupted"), *humour* (not something that's funny but a term related to renaissance physiology), *marry* (a corruption of the name of the Virgin Mary, and not a verb meaning to wed), *obsequious* (in the sense of showing respect for the dead as well as being generally obedient), *prefer* (where in *King Lear* 1.1.278 it means "recommend" not "like more"), and *presently* ("instantly," not as it means to us today: "soon").

◇ *Neologisms.* These are words which were first coined by Shakespeare, or words the meaning of which he subtly changed. This list includes *herblet* (or a little herb), *hobbyhorse* (in *Love's Labor's Lost* 3.1.30, the word means a prostitute), *oar* (to row), *revokement* (revocation), *exsufflicate* (inflated), *fair play* (which means exactly what the modern phrase denotes), *filthy* (in the sense of "murky" or "thick"), *forthright* (a noun meaning a straight path), *machine* (the body), and *pedant* (my personal favorite: in *Twelfth Night* 3.2.83, it means "teacher").

◇ *Unexplainable words.* These are words which scholars have not been able to define. The list includes *winnowed* (*Hamlet* 5.2.201, where the sense seems to mean "wise" but the metaphor is unclear), and *Lipsbury pinfold* (*Hamlet* 2.2.9, where the idea that it means "between the teeth," as some editors have suggested, seems far-fetched).

Advice

So much for the fascinating ways in which Shakespeare uses language subtly to render his depiction of reality. What is the contemporary student to do when faced with so varied a vocabulary? Here are several suggestions:

◇ Read the difficult or unusual words aloud. Shakespeare sometimes chooses a word rather than its synonym based primarily on its sound.

◇ Make a note of the words which Shakespeare uses in a different sense from the way we do, *and* write down an explanation of why, based on the etymology (or origin) of the word. *Modern*, for example, means "ordinary" for Shakespeare because the word ultimately derives from the Latin word *modus*, which means "a measure." So, *modern* can mean something which can be measured, something which is "ordinary." By contrast, the word *modern* for us has taken on the meaning of a related Latin word *modo*, which means "just now."

◇ Don't panic. If the experts don't know what an obscure phrase means, such as Edgar's "Turlygod" (*King Lear* 2.3.20) or the Fool's "Whoop, Jug! I love thee" (*King Lear* 1.4.222), why worry? It would be nice to figure it out, but you can understand the play without doing so.

◇ Enjoy newness. There are over 500,000 words in English. Most people operate with a 5000-word working vocabulary at best. Why not *add* to that list?

◇ Surprise your friends with a neologism or two at your next party. Call someone "nook-shotten" or "superserviceable." Tell someone to "sneck up." See what reaction you get.

◇ Make a note of the phrases that Shakespeare came up with or popularized. The list is an impressive one. You may not use the phrase "action-taking," but "lily-livered" (*King Lear* 2.2.17)? Doesn't that sound familiar? What about "blinking idiot"? That actually appears in *The Merchant of Venice* 2.9.54.

◇ Above all, have fun with his language. Shakespeare clearly did. Anyone who can invent Falstaff, a comic genius with words, thought language was a wonderful invention. Falstaff, you may remember, is one of only two characters to appear in *four* Shakespeare plays: *I Henry IV, 2 Henry IV, Henry V,* and *The Merry Wives of Windsor.* Admittedly, Falstaff's only *mentioned* in *Henry V,* but that's because the Oldcastle family was so upset at his popularity as a dramatic character that it sued to keep him out of the play. *The Merry Wives of Windsor* is, however, in all likelihood a play commissioned by Queen Elizabeth because she wanted Falstaff to appear on stage once again. Put simply, Falstaff is Shakespeare's favorite character because of his genius with words.

Rearranging Word Order

Students often find Shakespeare's syntax, the structure of his sentences, difficult. It's not hard to see why. The standard pattern of a sentence in English is often referred to as SVO: subject—verb—object. At it simplest, this type of sentence could read: "He hit the ball." "He" is the subject (the person performing the action); "hit" is the verb (the word describing the action); "the ball" (the object, which has the action performed on it). The first sentence in this paragraph is an SVO sentence: "Students" (subject); "find" (verb); "syntax" (object). Everything else in that first sentence simply modifies or further describes the meaning of the verb (the adverb "difficult" describes something about "find") or the object (the noun phrase "the structure of his sentences" explains what "syntax" means). So much for the essential grammar lesson.

There are several points to realize about Shakespeare's use of syntax:

1. Shakespeare uses the SVO order very frequently. In other words, most of his sentences are straightforward. If we look once again at the first scene in *King Lear,* such sentences abound. Here are just a few:
   ◇ "I cannot conceive you" (12)
   ◇ "I find she names my very deed of love" (71)
   ◇ You have begot me, bred me, loved me" (98)
   ◇ "Here I disclaim all my paternal care" (113)
   ◇ "I know no answer" (204)
   ◇ "Time shall unfold what plighted cunning hides" (284).

2. Shakespeare also uses several other sequences in the same scene (and, indeed, throughout his plays):

◇ VOS: "Attend the lords of France and Burgundy, Gloucester" (34)
◇ SOV: "That we our largest bounty may extend" (52)
◇ VS: "But goes thy heart with this?" (105)
◇ VSO: "So be my grave my peace" (125)
◇ OSV: "My life I never held but as a pawn" (156).

Indeed, the only permutation missing from the scene is OVS, and that occurs in *King Lear* 3.4.89–90: "Wine loved I/deeply."

3. Shakespeare delights in delaying the appearance of the important part of the sentence. Even when he does have a straightforward SVO sequence, he may begin with something else. Take, for example, the sentence, from the first scene in *King Lear*, in which Lear grants Goneril one-third of his kingdom:

> Of all these bounds, even from this line to this,
> With shadowy forests and with champains riched,
> With plenteous rivers and wide-skirted meads,
> We make thee lady (63–66).

On the face of it, the sentence looks really strange; in fact, it's a very common SVO sequence ("We make thee lady") preceded by three prepositional phrases ("Of all these bounds," "With shadowy forests and with champains riched," and "With plenteous rivers and wide-skirted meads") and one adjectival phrase ("even from this line to this").

4. Shakespeare loves to vary not only the order of the words in his sentences but also their length. On the one hand in this first scene of *King Lear*, he can write a short line that contains three separate sentences: "Nothing. I have sworn. I am firm" (1.1.249). On the other, in that same scene he can construct sentences that run to half a dozen lines or more: 1.1.48–53, 70–76, 109–16, and 221–26. Indeed, one by Cordelia runs to eleven lines: 1.1.227–37.

5. Shakespeare interrupts his sentences to achieve an appearance of casual conversation. In *The Merchant of Venice*, for instance, Tubal and Shylock are discussing Antonio's business as a sort of import-export merchant. Their conversation goes as follows:

TUBAL	Yes, other men have ill luck too. Antonio, as I heard in Genoa—
SHYLOCK	What, what, what? Ill luck, ill luck?
TUBAL	hath an argosy cast away, coming from Tripolis.

(3.1.93–95)

The exchange makes no sense (in fact, it even looks typographically odd) unless you see Shylock's interruption of Tubal as showing his intense wish that Antonio's merchant ships sink. If they sink, then Antonio will be unable to repay Shylock what he owes him (3,000 ducats), and under the terms of their agreement Shylock will be able to cut a pound of flesh from the region closest to Antonio's heart. Given Shylock's vengeful nature, no wonder he is eager to hear of Antonio's "ill luck."

6. Shakespeare matches the syntax to the emotional state of the speaker. At the end of Act I of *Hamlet*, Hamlet makes his friends swear not to reveal to anyone that he will pretend to be mad in order to buy himself time to decide how to avenge his murdered father. Hamlet is, however, so distraught by his recent conversation with his father's ghost that, despite all his learning and intellect, he can't construct correctly a complex sentence. See what he says to Horatio and Marcellus:

> But come;
> Here, as before, never, so help you mercy,
> How strange or odd soe'er I bear myself—
> As I perchance hereafter shall think meet   180
> To put an antic disposition on—
> That you, at such times seeing me, never shall,
> With arms encumbered thus, or this headshake,
> Or by pronouncing of some doubtful phrase
> As "Well, we know," or "We could, an if we would,"   185
> Or "If we list to speak," or "There be, an if they might,"
> Or such ambiguous giving out, to note
> That you know aught of me—this do swear,
> So grace and mercy at your most need help you
> (1.5.177–89).

The general sense is clear, but three characteristics of the speech betray Hamlet's terrible uneasiness: all the dashes; the absence of any word preceding "That" (182) which can be related to it; and the incomplete verb "shall" (182) linked incorrectly to the infinitive "to note" (187). It's wonderful, I think, that Shakespeare matches language to speaker in such a way.

7. Shakespeare uses syntax as a weapon, or to be more accurate, he has his characters do so. There's a wonderful example of political double-speak in *Richard III*. Let me give you a little context. Richard and his henchman Buckingham have just killed Hastings because he was a threat to them. They need to cover up the crime and also wish to get the Mayor of London to persuade the people of the city to support Richard's attempt to become king. How to accomplish both goals? Waffle them to death seems to be Buckingham's approach, and it works wonderfully. In 3.5.50–61, Buckingham speaks with the Mayor as follows:

> I never looked for better at his [Hastings'] hands   50
> After he once fell in with Mistress Shore.
> Yet had we not determined he should die
> Until your lordship came to see his end,
> Which now the loving haste of these our friends,
> Something against our meanings, have prevented;   55
> Because, my lord, we would have had you heard
> The traitor speak and timorously confess
> The manner and the purpose of his treasons,
> That you might well have signified the same
> Unto the citizens, who haply may   60
> Misconster us in him and wail his death.

He begins by damning the murdered Hastings for treachery (50–51) and then moves on to assert that both he and Richard wanted Hastings to live so that the Mayor could hear him confess his treason (52–53, 56–58) and persuade the people that Hastings deserved to die (59–60). Yet, the wonderful complexity of Buckingham's speech means that the Mayor can understand the gist of what he says but be unable to question him closely. One can imagine the Mayor thinking, "Say what?" The complexity of the speech is important because Buckingham's explanation wouldn't make sense if too closely examined. Who, for example, are "these our friends" to whom Buckingham alludes, and why does Buckingham think the common people will blame him and Richard for Hastings' murder? Isn't it a guilty conscience speaking? Shakespeare's audience would not have fully understood what Buckingham is saying, nor would a modern audience. That is precisely Shakespeare's intent. He needs to convey a general impression and not specific information. As a contemporary reader, can't you think of politicians whose sole intent seems to be to avoid a direct answer, to confuse rather than to clarify?

8. Shakespeare was very self-conscious about syntax. In *Twelfth Night*, Feste (Olivia's Fool or jester) remarks to Viola that "A sentence is/but a cheveril [kidskin] glove to a good wit. How quickly the/wrong side may be turned outward" (3.1.11–13). Surely that comment stands for Shakespeare's own attitude to the sentences he wrote, for their variety is extraordinary.

Faced with such an array of different sorts of sentences, the reader may well ask the simplest question of them all, "Why?" Why does Shakespeare offer such varied syntax? I think there are three principal reasons. Knowing them may help to decrease your perplexity, for it often helps in the understanding of meaning to understand a writer's intent.

1. Shakespeare realized that the attention of his audience depended on change. If a play of, say, 3500 lines in length and 3 hours duration were

written in essentially the same form, the audience would become catatonic. So, Shakespeare was always changing word order in minor ways
to keep his audience alert and involved.

2. Shakespeare wanted to create a drama that would move an audience
emotionally. One way to do that is to pay attention to the sounds of
words. Clearly the response to language is highly subjective, but it does
seem to me (and to all those who love Shakespeare's works) that the
beauty and subtlety of the plays lie in large measure in the playwright's
exquisite handling of language. Part of that handling involves word
order. Let's briefly return to the opening scene of *King Lear* for an
instance of what I mean. Just after disinheriting Cordelia, Lear turns to
his two sons-in-law (Cornwall and Albany) to explain the terms of the
agreement by means of which they have gained control of England. Lear
explains what he wants in return for such generosity:

> Only we shall retain
> The name and all th' addition to a king.
> The sway, revenue, execution of the rest,
> Belovèd sons, be yours, which to confirm,
> This coronet part between you (135–39).

The first sentence is fine. The second inverts the expected order in two
key places. You would expect the second sentence to read:

> The sway, revenue, execution of the rest,
> Be yours, belovèd sons, which to confirm,
> Part this coronet between you.

It doesn't read that way for one reason: Shakespeare wants to intensify
the impact of Lear's foolishness on the audience. He does so by throwing to the beginning of their respective lines two phrases of great significance: "Belovèd sons" and "This coronet." The first phrase shows
Lear's pettiness, for Lear wants to hurt the feelings of his favorite daughter, Cordelia. His two sons-*in-law* are now more precious to him than a
daughter of his own blood. The second phrase shows the audience what
is at stake: Nothing less than the crown itself. It also foreshadows for
the audience what will happen in the play: There will be civil war over
who should rule the kingdom. After all, one cannot literally divide a
crown in two without destroying it.

3. Shakespeare wanted to create a language that would mirror the complicated way in which people think. His syntax with all its inversions
reflects exactly the way in which people think and speak *especially when
under stress*. We would like to think that we are all wonderfully logical in

our thinking and impressively articulate in our speech. The reality is that we all tack back and forth around an idea until our audience understands it. In just the same way do Shakespeare's characters speak.

I'll emphasize this last point by analyzing one of the most syntactically complicated passages in all of Shakespeare: Henry V's speech shortly before the battle of Agincourt begins. On the one hand, Henry V wants to have God on his side to help his soldiers defeat the French; on the other, he wants God to forget the fact that his father, Henry IV, usurped the throne from the rightful king, Richard II. His anguished speech goes thus:

> O God of battles, steel my soldiers' hearts;
> Possess them not with fear! Take from them now
> The sense of reckoning, ere th' opposèd numbers
> Pluck their hearts from them. Not today, O Lord, 290
> O, not today, think not upon the fault
> My father made in compassing the crown!
> I Richard's body have interrèd new,
> And on it have bestowed more contrite tears
> Than from it issued forcèd drops of blood. 295
> Five hundred poor I have in yearly pay
> Who twice a day their withered hands hold up
> Toward heaven, to pardon blood; and I have built
> Two chantries, where the sad and solemn priests
> Sing still for Richard's soul. More will I do; 300
> Though all that I can do is nothing worth,
> Since that my penitence comes after all,
> Imploring pardon (*Henry V* 4.1.287–303).

The first three-and-a-half lines (287–90) go fine. They are *almost* regular SVO sentences. (To be completely regular, the second sentence should read: "Take the sense of reckoning from them now.") Then, faced with having to ask God to ignore his father's sinful usurpation of the crown, Henry V's language breaks down into the illogical repetition of "not's" followed by several OSV, OVS, SOV, and VS sentences. To show you what I mean, here are lines 293 to 303 rewritten in standard SOV order:

> I have interrèd Richard's body new,
> And have bestowed more contrite tears on it
> Than forcèd drops of blood issued from it. 295
> I have five hundred poor in yearly pay
> Who twice a day hold up their withered hands
> Toward heaven, to pardon blood; and I have built

Two chantries, where the sad and solemn priests
Still sing for Richard's soul. More I will do;   300
Though all that I can do is worth nothing,
Since that my penitence imploring pardon comes
After all.

All that can be said after reading Shakespeare's original and the "corrected" passage is "Thank God for syntactical inversion."

Advice

So faced with Shakespeare's virtuosity when it comes to syntax, what is a contemporary reader or viewer to do? Let me offer the following ideas:

◇ Always look for the main statement in any given sentence that is giving you difficulties. It may be delayed; it may be inverted; it will be there. Once you have found that, everything else falls into place.

◇ Read aloud particularly troublesome sentences. Shakespeare meant his words to be spoken to an audience rather than read silently, so sometimes simply reading them to an audience (even if that audience is only yourself) helps to clarify his meaning.

◇ Remember that Shakespeare never inverts syntax without reason. Often he wants to start a particular line with an important phrase or to have the words reflect the psychological state of the speaker. So, to understand a particular line in the play you need to be actively engaged in thinking about what has happened thus far in the action and how characters might be expected to react. You need to be sensitive to subtext.

◇ Remember that Shakespeare likes to play with language, so you need to remain flexible in your own ideas about word order.

◇ Pay careful attention to punctuation. Commas mean that one idea that is related to the next one in the same sentence has finished. Periods mean the end of a whole idea. Question marks mean that even in modern English you can expect some degree of inversion.

Verse and Prose

Once you have come to terms with the peculiarities of Shakespeare's language and the complexity of his sentences, you'll likely notice how his plays seem to consist of three sorts of language. There is prose, the sort of writing that you do in essays. It has no set rhythm, but each new line begins at the left margin. Then, there is poetry that doesn't rhyme but begins each line with a capital letter. This is called blank verse (unrhymed and nearly always in that rhythm called iambic pentameter). Finally, there is rhymed poetry, most of which is also written in iambic pentameter. It is impossible to explain entirely why Shakespeare uses prose at some points, blank verse at others, and end-rhymed poetry at still others. The following guidelines will, however, cover most of the cases you'll encounter:

◇ Prose is more colloquial. It is used to convey madness (Ophelia in *Hamlet* and Lady Macbeth in *Macbeth*) or drunkenness (Lepidus in *Antony and Cleopatra*). It is used to differentiate subplots from the main plots: the Edmund-Gloucester subplot in *King Lear*, for example, is largely in prose; the main plot, involving Lear and his daughters, is largely in poetry. Prose is spoken by the lower classes. It is used extensively in humorous scenes. It is the language of crude sexual jokes. It is *always* the form in which the many letters in Shakespeare's plays are written.

◇ Unrhymed poetry (blank verse) is more refined than prose. It is spoken by the upper class. It is used extensively in court scenes and when discussing serious issues. It is a form which Shakespeare could use very self-consciously. In *As You Like It*, for example, Jaques threatens to leave if Orlando doesn't stop speaking in blank verse:

ORLANDO   Good day and happiness, dear Rosalind!
JAQUES   Nay, then, God b' wi' you, an you talk in blank verse
                                                              (4.1.28–29).

◇ End-rhymed poetry is used in the form of a rhyming couplet (or pair of lines) to conclude scenes. It is used in songs and riddles. Sometimes, the single rhyming couplet becomes a pair of couplets (as in *The Merchant of Venice* 2.5.55–58). Sometimes, the rhyme can become very intricate (as in *The Merchant of Venice* 5.1.193–202, where nine out of the ten lines end with one word, "ring"). Sometimes, the rhyme can be deliberately bad (as in *As You Like It* 3.2.86–93, 99–110, where Touchstone competes with Orlando and Rosalind in the renaissance version of a poetry slam). Another proof, if one were needed, that Shakespeare loves language.

◇ When someone from the upper class talks with someone from the lower class, both usually speak in prose unless the play is one written entirely in poetry. Sometimes it can take a while for one character to adjust to the speech of the other. In *Macbeth*, for instance, Macduff begins by speaking blank verse to the Porter at 2.3.21–22. After the Porter's initial response, he switches to prose at 2.3.25.

There are some other characteristics of Shakespeare's handling of poetry and prose that might be helpful to you:

◇ Speeches in poetry sometimes share lines, so one speech ends with a partial line which is then completed by the next speech. In *Antony and Cleopatra* (4.4.3–7), for instance, there is this exchange between the two lovers as Cleopatra tries to assist Eros as he helps Antony into his armor:

ANTONY   Come, good fellow [Eros], put thine iron on.
                If fortune be not ours today, it is
                Because we brave her. Come
CLEOPATRA   Nay, I'll help too.
                What's this for?   *[She helps to arm him.]*
ANTONY   Ah, let be, let be! Thou art
                The armorer of my heart. False, false; this, this.

Cleopatra here responds to Antony's speech but keeps the line within the iambic pentameter requirement of ten syllables. In his turn, Antony does the same for Cleopatra's question: "What's this for?" Later, in the next scene (4.5.11), it takes three characters (Eros, Antony, and a Soldier) to complete an eleven-syllable line about what has happened to Enobarbus, Antony's faithful follower:

EROS   Sir, his chests and treasure
            He has not with him.
ANTONY   Is he gone?
SOLDIER   Most certain.

In *Richard III*, the collaboration is even greater at 1.3.234 where Richard and Queen Margaret exchange comments twice within one line and still keep the count at ten syllables:

RICHARD   Margaret.
QUEEN MARGARET   Richard!
RICHARD   Ha?
QUEEN MARGARET   I call thee not.

◇ Sometimes prose is used to highlight a particular idea or moment. In *The Merchant of Venice* 1.1.114–18, for example, Bassanio suddenly lapses into prose in a scene which is otherwise entirely in poetry. Why? Because he is poking fun at the long-windedness of a friend, Gratiano. In *Macbeth* 1.2, the Scottish king, Duncan, inserts a prose question (at line 34) between the very poetic speeches of a Captain who is reporting the battlefield exploits of Macbeth? Why? Because Shakespeare wants the description of Macbeth's bravery to stand out.

◇ Shakespeare wrote some plays entirely in poetry (blank verse and rhyme only, no prose): *King John* and *Richard II*. He wrote some plays with a great deal of blank verse but little end rhyme: *Titus Andronicus*, for instance, has 93 percent of its lines written in blank verse, but only five percent of that verse rhymes. He wrote some plays with a great deal of end-rhymed poetry: *A Midsummer Night's Dream*, for example, has 37 percent of its lines written in rhyme; *Love's Labor's Lost*, a remarkable 41 percent. He wrote some plays with a great deal of prose in them: *Twelfth Night*, for example, has 65 percent of its lines written in prose; *The Merry Wives of Windsor*, a remarkable 88 percent. Shakespeare clearly liked to experiment with language.

◇ Shakespeare's later plays have more prose in them than do his earlier plays. His first ten plays (from *3 Henry VI* to *Romeo and Juliet*) average about 370 lines of prose per play; his last ten (from *Measure for Measure* to *The Tempest*) average about 625 lines of prose.

So much for the guidelines and characteristics. They are useful, but should not be applied too faithfully. As always with Shakespeare, what matters are the particular circumstances in which the language occurs. Let's look briefly at the verse and prose issue in all its complexity; let's look at *Antony and Cleopatra* 2.7, the scene in which the Triumvirate celebrate their agreement with Sextus Pompeius (also known simply as Pompey).

The scene comprises 136 lines. Lines 1–16, 24–36, 42–53, 57, and 90–92 are in prose; lines 115–20 are in end-rhymed poetry; the rest is in blank verse. The explanation for the frequent switching among the three forms of language (eleven times in quite a short scene) is a complex one. The scene begins in prose because the first sixteen lines consist of a conversation between two servants. (Remember, it's prose for the lower classes and poetry for those with power.) It shifts to poetry when Antony enters with the two other members of the Triumvirate (Octavius Caesar and Lepidus) after a ceremonial trumpet call. We seem to be in the middle of a conversation between Antony and Lepidus, one in which Antony delivers a grandiose speech about the Nile.

The scene then returns to prose because the conversation begins to include Lepidus, who has no head for drink. (Remember prose is the language of drunkenness.) It shifts back to blank verse in the conversations between Menas and Pompey, presumably because the latter is determined to *sound* as impressive and important as the members of the Triumvirate and because the content of their conversations involves something of great significance: Menas's plan to murder the entire Triumvirate. Their conversation takes up the middle part of the scene (until line 90). It is followed immediately by a brief prose conversation between Menas and Enobarbus, in which the latter comments on the removal from the boat of Lepidus stupefied with drink. (That's prose and drunkenness again.) This brief prose interlude is followed at line 93 by more blank verse, and the scene continues in that mode until the end with only one interruption, for a song in three end-rhymed couplets (AABBCC) by a boy accompanied by one chorus of all the partygoers.

Table 1.1

Percentages of Prose, Blank Verse, and Rhymed Verse in Shakespeare's Plays[a]

Plays	Prose	Blank Verse	Rhymed Verse	Plays	Prose	Blank Verse	Rhymed Verse
Comedies				3 Henry VI	0	95	4
The Comedy of Errors	14	65	21	King Henry VIII[b]	1	99	0
				Richard III	2	93	4
A Midsummer Night's Dream	22	34	37	2 Henry VI	17	79	3
The Taming of the Shrew	24	71	6	Henry V	43	44	2
				1 Henry IV	47	51	2
The Merchant of Venice	24	71	5	Henry IV	53	41	2
The Two Gentlemen of Verona	28	66	6	**Tragedies**			
				Titus Andronicus	2	93	5
Troilus and Cressida	34	59	7	Julius Caesar	7	92	1
Love's Labor's Lost	38	21	41	Macbeth	7	80	5
Measure for Measure	41	56	3	Antony and Cleopatra	9	89	1
All's Well That Ends Well	50	41	9	Romeo and Juliet	15	69	15
As You Like It	58	32	8	Othello	21	76	3
Twelfth Night	65	28	6	Coriolanus	24	75	1
Much Ado about Nothing	74	23	3	King Lear	28	67	5
				Timon of Athens	29	64	7
The Merry Wives of Windsor	88	7	1	Hamlet	31	62	3
Histories				**Romances**			
King John	0	95	5	The Two Noble Kinsmen[b]	5	93	2
Richard II	0	81	19	Cymbeline	16	78	4
1 Henry VI	0	88	12	The Tempest	21	70	3
				The Winter's Tale	28	68	2
				Pericles[b]	30	68	2

Note: The data in this table is adapted from Campbell and Quinn, page 932. The three columns sometimes do not add up to 100 percent because some of the lines belong in none of the three categories.

[a] The plays are organized in genres. Within genres they are organized in ascending order according to the percentage of prose each contains.

[b] These percentages are based only on the part of the play generally attributed to Shakespeare.

So far so good: it's possible to come up with an explanation for *almost* all the various changes from prose to poetry. What remains unclear to me is why the drinking bout that occupies the early part of the scene (24–53) is in prose while the bout towards the end (93–114), which mirrors it, is in blank verse. The answer can't be that in the first bout one character (Lepidus) is drunk while in the second no one is since Lepidus is carried off the boat after line 89. Octavius Caesar explicitly admits to being somewhat the worse for wear in the second drinking bout, yet he manages to speak perfect blank verse:

> It's monstrous labor when I wash my brain
> And it grows fouler (100–01).

Antony is drinking fast enough to get closer and closer to drink-induced oblivion, to "soft and delicate Lethe" (11), yet he speaks perfect blank verse too. So, if drunkenness is not the explanation for the difference, what else could be? One might argue that Shakespeare is using the social distinction between prose and poetry to undercut Lepidus's importance. The partygoers speak prose when they converse with him and poetry after he leaves because they think so little of him. That theory is attractive, but it doesn't account for the poetry Antony is speaking as he enters (17–23)—poetry which is addressed directly to Lepidus. The answer is surely that despite all the guidelines governing when Shakespeare uses poetry and prose, the simple fact is that on quite a few occasions Shakespeare is idiosyncratic. It's useful to remember, after all, that he didn't make the guidelines; they are a scholarly construct created after the event. He didn't sit down and say, "Well, according to my rule book I ought to use poetry here." He can choose to write either poetry or prose according to taste, *his* taste. That is a sobering truth for those who wish to understand Shakespeare's achievement as dramatic poet.

Writing and Discussion Assignments

1. Choose any one speech with which you have difficulty from Shakespeare's plays. List the words that are unknown to you, and devise a strategy for coming to terms with such unknown words. (Isabella's speech in *Measure for Measure* 2.2.115–28 would work well for this exercise.)
2. Choose any one speech that you particularly enjoy from a Shakespeare play, and analyze it for its syntax. When Shakespeare departs from the normal SVO word order, what is he trying to do in each case? (Hermione's speech in *The Winter's Tale* 3.2.91–116 would work well for this exercise.)
3. Examine any single scene from Shakespeare's plays for its use of "you" and "thou." Based solely on such use, explain the relation among the characters in the scene. (*Henry IV 1* 2.3 would work well for this exercise.)

4. Examine any single scene in Shakespeare's plays for its use of verse (blank or rhymed) and prose. Work out an explanation for why the scene alternates as it does between the two (or three) types of dramatic language. (*Much Ado about Nothing* 2.3 would work well for this exercise.)

Further Reading

Brook, G. L. *The Language of Shakespeare*. London: Andre Deutsch, 1976.

Doran, Madeleine. *Shakespeare's Dramatic Language*. Madison: The U of Wisconsin P, 1976.

Houston, John Porter. *Shakespearean Sentences: A Study in Style and Syntax*. Baton Rouge: Louisiana State UP, 1988.

Hussey, S. S. *The Literary Language of Shakespeare*. London: Longman, 1982.

Joseph, Sister Miriam. *Shakespeare's Use of the Arts of Language*. New York: Hafner, 1966.

Kermode, Frank. *Shakespeare's Language*. New York: Farrar, Straus, Giroux, 2000.

Robinson, Randal. *Unlocking Shakespeare's Language: Help for the Teacher and Student*. Urbana, IL: ERIC Clearinghouse on Reading and Communication Skills and NCTE, 1989.

Vickers, Brian. *The Artistry of Shakespeare's Prose*. London: Methuen, 1968.

Chapter 2

Erect his statue and worship it,
And make my image but an alehouse
sign

2 Henry VI 3.2.80–81

Shakespeare's Imagery

Chapter Overview

◇ Defining the two kinds of imagery: literal and figurative.
◇ Distinguishing among the five literal appeals to the senses.
◇ Understanding the 14 major devices at work in figurative language (from *analogy* to *synecdoche*).

Scholars have devoted more time to studying Shakespeare's imagery than any other single topic in his plays. Rather than summarize their ideas here, I'll simply outline the major characteristics of his imagery and examine a famous speech that illustrates that imagery's tremendous power. Then, I'll suggest how you can read Shakespeare's language in such a way as to become sensitive to that power. The result of such sensitivity will be greater understanding, greater pleasure, greater appreciation.

A Definition of Imagery

Imagery consists of two qualities inherent in all language but most frequently found in poetry and in dramatic language. The first comprises literal statements which appeal to any or all of the five senses: sight, hearing, touch, taste, and smell. The second comprises figurative language, nonliteral statements which ask us to see something in some new or unusual ways. I'll clarify with a straightforward example. Imagine that you are drinking a cup of coffee. You say: "I like this cup of coffee. It has a deep brown color; it tastes rich; it smells delightful. I like the warm feel of the cup against my cold hands. I even like the sound of the espresso machine as it whips the milk into a froth." You've just used the first type of imagery by successively appealing to the senses of sight, taste, smell, touch, and hearing. Imagine, now, that you say to a loved one: "You're the cream in my coffee." You don't mean that literally but figuratively. You don't mean that the one you love is made of a particular part of milk; you mean something like, "You're special; you make my life richer and sweeter." At any event, you've used a metaphor, a type of figurative language where you see an identity between two different objects or ideas. A = B, or "my loved one" = "the cream in my coffee."

The important point to realize is that appeals to the five senses are everywhere in things we say; we use figurative language all the time. When we say someone is "a pig," we don't mean that person is literally an animal. We mean that the person is so slovenly that he or she reminds us of a pig. If we call someone "hot," we don't mean that he or she is literally overheated. We mean that we get aroused thinking about that person. When you "cram" for finals, the metaphor is of pushing information into the brain until it can hold no more.

There is nothing remarkable about imagery in general, then. We use it every day and don't give it a second thought. There are, however, a couple of things quite remarkable about *Shakespeare's* use of imagery. First, his language is so powerful and dense in its appeal to the senses. Second, his language is remarkable for its sustained insistence that readers of, or spectators at, his plays see the world around them in figurative terms. He wants to convey as much as possible in as few words as he can, and he wants us to see the world afresh, to see it stripped of its thick coating of habit and expectation.

Literal Appeals to the Senses

Let's look first at some examples of literal appeals to the five senses and then at the various sorts of figurative language Shakespeare uses. For the sake of continuity and clarity, the great majority of the examples will be drawn from one famous Shakespeare play, which we have not looked at much in this book until now: *Macbeth*.

First, the literal appeals:

Appeal to the Sense of Sight

When Macbeth shouts at Banquo's ghost: "Never shake/Thy gory locks at me" (3.4.50–51), we see a ghost with bloody, matted hair.

Appeal to the Sense of Hearing

When Lady Macbeth says, after her husband murders Duncan: "I heard the owl scream and the crickets cry" (2.2.16), we hear them too in our minds.

Appeal to the Sense of Touch

When Macbeth shouts at Banquo's ghost: "thy blood is cold" (3.4.95), we feel that sensation.

Appeal to the Sense of Taste

When Macbeth toasts his guests at the banquet, "I drink to the general joy o' th' whole table" (3.4.90), our taste buds are aroused.

Appeal to the Sense of Smell

When Lady Macbeth in her madness tries to remove the stain of her guilt for Duncan's murder by washing off Duncan's nonexistent blood from her hands, she grotesquely complains: "Here's the smell of the blood still" (5.1.49). We smell that blood too.

Figurative Language

Now, let's look at figurative language. I've arranged the discussion in an alphabetical sequence of fourteen key devices.

Figurative Language
14 Key Terms

Analogy	Litotes	Pun
Hyperbole	Metaphor	Simile
Image Strands	Metonymy	Symbol and its
Irony and its four	Onomatopoeia	two variants
variants (cosmic,	Oxymoron	(public and private)
dramatic, structural,	Personification	Synecdoche
and verbal)		

Analogy.   The description (usually developed at some length) of an idea by comparing it with other ideas which are more familiar. The distinction between an analogy and a simile is that in an analogy the framework of the comparison is emphasized.

Example: In *As You Like It,* Jaques compares the life of the individual to that of an actor playing many roles. He continues the analogy by describing the cycle of life to the act and scene divisions in a play:

> All the world's a stage,
> And all the men and women merely players.

They have their exits and their entrances,
And one man in his time plays many parts,
His acts being seven ages. At first the infant,
Mewling and puking in the nurse's arms.
Then the whining schoolboy, with his satchel
And shining morning face, creeping like snail
Unwillingly to school. And then the lover,
Sighing like furnace, with a woeful ballad
Made to his mistress' eyebrow. Then a soldier,
Full of strange oaths and bearded like the pard,
Jealous in honor, sudden, and quick in quarrel,
Seeking the bubble reputation
Even in the cannon's mouth. And then the justice
In fair round belly with good capon lined,
With eyes severe and beard of formal cut,
Full of wise saws and modern instances;
And so he plays his part. The sixth age shifts
Into the lean and slippered pantaloon,
With spectacles on nose and pouch on side,
His youthful hose, well saved, a world too wide
For his shrunk shank; and his big manly voice,
Turning again toward childish treble, pipes
And whistles in his sound. Last scene of all,
That ends this strange, eventful history,
Is second childishness and mere oblivion,
Sans teeth, sans eyes, sans taste, sans everything
                                    (2.7.138–65).

Commentary: In the speech, note the directness of the comparison and the obviousness of the organization. These qualities are characteristic of analogy in contrast to simile. Analogy, too, compares things that are essentially alike; simile things that are essentially different. So, for instance, if Jaques had compared human existence to a bowl of cherries or a leaky faucet, then he would have been using a simile.

Hyperbole (pronounced hy-**per**-bo-lee). An exaggeration for the sake of effect. It is not meant to be taken literally. Sometimes we say: "I don't understand a word you just said." That's rarely if ever true (as long as the person is speaking in our own language); we simply say it to point out that there was something wrong with the way an idea was expressed.
    Example: When Macbeth says to his wife:

> I am in blood
> Stepped in so far that, should I wade no more,
> Returning were as tedious as go oe'r (3.4.137–39),

he has himself murdered Duncan and his two guards as well as having had three murderers kill Banquo. Nonetheless, he has not killed so many men that he would have to *wade* through their blood as one would wade through a stream. The blood would have to be up to his knees or higher for him to have to do that.

Commentary: In fact, Macbeth is exaggerating in an effort to steel himself for more murder. The purpose of the hyperbole is, then, in part to characterize Macbeth's thinking at a particular moment. More generally, the value of hyperbole lies in its shock effect: exaggeration forces us to pay attention.

Image Strands. The image (or series of images) which dominate a play. The term *strand* is a useful one because it suggests that just as a strand of fabric can be seen throughout a piece of cloth, so an image strand occurs throughout a play.

Example: In *Macbeth,* as Caroline Spurgeon points out in her *Shakespeare's Imagery,* four image strands dominate: ill-fitting clothes, echoing sounds, images of light and dark, and sin as disease. When, for example, Macbeth is greeted by Ross as Thane of Cawdor (a title bestowed on Macbeth in his absence after the earlier Cawdor had been executed for treason), Macbeth replies: "The Thane of Cawdor lives. Why do you dress me/In borrowed robes?" (1.3.108–09). And when Banquo sees Macbeth talking to himself about the Witches' prophecy, he comments to Ross and Angus: "New honors come upon him,/Like our strange garments, cleave not to their mold/But with the aid of use" (1.3.146–48; see also 1.7.33–37; 2.4.37–38; 5.2.15–16; and 5.2.20–22).

Commentary: The purpose of image strands is to reinforce the major themes in a play and to comment on the action. So, in *Macbeth,* the ill-fitting clothes and the echoing sounds show the unsuitability of Macbeth for kingship; the contrasting images of light and dark show the struggle for the moral heart of Scotland; and the idea of sin as disease emphasizes the corrupting effect of Macbeth's usurpation of the crown.

Irony. A broad and sometimes overused term which comes in several varieties. What all examples of irony share is the realization of a significant gap between appearance and reality.

There are four main types of irony: **cosmic, dramatic, structural,** and **verbal.**

1. **Cosmic irony** reveals human beings to be at the mercy of a cruel fate.

   Cosmic irony occurs in *Macbeth* when Macbeth decides to make sure the Witches' prophecy that he will become king comes true. He becomes king, and is then assured by the Witches that no one will overthrow him unless two seemingly impossible events occur: Birnam Wood moves to Dunsinane, and someone *not* born of a woman harms him. It turns out, of course, that both events do occur. Malcolm (the rightful heir to the Scottish throne) has his soldiers disguise their numbers by chopping down boughs from the trees in Birnam Wood to hide behind as they move. Macduff, who kills Macbeth, was—when a baby—not delivered normally through the uterus but, rather, by Caesarian section. In a sense, then, Macduff was not "born of woman" (5.3.4). And so, Macbeth is tricked by a malign fate.

2. **Dramatic irony** creates tension by emphasizing the gap in knowledge between the audience and some or all of the characters on stage. The audience sees all the action on the stage; the characters are aware of only part.

   Dramatic irony, as you might expect, is the commonest form of irony in Shakespeare's plays. There are at least half a dozen examples in *Macbeth*. One of the best is when a messenger announces to Lady Macbeth that Duncan will visit Macbeth's castle to honor him for his bravery in defeating the Scottish rebels. The messenger says simply: "The King comes here tonight" (1.5.31). He means Duncan, but the audience (which has witnessed the Witches' prophesying Macbeth will be king) knows that Shakespeare means Macbeth as well as Duncan by the title "King."

3. **Structural irony** occurs when a *central* character in a work has a naïve view of the world that runs counter to the experiences of the other characters and the audience or reader.

   Structural irony does not (perhaps, cannot) occur in so pessimistic a play as *Macbeth*, where all the characters inhabit a world turned upside down by the destructive ambition of Macbeth. Only one character in the play is naïve, Macduff's young son. He does take part in a wonderful, brief exchange with his mother about the nature of innocence in a corrupt world, doing so shortly before both are murdered by Macbeth's hired killers. Yet, he is in no sense a *central* character in the play. He is not even important enough to be given a name.

   Hamlet, however, provides a good example of structural irony in the character of Ophelia. She draws much of her power from her naïveté in contrast to the cynicism of Claudius, the double-dealing of Polonius (her father), the machinations of Hamlet himself, and the worldliness of the audience or reader. There is tremendous power in the simplicity of Ophelia's typical response to a situation that is too complicated for her to understand. "I do not know, my lord, what I should think," she says to her father when he asks her what she makes of Hamlet's declaration of love for her (1.3.105). Faced by Hamlet's apparent madness and her father's mysterious death, she can only say: "I hope all will be well" (4.5.69).

4. **Verbal irony** is a toned-down form of sarcasm in which someone says one thing but means another. It is this last form that is most commonly used outside the context of literature. If, for instance, you go to a really boring party and, then, say to a friend after you've left: "I had a wonderful time!" you're being ironic (and you're also hoping that your friend understands the gap you're pointing out between appearance and reality).

Verbal irony can be seen frequently in *Macbeth*. One of the most sophisticated examples is Macbeth's reaction to the First Murderer's appearance before him with Banquo's blood on his face. Macbeth says simply: "Banquo's safe?" (3.4.25). What the word *safe* should mean in *almost* any context is that Banquo is alive and well. What Macbeth, of course, means is that Banquo is dead and, so, he—Macbeth—is safe.

Commentary: The value of irony is considerable in any literary work but greater in drama than in any other **genre** (or category). Drama is built upon the acceptance of illusion, and irony of any sort forces the audience to focus on the illusion itself. So, the drama becomes more profound because it is seen on many levels: literal, representational, symbolic. Irony in drama also forces the audience or reader to think about the connection between what happens on stage and in real life. So, for example, anyone seeing what happens in *Macbeth* is forced through irony to think how the action applies to his or her own life. None of us will ever, of course, be a medieval Scottish king, but many of us will be faced with temptation in our lives. Will we, as Macbeth does, give way to temptation?

Litotes (pronounced li-toe-tees). This device is the flip side to *hyperbole*; it's a form of understatement which denies the contrary. If you think someone is stupid and say "He's not the brightest person I know," you're using litotes. If you finish a good meal and say—as you push your plate away—"That wasn't half bad!" you're using litotes again.

Examples: In *Macbeth*, when Macduff is told of the murder of his wife and children, he shows little outward grief but responds:

> I cannot but remember such things were,
> That were most precious to me. Did heaven look on
> And would not take their part? (4.3.224–26).

What he means, of course, is that he will always remember his loved ones and the failure of the gods to come to their aid. Another classic example of litotes is in *Richard III* when Richard responds to Buckingham's ill-timed request for the preferment he was promised: "I am not in the giving vein today" (4.2.118). Translation? You blew your chance to help me; you won't get anything out of me; in fact, you are no longer a friend of mine.

Commentary: The strength of litotes in drama is simply that it gives the playwright more than one emotional gear with which to work. Drama is so much a matter of declaration, declamation, and expression that sometimes quietness is an effective way of highlighting the state of mind of particular characters and of emphasizing the importance of particular statements. Think, for example, how effective quiet passages are in music, whether classical, jazz, or rock.

Metaphor (pronounced **met-uh-for**).   This figure of speech is the single most important and frequently used emotional weapon at the disposal of the writer. The writer describes one idea or object in terms of another so there is an identity between the two. If you say you are "dirt poor," you are saying that you are so poor that the only thing you have is something of no value: dirt. Your state of poverty is identical to dirt. If you say that someone has a mercurial temperament, you are saying that person's personality has the qualities of mercury: rapid change, fragmentation, sensitivity. Again, that person's temperament is identical to mercury.

Examples: In *Macbeth*, when Lady Macbeth calls memory "the warder of the brain" (1.7.66), she is saying that the memory looks after the other parts of the mind in the same way that a prison guard looks after a prisoner. In *Macbeth* again, when Macbeth greets the three Witches with the insult: "you secret, black, and midnight hags" (4.1.48), he is identifying them with three qualities: secrecy, blackness, and the traditional witching hour. However, they are not literally secret (he and Banquo see them and talk with them); they are not black (although they may be very dirty); and it isn't midnight. Since Macbeth meets them during the day, they must be creatures of night *and* day.

When a metaphor takes place over more than a line or is developed at some length, it is labeled an *extended metaphor*. In *Macbeth*, Duncan and Banquo talk together after the rebels have been successfully defeated, and develop the same metaphor at length. Duncan begins with an agricultural metaphor: "I have begun to plant thee, and will labor/To make thee full of growing" (1.4.28–29). To which Banquo responds: "There if I grow,/The harvest is your own" (32–33). Duncan replies in kind with a metaphor suggesting the irrigation of crops: "My plenteous joys,/Wanton in fullness, seek to hide themselves/In drops of sorrow" (33–35).

What is particularly remarkable about metaphors is that they often nest inside each other. So, although Duncan's final comment suggests irrigation, it includes within itself a metaphor for tears: "drops of sorrow." In no way are such multiple metaphors unusual in Shakespeare. Take, for example, Macbeth's touching wish that the doctor prescribe his wife something to cure her insanity: "Canst thou not minister to a mind diseased [?]" he asks (5.3.42). He then continues with a series of metaphors in the next five lines: gardening ("Pluck from the memory a rooted sorrow"); writing ("Raze out the written troubles of the brain"); and purification, clothing and measurement ("Cleanse the stuffed bosom of that perilous stuff/ Which weighs upon the heart"). He concludes two lines later with a canine metaphor: "Throw physic to the dogs!" (49).

Commentary: The critical importance of metaphor lies in the need to have the words of the play spark connections in the audience quickly and memorably. Metaphor does this so well because it condenses every idea it expresses, and it does so in a way that makes the audience or readers look beyond the words to worlds created in their own mind. Think of the difference, for example, between Macbeth saying "I don't trust medicine" and "Throw physic to the dogs!" The first weakly registers an opinion; the second lets you see a startling image: of dogs tearing at food. In just such a way would Macbeth like to destroy medicine. It only has the value of leftover food anyway, and it deserves to be torn into.

Metonymy (pronounced meh-**tonn**-uh-me). This device substitutes an emotionally associated object for an idea. For instance, when you take your spouse's hand in marriage you are taking a great deal more, but the hand is focused on because it wears the ring that signifies faithfulness and love. When you refer to the "Stars and Stripes," you are substituting an associated object, the flag of the United States, for feelings of patriotism. Metonymy differs from **synecdoche** in that synecdoche (which substitutes a part for the whole or the whole for a part) doesn't depend directly on an emotional association. In practice, however, the two terms are closely related and sometimes conflated.

Examples: In 3.1 when Macbeth recalls the Witches' first prophecy, he bridles at the fact that he will not be able to pass on the kingship to his descendants because the prophecy said that the royal line would descend from Fleance, Banquo's son: "Upon my head they placed a fruitless crown/And put a barren scepter in my grip" (62–63). Metonymically speaking, they made him king, but the gift is worthless to him. Later, Macbeth reflects on his murder of Duncan and lists several metonyms for Duncan's being beyond the strife that characterizes the life of kings: "nor steel, nor poison,/Malice domestic, foreign levy, nothing/Can touch him further" (3.2.26–28). Not all of these terms are metonyms, but "steel" is associated with the sword, and "poison" with death.

Commentary: As with metaphor, metonymy's value is that it involves the audience even more directly in the action. It makes it think not in abstractions or in generalities but in specifics that it knows, relates to, and as a result understands better.

Onomatopoeia (pronounced on-o-mat-o-**pea**-uh). This device matches the sound of the word as closely as possible to what is being described. Words such as "buzz," "tick-tock," "hiss," and "crash" are supposed to represent the very sounds they describe. In truth, the connection is less real than it is conventional or traditional.

Examples: In *Macbeth*, the Third Witch's cry "A drum, a drum!" is intended to reinforce the sound itself (1.3.30). Later, the First Witch imitates the sound of a cat with the word "mewed" and the Second Witch the sound of a hedgehog with the word "whined" (4.1.1, 2). Then in the same scene, all three Witches reinforce the sound of boiling liquid with the refrain: "Double, double, toil and trouble;/Fire burn, and cauldron bubble" (10–11).

Commentary: The purpose of onomatopoeia is to reinforce the mood of a particular scene. It can be a useful device for the playwright, who lives by words and, so, needs every trick to help convince the audience or readers that what is shown on stage or page is a powerful representation of events that could happen in real life—and to them as well.

Oxymoron (pronounced oxy-**more**-ron). This device yokes together two contradictory ideas. The origin of the word reveals its intent, for it derives from two Greek words which together mean "sharp-dull." We use oxymora all the time without thinking how odd the combined terms are: "bittersweet," "close acquaintance," "deafening silence," "jumbo shrimp," "liquid paper," "nasty nice," "usually always." Sometimes the terms can be used sarcastically, as in "airline food" and "network news."

Examples: In *Macbeth*, the protagonist defends his murder of Duncan's guards with a string of oxymora: "Who can be wise, amazed, temp'rate and furious,/Loyal and neutral, in a moment?" (2.3.110–11). In *Romeo and Juliet*, Shakespeare has fun with the oxymoron as Romeo lists several, doing so almost as a game:

> Why, then, O brawling love, O loving hate,
> O anything of nothing first create,
> O heavy lightness, serious vanity,
> Misshapen chaos of well-seeming forms,
> Feather of lead, bright smoke, cold fire, sick health,
> Still-waking sleep, that is not what it is! (1.1.176–81).

Commentary: The purpose of oxymora is to show as intensely as possible the confused state of the speaker or, sometimes, the reality behind the words themselves. As so often with figurative language, oxymora allow the playwright to achieve an essential economy by saying more than one thing at once.

Personification. This figure of speech treats animals, ideas, or inanimate objects as if they were human. If we believe our pets have highly developed powers of reasoning, if we ask for mercy from the legal system, if we think our computer crashes because it can smell fear, we are personifying them. Personification is, then, used almost every day as a means of coming to terms with the world.

Example: In *Macbeth,* when Macbeth prepares to murder Duncan he is so nervous that he begs the earth not to betray him and say what he has done:

> Thou sure and firm-set earth,
> Hear not my steps which way they walk, for fear
> The very stones prate of my whereabouts (2.1.57–59).

Pet rocks notwithstanding, stones cannot literally talk (or "prate").

Commentary: The contribution that personification makes to the world created by the writer is to give it life. So, Shakespeare peoples his stage with characters for whom the world is alive in unusual ways. In the above example, Macbeth could simply have said that he was nervous, but that is not nearly as powerful in terms of drama as is his paranoid belief that the stones could talk and give him away.

Pun. A play on words with identical or very similar sounds but different meanings. Puns are important because of their ability to allow the user to say two things at once, and they do have serious literary value. They are, for instance, very important in the structure of James Joyce's *Ulysses,* one of the major novels of the twentieth century. Some, however, consider the pun the lowest form of humor. Yet, given the size of the English vocabulary (500,000 words and growing) and, so, the sheer number of words that sound the same, possibilities for puns are everywhere as an undeniable fact of language use: *I* and *eye, one* and *won, die* and *dye,* and so on.

Puns are used every day, sometimes with an unintended comic effect. The sentence, "Mary Rose sat on a pin; Mary rose" might get a smile from a reader or listener, but President Kennedy's infamous misuse of German when he said: "Ich bin ein Berliner" is humor of another kind. He meant to express solidarity with the citizens of West Berlin; what he actually said was *not* "I am a Berliner," but "I am a sweet roll (or doughnut)" since "ein Berliner" was local slang for a breakfast pastry.

Examples: Shakespeare uses puns frequently in his plays. A simple example is in *Macbeth* when the title character puns on the word *grave* (in the sense of both "serious" and "a tomb") as he talks with Banquo, whom he will soon have murdered. He says to him, "We should have else desired your good advice,/Which still hath been both *grave* and prosperous,/In this day's council" (3.1.21–23). A more subtle example occurs in *Hamlet* when the title character expounds in the opening of his first soliloquy: "O, that this too too sullied flesh would melt,/Thaw, and resolve itself into a dew!" (1.2.129–30). Hamlet wishes he could die and says so with a pun on "a dew" and "adieu." He also feels horribly corrupted by events and says so with a double pun on "sullied" as "solid" (as the 1623 Folio reads) and "sallied," that is, dirty (as the early quartos of the play have it).

Shakespeare's favorite pun in all his dramatic works is, however, the play on words of "son" and "sun." You can see it at work when Hamlet and Claudius first meet in that tragedy. Claudius tries to show that he and Hamlet can be close: "But now, my cousin Hamlet, and my son," he says (1.2.64). Hamlet picks up on the final word just a few lines later when he replies: "I am too much in the sun" (1.2.67). Where Claudius means that he wants them to be close, Hamlet means that he dislikes such royal favor if it means close scrutiny of his actions.

This same pun (on *son/sun*) is even more important in *Richard III*, where it becomes almost a **motif** (something which runs throughout the play as a comment on the action). The first two lines of the play, which are spoken by the future Richard III, read, "Now is the winter of our discontent/ Made glorious summer by this son of York." What more likely on a lovely summer's day than that the *sun* should shine? Within a hundred lines of his death in 5.5, the king remarks: "The sun will not be seen today;/The sky doth frown and lour upon our army" (5.3.282–83). So the play begins and virtually ends with that pun. In between, whenever Richard uses the word *sun* it echoes this initial pun and emphasizes the nature of his central complaint: that he is in the shade (away from the *sun*) because he is the youngest *son* of Richard Plantagenet, Duke of York and, so, least likely to succeed to the throne. The pun is even picked up by another character, Queen Margaret, when she complains about the death of her son, Edward, Prince of Wales. She complains that Richard has cast a shadow on the land and turned "the sun to shade" (1.3.266). She continues:

> alas, alas!
> Witness my son, now in the shade of death,
> Whose bright outshining beams thy cloudy wrath
> Hath in eternal darkness folded up (1.3.266–69).

Commentary: Shakespeare raises the use of puns to high art. He takes the initial value of this figure of speech (you can use it to open up with great economy two different, sometimes opposed, worlds of meaning) and transforms it into a device of great power because of the nature of drama *as it is acted.* When you read one of Shakespeare's speeches which includes a pun, you know what word is initially meant and so what word is being echoed. When you *listen* to that same speech, however, you cannot tell, precisely because the two words sound the same. In *Macbeth*, for example, when Macbeth says to his wife: "We are yet but young in deed" (3.4.145), do you hear it as "indeed" or "in deed"? The two possibilities change Macbeth's meaning in profound ways (he's either really naïve or, alternatively, unpracticed as a murderer), and the audience's sense of what he means will vary. Some will hear it one way, some another. The play will be the richer for such an ambiguity that is present *in performance* but not *on the page.*

Simile (pronounced **sim-uh-lee**). Along with its figurative cousin, the metaphor, simile is one of the commonest literary devices. Simile is a less powerful literary device than is metaphor, however. Where metaphor denotes an *identity* between two dissimilar things, simile denotes merely a likeness and does so using such introductory words as "like," "as," or "so." To clarify briefly: When one says "My love is like a rose," you're using a simile; if you were to say, "my love is a rose," that would be metaphor.

Examples: The second scene in *Macbeth* is a good example of the extraordinary frequency with which Shakespeare uses simile. In a scene of only seventy lines, there are *nine* similes. The first is also the most straightforward, a simile in which the toughness of one of the combatants is praised: Malcolm says to his father, Duncan, "This is the sergeant/Who like a good and hardy soldier fought/'Gainst my captivity" (3–5). A more complex example occurs shortly afterwards when the sergeant describes the battle: "And Fortune, on his [Macdonwald's] damnèd quarrel smiling,/Showed like a rebel's whore" (14–15). To make sense of his comment, you need to know that Fortune is always depicted as a woman. Once you know this, then you can see that the sergeant is colorfully complaining that good fortune deserted the king's side and favored the rebels' with the same speed that a prostitute goes from one customer to another.

Just as there are extended analogies and extended metaphors, so there are *extended similes.* There is no exact rule for how long or complex a simile has to be before it is labeled "extended," but the rule of thumb I use is that if it goes over more than two or three lines or gets picked up again after a break, then it's extended. That second scene in *Macbeth* has a couple of extended similes among the total of nine. The best example is the sergeant's comparison of the ebb and flow of battle to natural events such as storms and sunshine:

> As whence the sun 'gins his reflection
> Shipwrecking storms and direful thunders break,

So from that spring whence comfort seemed to come
Discomfort swells (25–28).

The initial simile of sun and storms (25–26) leads not to what it is describing but to another simile, of springs of water (27–28). Both are explained by the remaining five lines of the sergeant's speech, in which he describes the counterattack of the Norwegian forces against the briefly triumphant Scots:

No sooner justice had, with valor armed,
Compelled these skipping kerns to trust their heels
But the Norweyan lord, surveying vantage,
With furbished arms and new supplies of men,
Began a fresh assault (29–33).

Commentary: The importance of similes is three fold. First, they allow spectators and readers to see more than the story Shakespeare tells. Comparison broadens any play's spectacle. Second, they can underline the unity of the play. If similes of a particular kind (or, for that matter, any of the devices of figurative language) recur throughout the play, then they act to reinforce particular themes. In *Macbeth*, for example, there are many similes that involve darkness and light. Shakespeare's point in using them is that what is at stake for a Scotland under Macbeth's bloody rule is nothing less than the defeat of goodness by sin. Third, similes (and again all figurative language) can be specific to certain characters. So, the similes that are used define personality. Shakespeare has the sergeant in *Macbeth*, for example, use that rather confused extended simile in order to reveal his state of exhaustion. Ten lines after he finishes that simile, he is helped off to receive first aid. As he says, "I am faint. My gashes cry for help" (42). Anyone listening carefully to how he expressed himself would have known that.

Symbol. This device represents an abstract idea by means of a concrete (i.e. physical) object. Symbols can be divided for convenience into **public** (or universal) and **private** (or group-specific) types. The first of these can be illustrated well by a rose, a well-known symbol of love or the beloved. The rose works as a symbol of love or the beloved because it looks beautiful, is delightful to the touch, and smells nice. Like love, however, it is sometimes short lived and always has thorns. The second type of symbol can be illustrated by referring to the poetry of Sylvia Plath, a major twentieth-century American poet. For her, black shoes were evocative of her father, and plaster casts represented her fragile sense of self. Neither is a universal symbol; they can only be understood in the context of her poetry and life.

Some distinctions would be useful here. Symbol differs from metaphor and simile because whereas in metaphor and simile the relation is made clear, with a symbol the relation is never stated but only understood. It differs from metonymy and synecdoche because the symbol stands for itself as well as representing something else and because it has to represent an idea; by contrast, examples of metonymy and synecdoche can only be understood in relation to what they are substituting for and what they are substituting for is often another object and *not* an idea. It is important to remember, however, that particular instances of literary language can include within them several devices at once. It is possible for one statement to have value as symbol, synecdoche, and metonymy depending on how you read it.

Examples: Let's clarify the definitions made in the last paragraph by considering Yorick's skull in *Hamlet* 5.1.172–216, perhaps the most famous skull in all of literature. As a public symbol, the skull of Hamlet's jester represents death. An object (skull) has profound abstract significance (death). As a private symbol, Yorick's skull represents happiness, for Hamlet talks about the good times he and Yorick had together when he was a young boy and Yorick entertained the king. As synecdoche, Yorick's skull substitutes a part (the skull) for the whole man, but that substitution is a general one in that it could apply to any man or woman. In other words, every human has a skull that considered on its own represents the entire individual. As metonymy, Yorick's skull represents Yorick specifically and not the broader symbol of death because some characteristics of the skull remind Hamlet of the jester in particular. They have an emotional association for him. As he says, " Here hung those lips/that I have kissed I know not how oft," and jokes: "Not one now, to mock your own grinning?" (187–88, 191).

Some symbols gain power not (as does Yorick's skull) from their complexity but rather from their simplicity and frequency. Let's look briefly at how Shakespeare uses "gashes" as a symbol in *Macbeth*.

First, some data:

◊ The word appears in various forms five times in the play.
◊ The word appears once in each act: 1.2.42; 2.3.115; 3.4.27; 4.3.41; and 5.8.2.

The details of each use are these:

◊ The first is by one of Duncan's soldiers (he's referred to as both a sergeant and a captain): "But I am faint. My gashes cry for help."
◊ The second is by Macbeth and describes the awful appearance of the murdered Duncan: "his gashed stabs looked like a breach in nature/For ruin's wasteful entrance."
◊ The third is by the First Murderer and describes the awful appearance of the murdered Banquo: "Safe in a ditch he bides,/With twenty trenchèd gashes on his head,/The least a death to nature."

◇ The fourth is by Malcolm (Duncan's son) and describes the state of Scotland under Macbeth's rule: "I think our country sinks beneath the yoke;/It weeps, it bleeds, and each new day a gash/Is added to her wounds."

◇ The fifth and last is by Macbeth again and describes his determination to fight on to the bitter end: "Why should I play the Roman fool and die/On mine own sword? Whiles I see lives, the gashes/Do better upon them."

What can be the only conclusion from such data? What do the examples themselves so clearly point to? That the gash symbolizes the damage that has been done morally and physically to Scotland as a result of Macbeth's ambition. It is a wonderful symbol carefully used by the playwright, for the word itself is unusual enough even in Shakespeare's time to draw attention to itself. It is something physical which graphically describes the destruction it represents.

Synecdoche (pronounced suh-nek-duh-kee). This device is the close cousin of *metonymy*; some critics, indeed, come close to calling it an identical twin. But as I suggested when I talked about metonymy, they are different and the difference is worth preserving. Synecdoche occurs either when a part substitutes for the whole or when the whole stands in for a part. As so often with figurative language, we often use it in our everyday language without thinking twice.

When you say to a friend as you admire her new car, "I like your wheels," you are using the first type of synecdoche (in which a part stands for the whole). If you weren't, it wouldn't be a very impressive car at all; in fact, it wouldn't run. If you meant what you said literally, there would be just a few wheels (four, presumably) lying on the ground doing nothing. There wouldn't even be a tire in sight. Your friend, however, knows exactly what you mean.

Now, let's look at the other sort of synecdoche, in which the whole substitutes for a part. Suppose you get a loud knock on your door at three a.m. After your heart has stopped racing, you might call out: "Who's there?" The unidentified person replies: "It's the law." Now's your chance to impress. Before you ask for proof of identity and open the door, you could say "Nice use of synecdoche." Why? Because the police officer isn't the law; he or she is simply a single representative of that branch of government. He or she is a part representing the whole. If the law were literally there, it would get very crowded on your street. In fact, it would get very crowded in your town.

So what's significant about synecdoche if we use it all the time? In a sense, it's not actually that impressive. We're all much more creative users of language than we think. It is important, however, to see that writers use this figure of speech as they do all figurative language with more skill and deliberation than others do. They are also concerned to achieve a particular effect.

Examples: Let's return one last time to *Macbeth*. There is only one clear example in the play of the rarer sort of synecdoche: the whole representing the part. At the very end of the play, the future king of Scotland, Malcolm, praises his faithful followers and rewards them: "Henceforth be earls, the first that ever Scotland/In such an honor named" (5.8.64–65). Of course, Scotland hasn't named them, he has. The whole (country) representing the part (king). By contrast, there are several examples in the play of the commoner variety of synecdoche: the part representing the whole. Two memorable instances describe Scotland under Macbeth's rule: Lennox's statement, "this our suffering country/Under a hand accursed!" (3.6.49–50); and Macduff's more emotional phrasing, "New widows howl, new orphans cry, new sorrows/Strike heaven on the face" (4.3.5–6). In both, part represents whole. The most remarkable example occurs when Macduff (newly arrived at Macbeth's castle) asks the host whether King Duncan is awake. Since Macbeth has already killed Duncan, the honest answer is "No, and he never will awake again." Macbeth, however, cannot say anything of the sort and get away with the crime. All he can do is to offer to show Macduff where Duncan is staying. Yet, he cannot even bear to go near the threshold of the dead king's room. From a distance all he can manage to say is: "This is the door" (2.3.50). The part represents the whole: the door standing in for the entire room and what it contains, the body of the brutally murdered Duncan.

Commentary: Two qualities distinguish Shakespeare's handling of synecdoche. First, he uses the device often and does so always to condense his material. Were he to spell out all that he presents by synecdoche then the plays would be a great deal longer and all the dramatic tension would dissipate into long-windedness. Second, he often combines synecdoche with other devices in order to intensify the reader's or audience's reaction to events. In the case of the conversation between Macduff and Macbeth which I discussed in the last paragraph, synecdoche is combined with irony (the gap in knowledge between Macduff and Macbeth is *vast*) and astute psychological insight. If you had killed Duncan, would you like to go anywhere near the room where the body is lying?

Test Case #2: The Barge at Cydnus

I'll finish this chapter with a second test case to match the one from *Hamlet* with which I began the previous chapter. Now, however, you are armed with a much fuller knowledge of Shakespeare's figurative language and imagery, so rather than follow the excerpt (as I did earlier) with a series of observations about how to understand what Shakespeare is trying to do I'll simply mark all the devices he uses. I want to reinforce the material that was covered in this chapter, but I also want to show how dense Shakespeare's language is. It fairly bristles with figures of speech. In fact, there are more devices at work in the excerpt than I have marked, since some are the subject of the next chapter, on rhetoric.

The excerpt is from *Antony and Cleopatra*: Enobarbus's description of the first meeting between the legendary lovers. It appears in 2.2 and goes like this:

simile	The barge she sat in, like a burnished throne	200
metaphor	Burnt on the water. The poop was beaten gold;	
	Purple the sails, and so perfumèd that	
personification and metaphor	The winds were lovesick with them. The oars were silver,	
	Which to the tune of flutes kept stroke, and made	
personification and simile	The water which they beat to follow faster,	205
	As amorous of their strokes. For her own person,	
metaphor	It beggared all description: she did lie	
	In her pavilion—cloth-of-gold of tissue—	
	O'erpicturing that Venus where we see	
metaphor	The fancy outwork nature. On each side her	210
simile	Stood pretty dimpled boys, like smiling Cupids,	
	With divers-colored fans, whose wind did seem	
	To glow the delicate cheeks which they did cool,	
	And what they undid did.	
simile	Her gentlewomen, like the Nereides,	
	So many mermaids, tended her i' th' eyes,	
metaphor	And made their bends adornings. At the helm	
	A seeming mermaid steers. The silken tackle	
metaphor	Swell with the touches of those flower-soft hands,	220
metaphor	That yarely frame the office. From the barge	
personification	A strange invisible perfume hits the sense	
synecdoche and personification	Of the adjacent wharfs. The city cast	
	Her people out upon her; and Antony,	
	Enthroned i' the market-place, did sit alone,	225
personification	Whistling to th' air; which, but for vacancy,	
	Had gone to gaze on Cleopatra too,	
	And made a gap in nature.	
	Upon her landing, Antony sent to her,	
	Invited her to supper. She replied	230
	It should be better he became her guest,	
	Which she entreated. Our courteous Antony,	
hyperbole	Whom ne'er the word of "No" woman heard speak,	
hyperbole	Being barbered ten times o'er, goes to the feast,	
metaphor	And for his ordinary pays his heart	235
personification and metaphor	For what his eyes eat only (200-14; 216-28; 229-36).	

Shakespeare's language is as wonderfully dense as this marked-up speech shows.

Advice

So, what are you to do when faced with the blizzard of images in Shakespeare's plays? I offer several strategies:

◊ If you're one of those people who don't like to probe literature too deeply for meaning, remember that studying language carefully doesn't destroy the magic of literature. In fact, it enhances it because you understand better how it works.

◊ Always write down your observations; don't assume that you will remember them. If you can, mark and label instances of imagery wherever you see it in the play that you're reading.

◊ Don't rush to analyze what the language means figuratively. Always begin with the literal. What senses are being stimulated by the words themselves?

◊ Once you understand the literal meaning, then ask yourself what the images mean figuratively.

◊ Once you understand the figurative meaning, look at what devices are conveying the meaning. Metaphor? Simile? Personification? Metonymy? A combination of several devices?

◊ Now, look at the overall effect of the passage or passages you are examining: What point is Shakespeare making in relation to the play as a whole?

Writing and Discussion Assignments

1. Analyze the opening scene in any Shakespeare play for the appeals it makes to the senses. Does any particular sense predominate? Why?
2. Choose any one speech of a dozen lines or more that you particularly enjoy from a Shakespeare play, and analyze it for its use of two or three types of figurative language. What surprises you about your findings? (The Ghost's speech in *Hamlet* 1.5.43–92 would work well for this exercise.)
3. Examine any single scene from Shakespeare's plays for its use of image strands. How do such groups of images reinforce your sense of the overall meaning of the play? (*Othello* 5.2 would work well for this exercise.)
4. Examine Shakespeare's use of irony in *Othello*. How many sorts of irony are there in the play? What is their effect, individually and cumulatively?
5. Examine any Shakespeare play for its symbols. How effective is Shakespeare's use of them? Do you see their use change as the play develops? (*Titus Andronicus* would work well for this question.)
6. Take three Shakespearean scenes: one from an early Shakespeare comedy (e.g. *The Comedy of Errors*), one from a middle-period comedy (e.g. *Twelfth Night*), and

one from a late comedy (e.g. *Measure for Measure*). Examine the imagery in each of them. Do you see a development in Shakespeare's technique? Is the imagery denser? more complicated? more varied?

7. Imagine that you've been called in at the last moment to do a rewrite of a Shakespeare speech, specifically *Hamlet* 2.2.1–18. You've been told to pump it up a little. Take any half dozen lines or so from the speech and revise them so that they are full of Shakespeare's imagery.

Further Reading

Charney, Maurice. *Shakespeare's Roman Plays: The Function of Imagery in the Drama.* Cambridge: Harvard UP, 1963.

Clemen, Wolfgang H. *The Development of Shakespeare's Imagery.* London: Methuen, 1951.

Matthews, Honor. *Character & Symbol in Shakespeare's Plays. A Study of Certain Christian and Pre-Christian Elements in Their Structure and Imagery.* London: Chatto & Windus, 1969.

Spurgeon, Caroline. *Shakespeare's Imagery and What It Tells Us.* Cambridge: Cambridge UP, 1935.

Thompson, Ann and John O. *Shakespeare: Meaning and Metaphor.* Iowa City: U of Iowa P, 1987.

Webb, J. Barry. *Shakespeare's Imagery of Plants.* Hastings, E. Sussex, Eng.: Cornwallis P, 1991.

Chapter 3

Shakespeare's Rhetoric

Chapter Overview

◇ Defining the history and meaning of the term *rhetoric*.
◇ Understanding the 17 major rhetorical devices (from *adage* to *stichomythia*).
◇ Recognizing the three distinctive features of Shakespeare's rhetoric: pattern, repetition, and variation.

In this chapter, we will concentrate on Shakespeare's use of rhetoric, or the arts of persuasion in writing and speech. Just as with the discussion of Shakespeare's figurative language (in Chapter 2), if you can see how and why Shakespeare uses words in the way that he does then it will become much, much easier to understand what he is saying.

The History of Rhetoric

One tradition has it that rhetoric was invented in the fifth century BC in Sicily after the overthrow of the Syracusan dictators; another suggests it was developed by Gorgias in Athens towards the end of that same century. Whatever the truth of such traditions, rhetoric became a highly developed art in the Classical world under the care of such Greek rhetoricians as Socrates, Plato, and Aristotle, and their Roman descendants: Cicero, Cato, and Quintilian. The Classical five-part model for organizing any persuasive speech has come down to us today as the most effective method for convincing an audience of the validity of an argument or point of view. The five parts are

◇ **Invention.** This term means development of ideas. It rests on three concepts:

1. **Ethos** (or the character of the speaker)
2. **Pathos** (or appeals to the emotions of the audience)
3. **Logos** (or the structure of the ideas presented).

◇ **Arrangement.** This term refers to how the speech is organized. Ideally that organization is in seven parts:
   1. Opening
   2. Statement of background facts
   3. Definition of terms
   4. Statement of thesis or main idea
   5. Proof
   6. Refutation of the opposition's arguments
   7. Conclusion.

◇ **Style.** This term means fitting the language to the subject and to the audience. It depends on four qualities:
   1. Accuracy
   2. Clarity
   3. Appropriateness
   4. Colorfulness.

◇ **Memory.** This term refers to the ways in which the language itself provides the speaker *and his or her audience* with the means to remember the ideas presented.

◇ **Delivery.** This term refers primarily to the persuasive edge given to rhetoric by gesture and voice.

Classical authors even decided that rhetoric could be subdivided into three types:

◇ Deliberative (or political)
◇ Forensic (or judicial)
◇ Epideictic (or praising).

In the medieval period, rhetoricians (such as Alcuin, Isidore, and Dante) were concerned with the moral question of the relation between truth and lies. The question that mattered most to them was a moral one, and could be expressed as follows: How should we respond to a brilliant, convincing speech or argument given by someone we know cannot be trusted? In the Renaissance (and here we come back to Shakespeare and his age), rhetoricians were fascinated not with morality, but with style. One book, for example, Henry Peacham's *The Garden of Eloquence*, published when Shakespeare was just thirteen, lists no less than 184 separate rhetorical devices (or uses of language) available to the rhetorician. In the modern age, examples of all three types of rhetoric are everywhere. We see the deliberative in political speeches; the forensic in court cases; the epideictic in advertising (where praise is showered on things in an effort to get us to buy them).

And how does all this relate directly to Shakespeare and his plays? It does so in four main ways:

1. Rhetoric is everywhere in his plays, and so it becomes another useful means of seeing what Shakespeare is trying to do with language.

2. His style (in Classical rhetoric—as we've seen on page 67—the third major element in any persuasive speech) is remarkable, varying quite deliberately from the very simple to the impressively ornate. Sometimes this style trips up readers, but it shouldn't once you know what Shakespeare is doing. To that end, we shall see in a moment how he uses more than a dozen of the best-known rhetorical devices.

3. Shakespeare's characters make appeals based, with remarkable frequency, on ethos, pathos, and logos. Just think for a moment about the power of Henry V's speech at Harfleur (3.1.1–34), the famous one beginning "Once more unto the breach, dear friends, once more." That speech works because of a threefold appeal.
   ◇ It works because of ethos or the character of the king: He has suffered what his tired men have suffered.
   ◇ It works because of pathos or Henry V's appeals to the emotions of his soldiers (men whom he calls "dear friends," "noblest English" [17], and "good yeomen" [25]).
   ◇ It works because of the speech's logos or clear development (from request through several well-developed metaphors and similes to an appeal to patriotism and back at the end to that same request: Storm the town's defenses even against the odds).

4. The speeches that Shakespeare's characters make can be usefully divided into the deliberative (or political), the forensic (or judicial), and the epideictic (or praising). One need only think of John of Gaunt's "sceptred isle" political speech in *Richard II* 2.1.31–68, or of Portia's judicial defense of Antonio in *The Merchant of Venice* 4.1, or of Berowne's epideictic speech in praise of love in *Love's Labor's Lost* 4.3.285–339.

Shakespeare's Dramatic Rhetoric

Now let's look at Shakespeare's rhetoric in detail. I've arranged the discussion in an alphabetical listing of seventeen key terms.

Rhetoric

17 Key Terms

Adage	Caesura	Logos
Alliteration	Chiasmus	Pathos

(continued)		
Anaphora	Consonance	Rhyme
Antistrophe	Enargia	Soliloquy
Aside	Ethos	Stichomythia
Assonance	Isocolon	

Adage. A pithy or short saying very much like a proverb or aphorism. "A stitch in time saves nine" or "haste makes waste" are well-known adages.

Examples: In *Richard II*, John of Gaunt remarks to Bolingbroke, "There is no virtue like necessity" (1.3.278). Two scenes later, Ross replies to Northumberland's concerns about his courage: "Urge doubts to them that fear" (2.1.299). In *Hamlet*, Polonius is full of adages, most notably "Neither a borrower nor a lender be" (1.3.75) and "brevity is the soul of wit" (2.2.90).

Commentary: The persuasive effect of adages is that they emphasize in a memorable way the combined wisdom of an entire culture. They are everywhere in Shakespeare—so much so that he makes fun of people's reliance on them in the aphoristic debate between the Duke of Orleans and the Constable of France in *Henry V* 3.7.113–24.

Alliteration. The repetition of the same initial sounds (usually consonants) in successive or nearby words.

Examples: Bolingbroke's wonderful statement about the unpleasantness of being exiled from one's own country—"the bitter bread of banishment" (*Richard II* 3.1.21)—is a good example of alliteration at its simplest. Guildenstern's hope in *Hamlet* that he can help Gertrude find the cause of the change in her son's personality shows a more sophisticated use of the same device: "Heavens make our presence and our practices/Pleasant and helpful to him!" (2.2.38–39). Here, there is a double alliteration of "h" and "p" consonants with the first alliteration bracketing the second.

Commentary: The value of alliteration is that it emphasizes the idea being presented by making the sound of it memorable through repetition. In the medieval period in Britain, alliteration was used by many poets as a substitute for rhyme.

Anaphora (pronounced uh-**naf**-or-ra). The repetition of words at the beginning of successive clauses, lines, or sentences.

Examples: Shakespeare begins *Richard III* with Richard, Duke of Gloucester delivering his "Now is the winter of our discontent" speech. To give clear structure to the speech, Shakespeare has the Duke repeat "Now" at the beginning of lines 5 and 10, and "I" at or near the beginning of lines 14, 16, 18, 23, 24, 30, and 37. A more obvious example of anaphora occurs in *Henry V* when the King reveals his knowledge of Cambridge, Grey, and Scroop's intended treachery at Southampton. Four successive lines begin with the identical phrase: "Why, so didst thou" (2.2.128–31).

A more sophisticated example of this sort of patterning that is so typical of Shakespeare's rhetoric occurs in *As You Like It*. Here, the two pairs of apparently mismatched lovers (Silvius and Phoebe, and Rosalind and Orlando) talk about love and do so through a complex pattern of varied anaphora:

SILVIUS	It [love] is to be made of sighs and tears;
	And so am I for Phoebe.
PHOEBE	And I for Ganymede.
ORLANDO	And I for Rosalind.
ROSALIND	And I for no woman.
SILVIUS	It is to be all made of faith and service;
	And so am I for Phoebe.
PHOEBE	And I for Ganymede.
ORLANDO	And I for Rosalind.
ROSALIND	And I for no woman.
SILVIUS	It is to be all made of fantasy,
	All made of passion and all made of wishes,
	All adoration, duty, and observance,
	All humbleness, all patience and impatience,
	All purity, all trial, all observance;
	And so am I for Phoebe.
PHOEBE	And so am I for Ganymede.
ORLANDO	And so am I for Rosalind.
ROSALIND	And so am I for no woman.
PHOEBE	[to Rosalind]
	If this be so, why blame you me to love you?
SILVIUS	[to Phoebe]
	If this be so, why blame you me to love you?
ORLANDO	If this be so, why blame you me to love you? (5.2.81–102).

Commentary: The purpose of anaphora is to heighten the significance of the language (it is clearly carefully thought out) and to make it more memorable for the listener, reader, or watcher.

Antistrophe (pronounced **an-tee-strowf**). The repetition of words at the end of successive clauses, lines, or sentences. This device is, then, the reverse of the one above, **anaphora**. In *Macbeth*, for example, Macbeth, after he has killed Duncan, looks down at his bloodstained hands and comments, "This is a sorry sight." His wife, in an effort to snap him out of his shock, replies, "A foolish thought, to say a sorry sight" (2.2.24–25). Often, antistrophe is combined with anaphora. So, in *Richard III*, when the Duchess of York says goodbye sequentially to three of her relations (the Marquess of Dorset; Anne, Duchess of Gloucester; and Queen Elizabeth, Edward IV's widow), she does so in poetry where the beginnings *and* ends of lines repeat:

> Go thou to Richmond, and good fortune guide thee!
> Go thou to Richard, and good angels tend thee!
> Go thou to sanctuary, and good thoughts possess thee!
> (4.1.91–93).

Commentary: Antistrophe is less common than anaphora, but it nonetheless does occur often enough to be worth watching out for. Like anaphora, it makes the language more memorable for the audience by emphasizing its artificiality.

Aside.   This device is usually defined as a comment or short speech by one character to the audience or to another character which, by convention, is not heard by the other characters on stage. Such a definition, however, scarcely covers the wide variety of asides used by Shakespeare in his plays. As always, he likes to break the "rules" for the good of dramatic effect.

Examples: A typical aside is Viola/Cesario's remark in *Twelfth Night* to the audience when her/his beloved, Orsino, asks her/him to woo Olivia on his behalf. She responds: "Yet a barful strife!/Whoe'er I woo, myself would be his wife" (1.4.41–42). Yet, there are numerous exceptions to the definition of the typical aside. It is true that most of Shakespeare's asides are short, but Shylock in *The Merchant of Venice* directs a twelve-line aside to the audience when he first sees Antonio, the merchant (1.3.38–49) and Tamora, in *Titus Andronicus*, directs an aside of no less than 14 lines to the new emperor, Saturninus (1.1.443–56). It is true that most of Shakespeare's asides are inaudible to the rest of the characters on stage even though they have, of course, to be spoken loudly in order to be heard by the audience, but Lancelot's aside to Jessica in *The Merchant of Venice* is overheard by Shylock. He responds to Lancelot's lines with this comment: "What says that fool of Hagar's offspring, ha?" (2.5.45). Nor is the audibility of asides particularly unusual: Rosalind overhears Orlando in *As You Like It* (1.2.243), and Prince Edward overhears Richard's comment to Buckingham in *Richard III* (3.1.80).

It is true that some asides are the equivalent of throw-away remarks in movies, but sometimes they do achieve ritualistic power. In *Richard III* 1.3, Queen Margaret delivers a long series of asides to the audience to let it know that she is not at all fooled by Richard's machinations: six asides in less than 35 lines, each responding to Richard's part in a conversation with Queen Elizabeth (111–44). In *Love's Labor's Lost*, Berowne reacts in a series of asides to Dumaine's floridly expressed love for Kate (4.3.74–96). Sometimes, too, asides take the form of a conversation (*Hamlet* 2.2.381–87); sometimes, they rhyme (*Hamlet* 4.5.19–20); sometimes, they are directed at particular characters in a complex sequence (*The Tempest* 1.2.498–505).

Commentary: Shakespeare's use of asides is a wonderful example of his powers of invention. He takes a well-known dramatic device and greatly expands its function within drama. His purposes in so doing are many: sometimes, he intends humor; sometimes, he wants to emphasize the ritualistic quality of drama; sometimes, he wants to emphasize particular moments by slowing down the action. After all, while one character delivers a long aside, no significant stage business can go on. For that period of time, the audience is riveted on one character, and everyone else is little more than a tableau.

Assonance.   Repetition of vowel sounds in successive or nearby words where the consonants that follow the vowels and sometimes those that precede the vowels differ from each other.

Examples: In *Macbeth*, the Captain describes to King Duncan part of the battle against the rebels in terms of a simile: "As whence the sun 'gins his reflection/Shipwrecking storms and direful thunders break" (1.2.25–26). The "e" sounds in the word-pair "reflection" and "Shipwrecking," and the (different) "e" sounds in the word-pair "direful" and "thunders" are examples of assonance. Similarly, the Witches' chant at 1.3.32–37 employs assonance with the "i" sounds of "thrice" and "thine," "thrice" and "mine," and "thrice" and "nine."

Commentary: The effect of assonance is to increase the musicality and memorability of the lines the characters speak.

Caesura (pronounced see-jhor-ra).   A pause in a line of verse or prose. It usually occurs in the middle of the line or sentence, and is frequently signaled or emphasized by punctuation.

Example: In *King John* (4.1.13–24), Arthur reflects, in a speech to his custodian, Hubert, on his state of mind during his imprisonment:

> Methinks nobody should be sad but I.
> Yet I remember, when I was in France,
> Young gentlemen would be as sad as night,   15
> Only for wantonness. By my christendom,
> So I were out of prison and kept sheep,
> I should be as merry as the day is long;
> And so I would be here, but that I doubt
> My uncle [King John] practices more harm to me.   20
> He is afraid of me, and I of him.
> Is it my fault that I was Geoffrey's son?
> No, indeed, is 't not; and I would to heaven
> I were your son, so you would love me, Hubert (4.1.13–24).

The commas at lines 14, 19, 21, 24 create caesuras, as does the period at line 16 and the semicolon at line 23. The device is used again in Arthur's speeches at lines 41–58 (where question marks and periods provide the pause) and lines 75–83 (where a semicolon and a colon perform the same duty).

Commentary: Caesura is one of Shakespeare's favorite devices. He uses it to match the speed of delivery to the emotion of the speaker and to break up the long iambic pentameter lines that are the staple of his plays.

Chiasmus (pronounced ki-**az**-mus).   The sequence of two or more phrases in the first part of a sentence or line of poetry is reversed in the second half. Numerically, the sequence would be represented 1-2-2-1.

Examples: President John F. Kennedy's famous exhortation to the American people in his Inauguration Address is a classic example of chiasmus (combined in this case with anaphora): "ask not what your country can do for you; ask what you can do for your country" (Horner 322). In *Richard II*, the deposed king reflects on the mistakes he made in his life: "I wasted time, and now doth time waste me" (5.5.49). In *Antony and Cleopatra*, Octavia—newly wedded to Antony—sees herself as the means by which Antony and her brother, Octavius, can become friends. As she succinctly puts it, "Husband win, win brother" (3.4.18). And she believes she can be this means despite being herself powerless. As she remarks to Antony, using chiasmus once more: "The Jove of power make me, most weak, most weak,/Your reconciler!" (29–30).

Commentary: Shakespeare uses this device quite frequently in order to bind two statements together (1-2-2-1 is more unified than 1-2-1-2) as well as to force the reader to reflect on the meaning of such an inversion. In the example above from *Richard II*, the audience or reader cannot help but think how different the king's life is in prison from what it was before his deposition. Chiasmus stresses that difference as well as—in this case—focusing on the different meanings of the word *waste*: "to fritter away" and "to be consumed." With such a straightforward device, Shakespeare greatly increases the irony of Richard II's circumstances at the end of the play.

Consonance. Repetition of final consonant sounds in successive or near-by words in which the vowel sounds are different. This device does for consonant repetition what assonance does for vowels.

Examples: In everyday speech, the words "lad" and "tread" are an example of consonance. In *3 Henry VI*, the future Edward IV insults Henry VI and his queen, Margaret:

> But when he [Henry VI] took a beggar to his *bed*
> And graced thy poor sire with his *bridal* day,
> Even then that sunshine *brewed* a shower for him
> That washed his father's fortunes forth of France
> And heaped sedition on his crown at home.
> For what hath *broached* this tumult but thy pride?
> (2.2.154–59; emphasis added)

Three of the italicized words—bed, brewed, and broached—are an example of sustained consonance (as well, incidentally, of alliteration). Each ends in the same consonant (be*d*, brewe*d*, and broache*d*), but each time that consonant has a different vowel sound before it (b*e*d, br*e*wed, and br*oa*ched). Indeed, a fourth example in the same speech could almost be added to the list, for the word *bridal*, followed as it is by *day* has almost the same pattern as the other three. In *The Merchant of Venice*, the wordplay gets more complicated even than the example from *3 Henry VI*. In a dialogue between Portia and Bassanio, assonance gives way to consonance within three lines when the word *life* becomes *live* becomes *love* (3.2.34–36). Once more, Shakespeare has taken a straightforward rhetorical device and used pattern and variety to make it—in the best sense of the word—more sophisticated.

Commentary: As with assonance, consonance increases the musicality of the speeches in Shakespeare's plays as well as their artificiality. That is, the choice of these words by Shakespeare is anything but casual. The device elevates the language and makes it more memorable.

Enargia (pronounced en-ar-gi-a). The vivid description of something. The description is so powerful that it creates the illusion in the imagination of something that is not there.

Example: In *Richard III* (1.4.9–33), Clarence—who is about to be murdered on the orders of his brother, Richard of Gloucester—

describes to his jailer a nightmare that he has just had. In one part of the speech in particular, he recreates with astonishing power the experience of drowning:

> O Lord, methought what pain it was to drown!
> What dreadful noise of waters in my ears!
> What sights of ugly death within my eyes!
> Methought I saw a thousand fearful wracks;
> Ten thousand men that fishes gnawed upon;   25
> Wedges of gold, great anchors, heaps of pearl,
> Inestimable stones, unvalued jewels,
> All scattered in the bottom of the sea.
> Some lay in dead men's skulls, and in the holes
> Where eyes did once inhabit there were crept,   30
> As 'twere in scorn of eyes, reflecting gems,
> That wooed the slimy bottom of the deep
> And mocked the dead bones that lay scattered by
>
>   (1.4.21–33).

Look at the catalogue of sights and sounds: the "dreadful noise" of drowning as the water rushes in the ears; the "sights of ugly death" (the "fearful" shipwrecks, the bodies of men eaten by fish, the skulls where gems have replaced eyeballs); the "dead bones" strewn on the sea floor. These are so vividly described that as you listen to the speech or read it you can see what Shakespeare describes with absolute immediacy.

Commentary: In Chapter 6 (on Shakespeare's stagecraft), we will look at one particular aspect of his "word painting." Enargia is just the general rhetorical term for such a device. It is essential for the rhetorician because the mind is best persuaded by what it can *see, hear, taste, touch,* or *smell.* Ironically, Shakespeare does such a good job with enargia and the imagination is so powerful that the description of Clarence's nightmare is more terrible described than enacted on stage.

Ethos (pronounced e-thoss, or e-thowss).   The character of the speaker and, by extension, the match between the content of the lines spoken and the personality and worth of the speaker. The concept is a vital one in Shakespeare's plays because the audience needs to be able to judge whether to trust someone's words. Along with logos and pathos, it is one of the major forms of persuasion available to any dramatic character.

Example: The power of *Antony and Cleopatra* and *Othello* derives from the complex ethos of the central characters. Antony's later challenges to Octavius Caesar, after the defeat at Actium, lack conviction because he has become so much Cleopatra's plaything or "strumpet's fool" (1.1.13).

Cleopatra may say to Antony, "Not know me yet?" but that plea for trust is based on the weak ethos of her having betrayed him at the battle of Actium (3.13.160). Othello seems to be a general in command of all his faculties, but the speed with which he is crushed by doubt about Desdemona's fidelity infects the value of everything he says. Iago may say some wonderful things to Othello about the value of reputation, "Good name in man and woman, dear my lord,/Is the immediate jewel of their souls" (3.3.168–69, also 70-74); the audience, however, can't help but remember that only three scenes earlier he had said precisely the opposite to Michael Cassio: "Reputation is an idle and most/false imposition" (2.3.262–63).

Commentary: The concept of ethos is crucial to drama, for it allows the audience or reader to assess the validity of any given statement in a play. There are few characters in Shakespeare's plays whose ethos is *not* sometimes (or frequently) at odds with what they say. Even Henry V, whom Shakespeare clearly wanted to portray as the quintessential English hero, seems to invoke God rather too much when justifying his actions and to be a little too ready to slaughter the French prisoners after the battle of Agincourt. Heroic, yes, but also a little too sanctimonious and decidedly ruthless. Ethos is also valuable because it brings drama closer to real life for any audience. Aren't we always trying to match the words someone says with what we can judge of his or her character?

Isocolon (pronounced i-so-co-lon).   A very precise form of grammatical parallelism in which succeeding phrases or clauses are of the same length and structure.

Examples: This rhetorical device is very common in Shakespeare. Two examples will, however, suffice. In *Love's Labor's Lost*, Nathaniel praises Holofernes' conversation, and does so with this very precise form of parallelism:

> Your reasons at
> dinner have been sharp and sententious, pleasant
> without scurrility, witty without affection, audacious
> without impudency, learned without opinion, and
> strange without heresy
>
> (5.1.2–6).

The first pair are adjectives (*sharp* and *sententious*) separated by the coordinating conjunction *and*. The remaining five pairs are adjective-noun pairs separated by the adverb *without*. In *The Merchant of Venice*, Portia describes the intensity of her love for Bassanio in terms of two alternating pairs of a simple adjective followed by a hyphenated one: "doubtful thoughts"; "rash-embraced despair"; "shuddering fear"; and "green-eyed jealousy" (3.2.109–10).

Commentary: The primary value of an isocolonic structure is to empha-size the speaker's ideas through skillful repetition. A secondary value is to emphasize the intellect of the speaker. Even under the sort of emotional pressure that Portia experiences in the casket scene with Bassanio, the flu-ency of her speech never falters.

Logos (pronounced **low-goss** or **log-oss**).   The fit between thought and its expression as well as the appearance of clear development. Along with ethos and pathos, it is one of the major forms of persuasion available to any dramatic character.

Example: In *As You Like It*, Touchstone's explanation to Jaques of the seven causes of argument is a fine example of logos in dry reasoning with its accurate but pointless categories of "Retort Courteous," "Quip Modest," "Reply Churlish," "Reproof Valiant," "Countercheck Quarrelsome," "the Lie with Circumstance," and "the Lie Direct" (5.4.68–102). In *Richard II*, the deposed king amuses himself by drawing an extended analogy between the prison where he is held captive and the world outside (5.5.1–66). Difficult as such an analogy is "Yet," he says, "I'll hammer it out" (5.5.5). The way in which he does so offers a perfect fit between thought and expression. He tries very hard to stay focused on the analogy but is con-stantly drifting towards self-pity and sorrow. The struggle for self-control infuses every word he utters. In *Hamlet*, Claudius's first speech to the assembled court (1.2.17–50) shows a new monarch determined to be in charge and to have all his public discourse demonstrate that strength of leadership. His logically structured speech and the finality with which he moves from agenda item to agenda item are proof of that resolve.

Commentary: Logos is a crucial concept because it allows the audience or reader to judge the quality of any character's words. Where *ethos* describes the character of the speaker, *logos* defines the relation between thought and expression. At its simplest, how appropriate are the words to the ideas being expressed? For example, is Iago's sordid language describ-ing the physical relation between Othello and Desdemona (1.1.90–91, 113–14, 119–20) in keeping with the love they bear one another, or is there something more behind Iago's lurid imagination?

Pathos (pronounced **pay-thoss** or **pay-thowss**).   The emotion in a speech, dialogue, or entire play, the purpose being to move the audience to sorrow, compassion, and sympathy. On one end of the spectrum, pathos trails off into stoicism; on the other, into sentimentalism or bathos (the ridiculous). Along with ethos and logos, it is one of the major forms of persuasion avail-able to any dramatic character.

Examples: I'll cite two very different examples. In *Richard II* 3.2, the king realizes that his days of power are over after the death of Bushy, Green, and the Earl of Wiltshire. He delivers a speech that begins with a request,

"Let's talk of graves, of worms, and epitaphs" (145). He continues with a plea, "For God's sake, let us sit upon the ground/And tell sad stories of the death of kings" (155–56). The speech is beautiful and moving. Moreover, just as he is about to tip the scales down into sentimentalism, he moves instead towards generalization with an extraordinary statement of the vulnerability, the essential humanity, of any monarch:

> For within the hollow crown
> That rounds the mortal temples of a king
> Keeps Death his court, and there the antic sits,
> Scoffing his state and grinning at his pomp,
> Allowing him a breath, a little scene,
> To monarchize, be feared, and kill with looks,
> Infusing him with self and vain conceit,
> As if this flesh which walls about our life
> Were brass impregnable; and humored thus,
> Comes at the last and with a little pin
> Bores through his castle wall, and—farewell, king!
>
> (3.2.160–70).

It is surely impossible not to sympathize with someone who understands so deeply and expresses so well the fragility of the human condition. Richard II in this speech uses pathos to make his rhetoric absolutely persuasive.

In a very different dramatic moment, Othello is equally persuasive because he knows how to use pathos to good effect. In his last speech, delivered just before he kills himself, he has one final chance to redeem his blighted reputation. He takes that opportunity, and succeeds in moving an audience who knows full well that he has just murdered the innocent Desdemona. He says to the assembled Venetians:

> Soft you; a word or two before you go.
> I have done the state some service, and they know 't.
> No more of that. I pray you, in your letters,
> When you shall these unlucky deeds relate,
> Speak of me as I am; nothing extenuate,
> Nor set down aught in malice. Then must you speak
> Of one that loved not wisely but too well;
> Of one not easily jealous but, being wrought,
> Perplexed in the extreme; of one whose hand,
> Like the base Indian, threw a pearl away
> Richer than all his tribe; of one whose subdued eyes,
> Albeit unusèd to the melting mood,
> Drops tears as fast as the Arabian trees

Their medicinable gum. Set you down this;
And say besides that in Aleppo once,
Where a malignant and a turbaned Turk
Beat a Venetian and traduced the state,
I took by th' throat the circumcisèd dog
And smote him, thus (5.2.348–66).

Why is this such an extraordinarily affecting speech? In part because of the caesuras that show the power of Othello's emotion; in part because of his concern with having the events recalled accurately ("I pray you . . . Speak of me as I am"; "Then you must speak"; "Set you down this"); and in part because of the manifest love he has for Desdemona and the clarity of the realization of what he has lost (he knows he has thrown away a "pearl" of extraordinary value).

Commentary: Pathos as a persuasive device is wonderfully effective because it targets the ways in which all human beings are fundamentally the same. At the deepest level, we all have the same sense of unfulfilled desire, the same feeling of regret, the same fear of death. It is perhaps instructive to see how well pathos persuades by looking at an example of the failure of a character to achieve a pathetic response. In *Richard II*, shortly after his highly emotional speech about kingship, the king tries one too many times for a sympathetic response from the audience. He launches into a tribute to his horse, Barbary, which had the bad taste to accept being ridden by the usurping king, Henry IV (5.5.84–94). It leads to a simile in which he sees himself as an ass ridden by the new king.

The speech fails as pathos for three reasons.

1. There is something slightly ridiculous (or anticlimactic) about a tribute to a horse.
2. The speech seems contrived so as to finish with the simile of Richard II as ass and Henry IV as rider.
3. The speech is unfortunately reminiscent of a couple of other moments in Shakespearean drama: the deliberately absurd tributes by the Dauphin in *Henry V* 3.7 to his horse; and one of the worst lines in all of Shakespeare, Hotspur's comment in *1 Henry IV* that he has chosen a particular horse on which to ride, "That roan shall be my throne" (2.3.70).

Rhyme. The repetition of identical stressed vowel sounds in words as well as all the sounds after the stressed vowel. Rhyme can be thought of as a combination of assonance and consonance, and most often refers to words at the ends of successive lines that match in the way I've just described. Such an instance of rhyme is strictly called end rhyme, but there are many examples in Shakespeare and other poets of internal rhyme, that is rhyme used elsewhere in lines of poetry or prose.

There are three types of rhyme, depending on the number of syllables that rhyme:

1. Masculine (or single) rhyme, in which the rhyme involves only one stressed syllable (*run* and *fun*).
2. Feminine (or double) rhyme, in which both the stressed syllable and the syllable following have the same sound (*thunder* and *wonder*).
3. Triple rhyme, in which the stressed syllable and the two syllables that follow all have the same sound (*glorious* and *furious*).

Examples: Let's start with the basic types of rhyme. There is internal rhyme (Feste's "Like a mad lad" in *Twelfth Night* 4.2.130); masculine end rhyme (*cries* and *eyes*, for example, in *Love's Labor's Lost* 4.3.137–38); feminine end rhyme (*fashion* and *passion*, for instance, which occurs just two lines earlier in *Love's Labor's Lost*); and even something close to triple end rhyme (*transgression* and *confession* in *Love's Labor's Lost* 5.2.432–33).

However, as you might expect with so fine a craftsman as Shakespeare, he goes far beyond these basics to great effect in his plays. Scenes in his plays often end in a rhyming couplet (or pair of lines) in order to give the audience a sense that a dramatic series of events has come to an end. The end of the first scene in *Richard III* is a good example of this common use of rhyme: Richard concludes, "Clarence still breathes, Edward still lives and reigns;/When they are gone, then must I count my gains" (1.1.161–62). Sometimes, Shakespeare varies the norm with a brief line that follows the ending couplet. So, Hamlet comments, "The time is out of joint. O cursèd spite/That ever I was born to set it right!" and then concludes by turning to Horatio and Marcellus and saying deferentially that they should exit at the same time, "Nay, come, let's go together" (1.5.197–99). Sometimes, as in *The Merchant of Venice* 2.5, the single rhyming couplet becomes a pair of couplets: Shylock says as he leaves, "Fast bind, fast find—/A proverb never stale in thrifty mind," and his daughter, Jessica, responds after he has left, "Farewell, and if my fortune be not crossed,/I have a father, you a daughter, lost" (55–58).

It is, however, in the poems, songs and riddles that Shakespeare uses rhyme with the greatest flexibility. In *As You Like It*, Rosalind and Touchstone deliberately indulge in bad rhyming for comic effect with Rosalind's name echoing with a long succession of end words: *Ind, wind, lined, mind, hind, kind, bind, rind,* and *find* (3.2.86–110). Quite correctly, Touchstone himself complains that such rhymes constitute "the very false gallop of verses" and "bad fruit" (111, 114). Rosalind (also quite correctly) suggests that they are love verses (in this case, bad poetry by her admirer, Orlando). Similar examples of close rhyming occur in the rhyming "casket" riddles in *The Merchant of Venice*: 2.9.63–72; 3.2.63–72; and 3.2.131–38.

Then at the end of that play, in an extraordinary dialogue, Bassanio and Portia deliver nine lines of rhymed iambic pentameter all of which end with the same word, "ring" (5.1.193–97, 199–202).

Commentary: Rhyme is the greatest mnemonic device that the poet has to work with because the mind instantly picks up on the repetition of identical sounds. The value of rhyme, then, as rhetoric is that it persuades by emphasizing particular words or ideas. It also provides something else that I mentioned at the beginning of this list of rhetorical devices: variety. It is essential that Shakespeare avoid doing the same thing twice or boring the audience by delivering speeches in uniform prose. His solution? To intersperse his plays with rhyme.

Soliloquy. A speech delivered to the audience by a character when alone on stage. The content of the speech is of one of two kinds: either the character reveals his/her innermost thoughts, or he/she previews the coming action by letting the audience know what his/her intentions are. Sometimes, a soliloquy (such as Iago's in *Othello* 1.3.383–405) combines both purposes. Although Shakespeare's most famous soliloquies come from his great tragedies, he wrote them throughout his career: from an early play such as *Titus Andronicus* to a late play such as *Cymbeline*.

Examples: A classic example of the introspective soliloquy is Hamlet's famous "To be, or not to be" speech (3.1.57–91) in which he thinks of suicide as an escape from his misery. We looked at this soliloquy in Chapter 1 (23–27). A good example of the previewing soliloquy is Aaron's speech in *Titus Andronicus* that begins the second act (2.1.1–25). Here he predicts that his affair with Tamora will continue and bring down Saturninus's empire.

Yet, as you might expect, Shakespeare bends the frame of the soliloquy—just as he did with the aside—to suit his needs as a dramatist. Given the moral or dramatic seriousness of the soliloquy, blank verse is the preferred form in which to deliver the ideas. Such a form avoids the lightness of rhyme and the triviality of prose. In *The Merchant of Venice*, however, Shakespeare breaks this custom by having Lancelot Gobo (of all things, a clown) open a scene with a lengthy prose soliloquy (2.2.1–29). In *Twelfth Night*, Malvolio (like Lancelot Gobo, a comic figure) soliloquizes, also in prose, about the evidence he has which shows Olivia loves him (3.4.66–85).

Given the importance of the soliloquy (to have one actor on stage and no action is riveting as spectacle), the convention is that the soliloquy contains the truth. It is an opportunity for the audience to know a character's innermost thoughts or intentions. In *Othello*, however, Shakespeare transgresses that convention by having Iago begin a soliloquy with something that he knows to be false: Cassio loves Desdemona. Presumably in an effort to persuade the audience that there is some justification for his plot against Othello, he remarks: "That Cassio loves her, I do well believe 't;/ That she loves him, 'tis apt and of great credit" (2.1.287–88).

In other ways, too, Shakespeare plays with the soliloquy as a rhetorical device. Sometimes he has speeches that are delivered by characters while alone on stage but which don't look like soliloquies. Oliver's brief speech in *As You Like It* 1.1.82–84 seems more like an aside, but it isn't labeled as such and it does contain an important reflection about the stage action. Claudius's speech in *Hamlet* 3.3.36–72 and 97–98 is an interrupted soliloquy. He delivers 37 lines of confession seeking God's forgiveness for his murder of old Hamlet. Then, young Hamlet enters, sees his uncle/stepfather praying, and delivers his own soliloquy of 23 lines, on another part of the stage, in which he debates whether to kill Claudius. Once Hamlet has exited after deciding that Claudius would go to Heaven if he killed him now, Claudius finishes his prayer with a couplet: "My words fly up, my thoughts remain below./Words without thoughts never to heaven go" (3.3.97–98). It's a brilliant piece of staging by Shakespeare because now the audience knows something Hamlet does not: he could have killed Claudius successfully because he would have gone straight to Hell.

Commentary: Soliloquy is Shakespeare's single, most concentrated, device for accomplishing two goals: moving the story forward or revealing the personality of a key character. If you think for a moment of the dramatic power of having one actor turn on the stage to face the audience, and of that actor speaking for a minute or two solely to that audience, then it becomes obvious why Shakespeare came to rely on the soliloquy as his greatest weapon and why he refined its effects throughout his career.

Stichomythia (pronounced **stik-o-mith-ea**). A dialogue in which two characters dispute with each other in short alternating lines.

Example: One of the best examples in all of Shakespeare is the dialogue between Richard III and Queen Elizabeth, the widow of Richard's brother, Edward IV, in *Richard III* 4.4. The topic of their dispute is Richard's wish to marry the Queen's daughter, Elizabeth of York. Richard begins by pointing out that she is the daughter of a king, and the dialogue unravels from there because the queen knows that Richard has a reputation for killing those who get close to him, not least his previous wife, Lady Anne. The king opens the rapid-fire dialogue itself by stating that Elizabeth of York "is a royal princess," and the debate continues:

QUEEN ELIZABETH
> To save her life, I'll say she is not so.

KING RICHARD
> Her life is safest only in her birth.

QUEEN ELIZABETH
> And only in that safety died her brothers [the princes in the Tower].

KING RICHARD
> Lo, at their birth good stars were opposite.

QUEEN ELIZABETH
> No, to their lives ill friends were contrary.

KING RICHARD
> All unavoided is the doom of destiny (213–18).

This stichomythic dispute then modulates into the lengthier speeches typical of Shakespeare's characters, but resurfaces at three other points in the scene: 265–69, 343–68, and 418–31. The result? A tactical withdrawal by the Queen ("I go. Write to me shortly,/And you shall understand from me her mind" [428–29]) which Richard interprets as a victory: "Relenting fool, and shallow, changing woman!" (431).

Commentary: The effect of stichomythia is startling: to go from the mannered artificiality of Shakespeare's typical speeches (wonderful language, but do people really *ever* talk like that?) to the *appearance* of something approaching real dialogue. Of course, such an appearance is false, for stichomythia is in its own way quite as artificial as, say, the aside or the soliloquy. People do tend to speak in short sentences, but they also rarely give each other alternating lines. So, what is Shakespeare's purpose? To change the tempo of his plays and to emphasize the importance of particular concerns by the alternating rhythm of stichomythia. Stichomythia is simply one more way in which Shakespeare varies his rhetoric to make his dramatic point more persuasively.

Pattern, Repetition, Variation

So much for the specifics of Shakespeare's masterful dramatic rhetoric. The overall effect of that rhetoric needs to be examined, too, and that effect can best be summed up in three words: **pattern**, **repetition**, and **variation**. Let's look at each of these key terms in some detail.

Pattern

Pattern is most obvious in such devices as stichomythia and rhyme, but it also appears in an aspect of Shakespeare's rhetoric that is less obvious but ultimately more significant: many of his major characters use language in a particular, individual way. To use the technical term, each of them has an *idiolect* that is as unique as a fingerprint. Horatio, Hamlet, Polonius, Othello, Iago, Falstaff, Antony, Cleopatra, Octavius, and Cordelia each have an idiolect.

◆ Hamlet is the intellectual who enjoys bamboozling Rosencrantz and Guildenstern with wordplay and—at 1.2.76—toys with the meaning of the word "seems."

◆ Cleopatra is the seductive manipulator who is "cunning past man's thought" (1.2.152). At one moment, she can tell a dirty joke. "I take no pleasure/In aught an eunuch has," she remarks to Mardian (1.5.10–11). At the next, she can deliver a beautifully balanced speech about her naïveté when she was young: "My salad days,/When I was green in judgment, cold in blood,/To say as I said then" (76–78). So sensitive is she to language that she can easily spot the effort at manipulation by others. When Caesar tries to fool her into trusting him after Antony's death, she turns to her maidservants and comments: "He words me, girls, he words me" (5.2.191).

◆ Othello's pattern of speech can be identified by its grandiloquence combined with coldness of imagery. Only Othello among all of the many hundreds of Shakespeare's characters would say (of Desdemona):

> Nay, had she been true,
> If heaven would make me such another world
> Of one entire and perfect chrysolite,
> I'd not have sold her for it (5.2.148–51).

Indeed, "chrysolite" is used only once in all of Shakespeare's works, but it has the combination of magnificence and coldness that is the hallmark of Othello.

◆ Iago is also instantly recognizable from his word choice. In his case, the profane, the sacred, and the simple mix at will. At one moment he can talk of Othello and Desdemona "making the beast with two/backs" (1.1.119–20); at another, he can talk of reputation as "the immediate jewel" of a person's soul (3.3.169); at yet a third, he can say with astonishing directness to Roderigo, "I am not what I am" (1.1.67).

And so the list continues, with Shakespeare intent on making sure that his audience recognizes important characters not simply by face or dress or voice, but by language. By their *pattern* of speech.

Repetition

Repetition is evident in many of the rhetorical devices Shakespeare used: *alliteration, anaphora, antistrophe, assonance, caesura, chiasmus, consonance, isocolon, rhyme,* and *stichomythia* are all, at heart, forms of repetition. Yet, Shakespeare is much more subtle in his use of repetition than the manuals of rhetorical devices can easily describe.

◇ There is the simple repetition in prose of a key term. In *Othello*, for example, there is Iago's constant return to the word *money* in his speech to Roderigo where he successfully convinces him to continue trying to seduce Desdemona. In only 27 lines of prose (1.3.337–63), he repeats the word seven times and even uses the same phrase five times: "Put money in thy purse" (342); "I say,/put money in thy purse" (343–44); "put/money in thy purse" (345–46); "put but money in thy purse" (348); "fill thy/purse with money" (349–50); "Therefore/put money in thy purse" (354–55); "Make/all the money thou canst" (356–57); and "Therefore make money" (360).

◇ There is the intricate alternating repetition of objects and their qualities. You can see this sort of repetition clearly in Puck's speech in *A Midsummer Night's Dream*:

> Sometimes a horse I'll be, sometimes a hound,
> A hog, a headless bear, sometimes a fire;
> And neigh, and bark, and grunt, and roar, and burn,
> Like horse, hound, hog, bear, fire, at every turn
>
> (3.1.103–06).

Here the persuasive value is in both the repetition itself and in the attention required of an audience to match up one list with the other.

◇ There is the repetition in duet form where two characters show their closeness by being almost of one voice. So, in *The Merchant of Venice*, the two lovers (Lorenzo and Jessica) show their mutual affection by each echoing the same phrase across 24 lines. Eight times they interweave the words, "In such a night" (5.1.1–24).

◇ There is the repetition across the scenes of a play, a rhetorical device which ties together the action of a play just as a melody gives coherence to a piece of music. So, in *The Merchant of Venice*, the Prince of Morocco's worry at 2.1.1 that he will be rejected by Portia because of the color of his skin ("Mislike me not for my complexion," he says) is echoed six scenes later by Portia's closing couplet spoken on an empty stage after the Prince, unsuccessful in his wooing of her, has left: "A gentle riddance. Draw the curtains, go./Let all of his complexion choose me so" (2.7.78–79). The same sort of repetition occurs in *Twelfth Night* when Orsino likens the power of Olivia's beauty to the power needed to purge "the air of pestilence" (1.1.19) while Olivia herself compares the suddenness of her love for Viola/Cesario to coming down with the plague: "Even so quickly may one catch the plague" (1.5.290). In *Hamlet*, too, Shakespeare echoes the phrase "mind's eye" across successive scenes: 1.1.116 and 1.2.185.

◇ There is even repetition among plays, a rhetorical trace which suggests Shakespeare's affection for certain words, ideas, or previously successful dramatic strategies. So, in *As You Like It*, a wrestler named Charles tells Oliver that his brother, Orlando, naïvely believes he can beat him in a wrestling match scheduled for the following day. He calls Orlando, "young and tender" (1.1.123). In *King Lear*, the King is angered at the beginning of the play by the refusal of his beloved daughter, Cordelia, to say effusively how much she loves him. His words: "So young, and so untender?" (1.1.106).

Such a repetition is even used to emphasize the philosophical heart of a play. In *Hamlet*, the prince realizes just before his ill-fated duel with Laertes that the most important thing a human being can do is to be prepared to die: "The readiness is all" (5.2.220). In *King Lear*, Edgar comforts his father, Gloucester, after the defeat of the rebellion against Regan and Goneril with the same observation as Hamlet's: "Ripeness is all" (5.2.10).

Variation

Shakespeare's most persuasive device is one that stresses the range of his powers as a wordsmith by juxtaposing the two ends of the spectrum of language: sometimes, simplicity and complexity; sometimes, straightforward word choice and grandiloquence. Again and again, he achieves variety in his plays by having a simple statement follow a complex one. The effect of such variation is two-fold. On the one hand, he highlights by means of contrast both of the ideas he presents. On the other, he ensures that his audience or reader is never able simply to coast through his dramas by being lulled into somnolence through the monotony of sameness. Let's look at three examples:

◇ In *Macbeth*, Macbeth wonders whether the stain of Duncan's murder can ever be washed off his hands. Shakespeare has Macbeth begin his answer to that question with long impressive-sounding words and then repeat himself in a simpler, shorter way:

> Will all great Neptune's ocean wash this blood
> Clean from my hand? No, this my hand will rather
> The multitudinous seas incarnadine,
> Making the green one red (2.2.64–67).

◇ In *Antony and Cleopatra* (4.15.71–76), Cleopatra's attendants, Charmian and Iras, try to revive their mistress when she faints after Antony's death. They try the simple approach, "Lady" (twice) and "Madam" (no less than four times). When that fails, they try grandiloquence: "Royal Egypt, Empress!" That finally works, and Cleopatra stirs into consciousness.

◇ In *Richard II* (2.1.153–62), the King begins with a comment on the recent death of his uncle, John of Gaunt, that uses metaphor ("ripest fruit first falls" and "pilgrimage"). He follows that with the most brusque of statements, "So much for that." He then returns to grandiloquence in his talk of the war in Ireland ("rug-headed kerns" who are full of "venom") only to finish with avaricious simplicity by focusing on his decision to seize the goods of the dead John of Gaunt (his "plate, coin, revenues, and movables").

Test Case #3: Portia's Defense of Antonio

I began this chapter with a brief discussion of the history of rhetoric. I mentioned how during the Classical period, rhetorical speeches were divided into three types: deliberative (or political); forensic (or judicial); and epideictic (or praising). As a conclusion to this chapter, let's look at one example of rhetoric in action. Let's examine the best known judicial speech in Shakespeare: Portia's defense of Antonio in *The Merchant of Venice* 4.1.

Before Portia (disguised as the lawyer Balthasar) enters the courtroom, everything seems lost for Antonio. Shylock is simply enforcing a legal contract: a pound of Antonio's flesh as compensation for the money (3000 ducats) Antonio has borrowed from Shylock. Although the judge (the Duke of Venice) could save Antonio by dismissing the court, to do so would be to bring Venetian law into disrepute.

So, how does Portia save the day? By invoking the power of rhetoric.

- ◇ First, she displays impeccable ethos (character) by coming in the guise of a well-respected lawyer. She even has her maidservant, Nerissa, disguised as a lawyer's clerk to vouch for her and to present to the Duke a letter from Bellario (another highly regarded jurist). The letter explains Bellario's absence (he's sick), and then praises Balthasar/Portia's greatness of learning despite his/her youth ("I never knew so young a body with so/ old a head" [162–63]). So, it appears as if the letter is genuine and as if one great lawyer is praising another.
- ◇ Second, she shows wonderful pathos (appeal to the emotions) in her request for Shylock to be merciful. The audience and (Balthasar hopes) Shylock will surely be moved to sorrow for Antonio's plight (he surely doesn't deserve such punishment for a failure to pay a debt), compassion for the mistakes that all humanity commit (how far short all of us fall from God's mercy), and sympathy for Shylock's confusion of justice and mercy (he does have a right to his money, but forgiveness is nobler).
- ◇ Third, she shows logos (structure of ideas presented) by the mild tone of her speech (in keeping with the seriousness of the occasion) and the organization of her ideas. Here, the movement of thought is circular (from heaven down to earth and back to heaven again) just as mercy should be: we are merciful to others so that they will be merciful to us in their turn.

◊ Fourth, Portia's speech is a masterpiece, too, because of the rhetorical devices she uses. I've marked the major ones in the margins of the speech below:

adage	The quality of mercy is not strained)	
assonance	(It) droppeth as the gentle rain from heaven	
anaphora	Upon the place beneath. (It) is twice blest:	
alliteration	(It) blesseth him that gives and him that takes.	185
repetition	'Tis (mightiest) in the (mightiest;) it becomes	
alliteration	The thronèd monarch better than his crown.	
alliteration	His scepter shows the force of temporal power,	
	The attribute to awe and majesty,	
	Wherein doth sit the dread and fear of kings.	190
alliteration	But mercy is above this sceptered sway;	
anaphora	(It) is enthronèd in the heart of kings;	
	(It) is an attribute to God himself;	
	And earthly power doth then show likest God's	
assonance	When mercy seasons justice. Therefore, Jew,	195
	Though justice be thy plea, consider this,	
assonance	That in the course of justice none of us	
alliteration	Should see salvation. We do pray for mercy,	*caesura*
	And that same prayer doth teach us all to render	
antistrophe	The deeds of mercy. I have spoken thus much	200
	To mitigate the justice of thy plea,	
	Which if thou follow, this strict court of Venice	
consonance	Must needs give sentence 'gainst the merchant there (182-203).	

◊ Finally, when even her best rhetorical appeals fail, Portia brilliantly refutes Shylock's arguments in favor of his taking a pound of Antonio's flesh in compensation for the 3000 ducats he owes. She points out that the agreement between the two men specifies exactly a pound of flesh. So, Shylock would be guilty of a serious infraction of the law if he cut more or less than a pound of flesh from Antonio's body. He will have to be accurate to "the twentieth part/ Of one poor scruple" (327–28). The agreement also mentions nothing about blood. So, Shylock would have to perform a miraculous operation: remove the pound of flesh without drawing blood!

The end result of Portia's powers of persuasion? Defeat for Shylock and victory for Antonio. After her brilliant performance, Bassanio's praise seems understatement: "Most worthy gentleman, I and my friend [Antonio]/ Have by your wisdom been this day acquitted/ Of grievous penalties" (406–08).

Writing and Discussion Assignments

1. Take a careful look at John of Gaunt's "sceptred isle" political speech in *Richard II* 2.1.31–68. What rhetorical devices does he use? How persuasive is it from your point of view? From Richard II's?
2. Take a careful look at Berowne's epideictic speech in praise of love in *Love's Labor's Lost* 4.3.285–339. What rhetorical devices does he use? How convincing is his praise? How could it be more convincing?
3. The exchanges between Polonius and Gertrude in *Hamlet* 2.2.86–113 are examples of failed rhetoric. What is wrong with Polonius's use of language? How could his rhetoric be improved?
4. Examine Ulysses' speech on "degree" in *Troilus and Cressida* 1.3.75–137. Describe what he means by the term and explain how important it is to him.
5. Shakespeare uses the word *rhetoric* six times in his plays: *Love's Labor's Lost* 2.1.229, 3.1.62, 4.3.56, 235; *The Taming of the Shrew* 1.1.35; and *As You Like It* 5.1.40. Examine each of these uses, and construct a generalization about Shakespeare's attitude to rhetoric. In what contexts does the word appear? What are its uses? How much does Shakespeare seem to value it?
6. Imagine that you are Isabella in the exchange between Angelo and Isabella in *Measure for Measure* 2.1, and imagine that this is real life, not drama. How well do you defend yourself against Angelo's request? How else might you have responded?

Further Reading

Desmet, Christy. *Reading Shakespeare's Characters: Rhetoric, Ethics, and Identity.* Amherst, MA: U of Massachusetts P, 1992.

Dixon, Peter. *Rhetoric.* London: Methuen, 1971.

Edwards, Philip, Inga-Stina Ewbank, and G.K. Hunter, eds. *Shakespeare's Styles.* Cambridge: Cambridge UP, 1980.

Joseph, Sister Miriam. *Shakespeare's Use of the Arts of Language.* New York: Columbia UP, 1947.

Lanham, Richard A. *A Handlist of Rhetorical Terms.* 2nd ed. Berkeley: U of California P, 1991.

Vickers, Brian. *The Artistry of Shakespeare's Prose.* London: Methuen, 1968.

Chapter 4

Let me play the fool.
With mirth and laughter let old wrinkles
come

The Merchant of Venice *1.1.79–80*

Shakespeare's Humor

Chapter Overview

◇ Understanding Shakespeare's crude humor.
◇ Understanding Shakespeare's cultural humor: his French and British jokes.
◇ Understanding Shakespeare's linguistic humor (malapropisms).
◇ Understanding Shakespeare's slapstick humor.
◇ Understanding Shakespeare's cosmic humor.

In this chapter, I'll focus on one final aspect of Shakespeare's language: his humor. I'll start with an acknowledgment: Shakespeare's humor can sometimes be difficult to understand. In part, this difficulty afflicts any discussion of humor. First of all, what's funny is often culturally specific. The English have a very different sense of humor from Americans, for example. The former enjoy the ludicrous and the crude; the latter laugh more readily at situational comedy. So, in my experience, the English comedian Rowan Atkinson (when playing the character Mr. Bean) sends the average Englishman into paroxysms of laughter but leaves many Americans puzzled. The reverse could be said of Jim Carrey. Also, it can be peculiarly frustrating to analyze humor. Once you've said something is funny, it gets noticeably *less* so when you start to show why it provokes laughter.

There are other reasons students may find Shakespeare's humor difficult:

1. Sometimes they fail to understand a joke because the language in which it is framed is so topical.
2. Sometimes they can't believe so great a playwright can be so crude in his humor.

3. Sometimes they don't understand how the humor acts as a counterpoint to the serious tone of a play.
4. Sometimes they forget to visualize what a particular action would look like on stage.
5. Sometimes they don't appreciate that Shakespeare's humor is cosmic (or descriptive of the human condition) in its reach. For Shakespeare, humor is sometimes the only response to the absurdity of life.

This chapter attempts to show the range of what makes us laugh in Shakespeare. You may not find every example funny, but hopefully you will get a better sense of the extraordinary range of Shakespeare's language.

Shakespeare's Crude Humor

Probably by disposition (he seems to have been both clown and philosopher) and certainly in order to achieve success as a playwright, Shakespeare needed to write intellectually sophisticated plays that would also appeal to the uneducated. Shakespeare could not have made money had he written plays of interest only to university men and aristocrats. Thomas Sackville and Thomas Norton had proved that a generation earlier with their earnest and extraordinarily dull play, *Gorboduc* (1562). So Shakespeare laces almost every play with jokes designed to make the groundlings (the Elizabethan and Jacobean equivalent of the great unwashed) laugh aloud. Most of them are clearly sexual.

In *Twelfth Night*, when Sir Andrew Aguecheek becomes sensitive about his long, lank, blond hair, Sir Toby Belch cannot resist such a marvelous chance for a crude joke at his friend's expense. Sir Andrew looks for reassurance (My hair "becomes me well enough, does't not?" he asks Sir Toby) only to get back an example of vintage Sir Toby humor: "Excellent. It hangs like flax on a distaff; and I/ hope to see a huswife take thee between her legs and/ spin it off" (1.3.100–02). Here, the "distaff" (or pole used in weaving) symbolizes Sir Andrew's penis and the wool on one end, his pubic hair. What he is humorously suggesting is that Sir Andrew may be lucky enough to have wonderful sex with a woman.

In *Twelfth Night*, a comedy, one might expect such humor, of course. Shakespeare, however, liked above all else to keep his audience guessing, so crude humor crops up in the least likely places. *The Merchant of Venice*, for example, is categorized as a comedy only because it includes three marriages. It is so serious a play, in fact, that one character (Antonio) almost has his heart cut out by another (Shylock). Nevertheless, the very last lines of the play present a sexual pun. Gratiano remarks on the importance of being faithful to his wife, Nerissa, but he can't resist being vulgar by referring obliquely to

Nerissa's vagina: "Well, while I live I'll fear no other thing/So sore as keeping safe Nerissa's ring" (5.1.306–07). The primary meaning is the ring which symbolizes faithfulness in marriage, but the secondary meaning is sexual.

In *Hamlet*, too, Shakespeare inserts some very effective crude humor into "The Mousetrap" scene, even though the play itself is one of Shakespeare's greatest tragedies. Hamlet indulges in some banter with Ophelia while they watch the play within the play:

HAMLET	Lady, shall I lie in your lap?
	[*Lying down at Ophelia's feet*]
OPHELIA	No, my lord.
HAMLET	I mean, my head upon your lap?
OPHELIA	Ay, my lord.
HAMLET	Do you think I meant country matters?
OPHELIA	I think nothing, my lord.
HAMLET	That's a fair thought to lie between maids' legs.
OPHELIA	What is, my lord?
HAMLET	Nothing.
OPHELIA	You are merry, my lord.
HAMLET	Who, I?
OPHELIA	Ay, my lord (3.2.110–22).

The pun on "country" (which sounds so much like the vulgar word for "vagina") as well as the vaginal symbolism of "Nothing" between "maids' legs" is clearly intentional. Each reinforces Hamlet's initial comment to Ophelia that he wishes to have sex with her: "Lady, shall I lie in your lap?" And Shakespeare makes sure that the audience gets the crude joke by having Ophelia fail initially to understand the joke ("What is, my lord?") and then acknowledge understanding it ("You are merry, my lord"). The effect of the crude joke? In part, it relaxes the tension of the scene. In part, it suggests that the relationship between Hamlet and Ophelia has progressed beyond their innocent love earlier in the play.

Shakespeare's Cultural Humor

Shakespeare and All Those French Jokes

Most of Shakespeare's crude jokes are fairly easy to spot and to understand. What is perhaps less easy to comprehend for anyone not English is Shakespeare's delight in jokes at the expense of the French. What needs to be remembered is that since 1066, when William of Normandy beat Harold at the Battle of Hastings (by devious means, the English would say), England and France have been at odds with each other. Close proximity has bred a rivalry that continues to this day. What needs to be remembered, too, is that Shakespeare was not unusual in cracking jokes about the French. There are several expressions in English slang that explicitly criticize them. The politest is "French leave," which means to make an exit rudely from a party by not thanking the hosts. Then there are "French kisses" (which no polite Englishman would ever indulge in) and even "French letters" (which are, of all things, condoms).

Shakespeare's jokes at French expense frequently focus on disease. Again and again, allusions to syphilis, to what contemporaries colloquially referred to as the "French disease," crop up in his plays. Often, such allusions are linked to one of the best-known signs of the disease: baldness, or the "French crown." Two of the best examples occur in *A Midsummer Night's Dream* and *Pericles*. In the former, Quince and Bottom discuss the available roles in the play they mean to put on to celebrate Theseus's wedding. Bottom says that he can play a part in a "French-crown-color beard," that is in one that's yellow. Quince jokes about the French being syphilitic: "Some of your French crowns have no hair at all,/ and then you will play barefaced" (1.2.86, 88–89). In the latter, Bolt (a pimp) and Bawd (Pander's wife) clearly allude to syphilis as French in origin, and talk about its unpleasant effects. (To appreciate the joke all you need to know is that the name "Verolles" is derived from the French word *verolé* meaning "syphilitic.")

BOLT	But, mistress, do you know the French knight that cowers i' the hams?
BAWD	Who, Monsieur Verolles?
BOLT	Ay, he? He offered to cut a caper at the proclamation, but he made a groan at it, and swore he would see her [Marina] tomorrow.
BAWD	Well, well, as for him, he brought his disease hither; here he does but repair it. I know he will come in our shadow, to scatter his crowns in the sun (4.2.102–10).

I don't claim for a moment that such a dialogue is tremendously funny for us, but Shakespeare's contemporaries would have laughed at it, and even we may smile at its knowing cleverness. What is useful to note as well is that the two examples just presented date from very different periods in Shakespeare's career. *A Midsummer Night's Dream* was written in about 1595; *Pericles* in about 1607. The first is early Shakespeare; the second late. Some thirteen years separate them, and yet the playwright is still returning to the same source—the "French disease"—for laughs.

You should not think, however, that Shakespeare's humor at French expense focuses only on their being disease-ridden. Shakespeare offers a full range of jokes:

◇ **Straightforward insults.** In *1 Henry VI*, the English general, Talbot, talks disparagingly of the enemy as "a yelping kennel of French curs!" (4.2.47). In *King John*, the king's mother, Queen Eleanor, labels an instance of treachery, a "foul revolt of French inconstancy!" as if, somehow, the word *French* were itself an intensifier (3.1.322). In *Henry V*, the king admits that his troops, who are suffering terribly from bad food and bad water, are "Almost no better than so many French" (3.6.147).

◇ **Complaints about food.** In *All's Well That Ends Well*, Parolles, a friend of Bertram, debates the value of virginity with Helena, the ward of Bertram's mother. For him it has no value, and he makes his point by once again cutting down all things French: "your old virginity," he says, is "like one of our/ French withered pears—it looks ill, it eats drily. Mar-/ry, 'tis a withered pear; it was formerly better; marry,/ yet 'tis a withered pear. Will you anything with it?" (1.1.161–64). Here, it's worth noting, Shakespeare cannot resist a sexual element in the joke.

◇ **Complaints about effete French manners.** In *Richard III*, Richard of Gloucester suggests that his political enemies at court are taking advantage of his roughness of manner to turn his brother, Edward IV, against him. And what example does he use of the smoothness he lacks? A French one, of course. He is a "rancorous enemy" simply because he cannot "Duck with French nods and apish courtesy" (1.3.50, 49). In *Hamlet*, Osric delivers Laertes' challenge to Hamlet by announcing that the bet includes "six French rapiers and poniards with their assigns,/as girdle, hangers, and so." Hamlet is unimpressed by such frippery and cuts down his bombast to "six French swords" (5.2.148–49, 160).

◇ **Complaints about the French language.** In *Richard II*, the Duchess of York denounces her husband's use of the affected "pardonne moy" by rejecting his example of "chopping French" and insisting that she will "[s]peak 'pardon' as 'tis current in our land" (5.3.119, 124, 123). In *1 Henry VI*, Sir William Lucy refuses to consider a surrender by the English forces at the battle of Bordeaux. Why? Because "Submission," he tells the French herald, "['t]is a mere French word./ We English warriors wot not what it means" (4.7.54–55). In *2 Henry VI*, Jack Cade, the rebel leader, goes one step further, by arguing that even the act of speaking French is traitorous. His first complaint against Lord Saye, one of the king's supporters, is that he "hath gelded the commonwealth and made/ it an eunuch." Worse than that, "he can speak/ French, and therefore he is a traitor" (4.2.160–61, 161–62).

Shakespeare also offers us French characters whose only purpose is to make the audience or reader laugh. The Dauphin in *Henry V* fulfills that role well, but it is Doctor Caius, a Frenchman, in *The Merry Wives of*

Windsor who does so with true brilliance. As early as 1.4, Mistress Quickly, the Doctor's housekeeper, lets everyone know what is in store by promising that when he appears there will be "an/ old abusing of God's patience and the King's English" (4–5). The Doctor doesn't disappoint.

◇ He begins by looking in his cupboard for some herbs that he needs (what he calls "some *simples*" "dat I vill not/ for the varld I shall leave behind" [58–59; emphasis added]). And what does he find hiding in there? One Peter *Simple*, the servant of Abraham Slender.

◇ He then threatens Sir Hugh Evans with castration, but delivers the threat in damaged, humorously illogical English: "I will cut *all*/ his two stones [testicles]" (105–06; emphasis added). Within one line these testicles (two or three?) magically disappear as Evans "shall not have a stone to/ throw at his dog" (106–07).

◇ Three scenes later he's beside himself with anger that Evans has not appeared to duel with him over his encouragement of Slender's courtship of Anne Page. This time, however, it's not so much that he fractures the language to good comic effect (although he doesn't seem too good at counting the time he has waited for Evans: "six or/ seven, two, tree [sic] hours" [2.3.32–33]). It's more that the English have fun insulting him without his knowing. The Host of the Garter Inn derides his medical profession by apparently praising him as "Castilian King-Urinal" and "Monsieur Mock-water [urine]" (30, 51). When the Doctor looks puzzled, the Host defines the two phrases: the first supposedly means "Hector of/ Greece" (not Troy!) and the second means "valor" "in our English tongue" (30–31, 54–55).

◇ One scene later, when Evans and the Doctor finally meet, Shakespeare cannot overlook the chance for one more medical joke, for he has Evans insult the Doctor in the now-familiar manner: "I will knog your urinal about your/ knave's cogscomb for missing your meetings and appointments" (3.1.83–84).

◇ Then, Shakespeare decides it's time to get some laughs out of the Doctor's accent. When Master Page invites Master Ford to go birding with him, Evans pipes up and invites himself: "If there is one, I shall make two in the company" (3.3.214). Not to be outdone, the Doctor follows suit, but mangles English once more: "If there be one or two, I shall make-a the turd" (215).

◇ Finally, Shakespeare designs one last humiliation for the French Doctor. The Doctor wishes to marry Anne Page, but she intends otherwise. She wins and marries the one she loves, Fenton. The Doctor is tricked into marrying a boy! As he ruefully announces: "I am cozened! I/ ha' married *un garcon* [or "boy," in French], a boy; *un paysan* [or "young peasant lad," in French], by gar, a boy" (5.5.200–01).

No one, however, can accuse Shakespeare of not being able to adapt his humor to the needs of his drama and his audience. So, in *Henry V*, despite all the occasions in his other plays where he pokes fun at the French, he includes one scene which is almost entirely in French (3.4) and one scene which includes significant amounts of French dialogue (5.2). Why? Not because he's hypocritical, but because the historical Henry V married a French princess, Katharine of Valois. What more natural, then, than that the king and his bride-to-be would converse some of the time in her language.

There is, however, more to it than this explanation suggests, for the scene that is almost entirely in French does not feature the king at all. That scene, in which Katharine demonstrates to her lady-in-waiting, Alice, her progress in learning English, is a tour de force for Shakespeare. It shows, too, how frequently he returns to crude humor to get his laughs. This time he does so in such a way as to appeal both to his learned audience and to the groundlings. The first would have got both parts of the joke because they understood French; the latter would have had to rely, in part, on stage gestures.

Let's take the joke apart. Katharine shows her progress in learning English by naming the parts of the body. As she does so, she points to herself. Then she asks Alice what the English call "le pied" (the "foot" in English) and "la robe" (or "gown" in English). You can almost see the joke coming as Alice replies, "Le foot, madame, et le count." Katharine is outraged because she hears *foutre* (the French word for "fornicate"). Shakespeare's educated theatergoers would laugh here. Katharine also mishears the word *count* (Alice meant to say gown?) as the slang English word for *vagina*. All of Shakespeare's audience, educated and groundling, would have laughed at this one.

Shakespeare and All Those British Jokes

By now, it's pretty clear that Shakespeare is hardly politically correct when it comes to his low humor. It's worth noting, though, that he doesn't hold up only the old enemy, the French, to ridicule. On the contrary, anyone with a funny accent is fair game because he wants his audience above all else to have reason to laugh. The three British nationalities other than English (the Irish, the Welsh, and the Scots) are often the particular focus of his humor, most notably in *Henry V* and *The Merry Wives of Windsor.*

In the first of these plays, it's all three ethnic groups—the Irish, the Welsh, and the Scots—who are played for laughs. Captain Fluellen is Welsh; Captain Macmorris is Irish; and Captain Jamy, Scottish. The first of these has a comically exaggerated Welsh accent, a delight in pedantry, and so strong a sense of national pride that in 5.1 he forces Pistol to eat the Welsh national symbol, the leek. The second also has a comically exaggerated accent, an Irish one this time, and is so proud of his ancestry that he and Fluellen almost come to blows over it. The third, again with a funny accent played for laughs, is long-winded even as he announces his courage. The three men appear in the so-called "international scene" (3.2), and the comedy at their expense is made more obvious by the presence of an English officer, Captain Gower, whose most notable characteristic is bland competence.

So, Fluellen talks again and again about military tactics: "the true disciplines of the wars" (71). Macmorris talks repeatedly about his nation in very defensive terms: "Of my nation? What ish my nation? Ish a/ villain, and a bastard, and a knave, and a rascal? What/ ish my nation? Who talks of my nation?" (121–23). Jamy talks as if one word were going out of fashion: "gud," that is, "good." He has only eleven lines in the play (and all in this scene), but he manages, nevertheless, to use "gud" an astonishing six times, including four times in only two lines: "I sall be vary gud, gud feith, gud captens bath,/ and I sall quite you with gud leve" (101–02). And the Englishman Gower? The best he can manage when he gets a word in edgeways is to act as a stage director: "The town [of Harfleur] sounds a parley" (135). It does, but Fluellen, Macmorris, and Jamy go on squabbling anyway.

In *The Merry Wives of Windsor*, the comedy is carried on the shoulders of Sir Hugh Evans, a Welsh clergyman and schoolmaster. The humor in his appearances comes mainly from the creative way he mangles English. After he has altered *cheese* and *butter* into *seese* and *putter*, Falstaff (who has suffered Evans's slaughter of the English language through five acts) memorably complains, "Have I lived to stand/at the taunt of one that makes fritters of English?" (5.5.141–42). Evans also is funny for his confusion of popular and religious songs in 3.1.

He is at his best, however, in the "Latin" scene (4.1), a set piece in which he tests his pupil's knowledge of Latin. This set piece is particularly interesting because it is humorous only to a particular part of Shakespeare's contemporary audience: the well-educated ones who knew Latin. (Similarly, the scene in *Henry V* [3.4] in which Katharine of Valois tests her knowledge of English works as comedy largely for a particular Shakespearean audience: those who knew French.) When Evans tests William Page, bilingual word jokes abound. *Pulcher* (the Latin for "beautiful") sounds to Mistress Quickly like "polecats" (24–25). When Evans gives the three forms of the object case for the Latin word *hic* (which means "this"), what should have been *hunc, hanc, hoc* comes out as *hung, hang, hog*. At which point, Shakespeare, through Mistress Quickly, can't resist a joke: "'Hang-hog' is Latin for bacon, I warrant/ you," she says (44–45). It gets worse. *Caret* sounds like "carrot" in Evans' mouth, so Mistress Quickly makes a joke about vegetables (49–50). *Horum* sounds like "whore," so Mistress Quickly gets upset at what Evans may be teaching the boy (57–58). She says it's bad enough that he teaches him the words "hick" and "hack" (which were

Renaissance slang for "drink" and "have sex" and sound identical to two other forms of the Latin word for "this": *hic* and *hac*). To mention the word "whore," however, is too much. "Fie upon you!" she says as she denounces Evans (61–63). Evans, of course, in his broken English has no defense but to mangle the language even more: "Thou art as foolish Christian creatures as I/ would desires" (66–67).

Before I finish this section on Shakespearean humor at the expense of nationality, it's important to note that to his credit Shakespeare makes fun not only of the French, the Irish, the Scots, and the Welsh, but of the English as well. He wants his audience not only to laugh at others but at themselves also. Such a sense of humor is implicit in the character of Captain Gower in *Henry V*. It is *explicit* in *Hamlet, Othello, The Tempest* and in several other plays.

In *Hamlet*, the First Clown (or gravedigger) tells Hamlet (whom the First Clown doesn't recognize) that Hamlet has been sent to England because he's mad, and in that country it doesn't matter much whether he recovers his sanity or not. Hamlet, playing the straight man, gives the cue line for the joke: "Why?" (5.1.153). The Clown replies: "'Twill not be seen in him there. There the/ men are as mad as he" (154–55).

In *Othello*, Cassio serves as Iago's straight man. Iago begins by remarking that the English are heavy drinkers, that is "are most potent in potting" (2.3.73). According to Iago, "Your Dane, your German, and/your swag-bellied Hollander . . . are noth-/ing to your English" (73–75). Cassio wants to hear more: "Is your Englishman so exquisite in his drinking?" (76). And Iago obliges: "Why, he drinks you, with facility, your Dane/dead drunk; he sweats not to overthrow your Almain [German];/ he gives your Hollander a vomit ere the next pottle can be filled" (77–80).

In *The Tempest*, the joke at the expense of the English occurs when the jester, Trinculo, first catches sight of Caliban. His initial reaction is puzzlement: "What have/ we here, a man or a fish?" he asks (2.2.24–25). Then he answers his own question by talking to himself about how such a creature would be received in England: "Were I in England now, as once I was, and had but/ this fish painted, not a holiday fool there but would/ give a piece of silver. There would this monster make/ a man. Any strange beast there makes a man" (28–31).

Shakespeare's Linguistic Humor

As I have suggested elsewhere in this book, Shakespeare lives and dies as a dramatist on the strength of his language. Given the limited special effects available to him on the Renaissance stage, it could not be otherwise. As a result, much of his humor depends on wordplay. He loves jokes on people's names. There's Sir Toby Belch in *Twelfth Night*—a perfect name for a drunkard. There's Sir Oliver Mar-Text in *As You Like It*—ideal for a country clergyman inclined to misinterpret the Bible out of ignorance. There's that wonderful group of sergeants and country soldiers in *2 Henry IV*: Fang; Snare; Moldy; Shadow; Wart; and Feeble.

He loves jokes, too, that depend on the audience spending time considering what words really mean and how complex are the uses humans put them to. In *Much Ado about Nothing*, he devotes six lines to the role of thought in love. Beatrice asks Margaret, Hero's gentlewoman, a sharp question about Benedick, and she responds:

> You may think
> perchance that I think you are in love. Nay, by'r Lady,
> I am not such a fool to think what I list, nor I list not to
> think what I can, nor indeed I cannot think, if I would
> think my heart out of thinking, that you are in love or
> that you will be in love or that you can be in love
> (3.4.75–80).

Seven times she uses forms of the word *think;* four times she uses the word *love.* Impressive in a speech of only six lines. It's a hard speech to understand because Shakespeare (through Margaret) is simply having fun with words. Margaret's statement is straightforward—she can't believe that Beatrice could ever be in love—but she's determined to get to it the long way around.

Shakespeare also loves puns, and did right from the beginning of his career. In one of his very earliest comedies, *The Comedy of Errors*, which may well date from 1589, he offers his audience or reader a plethora of them: *deer* and *dear* (2.1.99); *sconce* as head and battering ram (2.2.34–35); *bald* as hairless and straightforward (105–07); *bondman* (as servant) and *unbound* (as having one's hands untied) (5.1.289, 291).

The Malapropism

Above all forms of wordplay, however, Shakespeare loved the malapropism. A malapropism is a comical, confused misuse of a word, often a long one. The term is derived from a character named Mrs. Malaprop in Richard Sheridan's play *The Rivals* (1775), with Sheridan simply rendering into English the French phrase *mal à propos*, which means "inappropriately." In *Romeo and Juliet*, the Nurse tells Romeo that she would like to speak with him, but confuses the words *conference* and *confidence*: "If you be he, sir, I desire some confidence/ with you" (2.4.125–26). Romeo's friend, Benvolio, can't resist the chance for a joke, and comments: "She will indite [sic] him to some supper" (127). In *Measure for Measure*, Elbow, a constable, confuses the words *benefactor* and *malefactor, profanation* and *profession* when speaking to Angelo's deputy, Escalus (2.1.50–52, 55). In *A Midsummer Night's Dream*, Bottom gets the words *exposition* and *disposition* tangled up

(4.1.38). Sometimes, a malapropism is deliberate on the part of a character, and is meant by Shakespeare to be both funny and profound at the same time. In *Richard III*, for example, Richard, Duke of Gloucester calls himself and Clarence, "the Queen's abjects" (1.1.106). In one word, he suggests his frustration at not being in power. He is not a "subject" but an "object" and a lowly or "abject" one at that.

There are, however, two outstanding devotees of the malapropism in Shakespeare, characters whom I haven't thus far mentioned: Mistress Quickly in *1 Henry IV, 2 Henry IV, Henry V,* and *The Merry Wives of Windsor,* and Dogberry in *Much Ado about Nothing.* It's difficult to decide who is the champion; they are both extraordinarily talented at using the wrong word in the wrong place. Dogberry provides us in one scene with *desartless* instead of *deserving* (3.3.9), *senseless* instead of *sensible* (22), *tolerable* for *intolerable* (36), *vigitant* for *vigilant* (93). In his murder of English, he is joined by his colleague, Verges, who says *salvation* when he means *damnation* (3). A short time later, Dogberry reappears in equally good form with *confidence* instead of *conference* (3.5.2), *decerns* instead of *concerns* (3), *exclamation* for *acclamation* (24), *comprehended* for *apprehended* (44), *aspicious* for *auspicious* (44), *suffigance* for *sufficient* (50), *excommunication* for both *communication* and *examination* (61–62). His best work? Probably "Comparisons are odorous" for "Comparisons are odious" (3.5.15).

Mistress Quickly is equally dangerous with words and, since she appears in four plays to Dogberry's one, has even more opportunity to kill words stone dead. She is also more imaginative in their use. She has the best bawdy malapropism: *erection* for *direction* when she is talking to—of all people—Falstaff (*The Merry Wives of Windsor* 3.5.38). She also has the best extended malapropism in all of Shakespeare. It occurs in *2 Henry IV.* In that play, she tries to get Falstaff to live up to his promise to marry her. An officer, Fang, draws his sword on Falstaff to arrest him; Falstaff does likewise in his own defense. Mistress Quickly denounces him as a "honeysuckle villain!" a "honeyseed" and a "hempseed" (2.1.49, 51, 57). What does she mean? *Homicidal* and *homicide.* That surely tops the crudity of her malapropism in *The Merry Wives of Windsor,* where she calls Mistress Page a "fartuous" instead of a "virtuous" wife (2.2.92).

Malapropisms are undoubtedly funny, but why? The answer is fairly straightforward. People like to laugh at others more than at themselves, and what better than to laugh at someone who can't even use correctly what should come as naturally to us as breathing: words. Such an explanation fits well, too, with Shakespeare as dramatist. It neatly explains why it is his favorite linguistic joke. On the one hand, the limits of available staging meant that he had to emphasize language. On the other, language in the late sixteenth and early seventeenth centuries was in such a state of flux that malapropisms were much easier to commit. As a literary device, the malapropism gave Shakespeare the most wonderful opportunity for invention. It may even be that some of his malapropisms are unintentional.

Shakespeare's Slapstick Humor

If you think back through the plays you've seen and read, you may not be able to think of many occasions when Shakespeare uses visual humor, or slapstick, to make people laugh, for they are few in the canon of his works. Nonetheless, they do exist, and their very rarity increases their dramatic importance.

Shakespeare's slapstick is of two kinds: **reported** and **performed**. The first describes slapstick that would have been impossible to stage during Shakespeare's time and difficult to manage even now. The second shows **slapstick** that is simpler and, so, capable of being performed.

Let's look briefly at the first kind—reported slapstick—by analyzing a couple of excerpts, one from *The Merry Wives of Windsor* and one from *The Comedy of Errors*. The example from *The Merry Wives of Windsor* naturally involves Falstaff, Shakespeare's greatest comedic figure. He comes up with a scheme to make money by sleeping with Mistress Page and Mistress Ford. Neither is in any way interested, and both agree to punish him for his arrogant foolishness. Mistress Ford plans to have him hide in a laundry basket to escape her jealous husband. Then, two of her servants are to take him to Datchet Mead, and dump him in a waterlogged ditch beside the Thames. Clearly some of this stage business is impossible to show, but Shakespeare, through Falstaff, does a wonderfully funny job of telling what happens. The women's plan succeeds perfectly, and Falstaff returns to tell his story—and to tell it not once, but twice. The first time it's to Bardolph that he complains:

> The rogues slighted me into the river with as little remorse as they would have drowned a blind bitch's puppies, fifteen i' the litter! And you may know by my size that I have a kind of alacrity in sinking; if the bottom were as deep as hell, I should down. I have been drowned, but that the shore was shelvy and shallow—a death that I abhor; for the water swells a man, and what a thing should I have been when I had been swelled! I should have been a mountain of mummy (3.5.8–17).

Only another 70 lines or so go by before he's telling the story again to Mistress Ford's husband, who is disguised as Master Brook. This time he's not so concerned about almost drowning and swelling up to an even larger size. What scares him was the possibility of catching cold. He was, he says:

> thrown into the Thames and cooled,
> glowing hot, in that surge, like a horseshoe! Think of
> that—hissing hot—think of that, Master Brook!
> (111–13).

So, the audience can imagine what it must have been like, and Falstaff gets the chance to tell his tale twice, undoubtedly with appropriate, exaggerated gestures and sounds. He may, for example, have mimed the size of his belly or the action of rising to the surface of the water. As for sounds, he wouldn't have missed the chance to make the loud hissing sound of a red-hot horseshoe being dunked into cold water.

The example of reported slapstick from *The Comedy of Errors* is more complex and, for a modern audience, ambivalent. Antipholus and Dromio of Ephesus are wrongly imprisoned because of their supposed insanity and for a debt of 200 ducats. They escape, and Antipholus's servant brings the news to Adriana, his wife. He describes their treatment of one of their jailers, Doctor Pinch, in detail:

> My master and his man are both broke loose,
> Beaten the maids a-row, and bound the doctor [Pinch],
> Whose beard they have singed off with brands of fire,
> And ever as it blazed they threw on him
> Great pails of puddled mire to quench the hair.
> My master preaches patience to him, and the while
> His man with scissors nicks him like a fool;
> And sure, unless you send some present help,
> Between them they will kill the conjurer (5.1.169–77).

Clearly, such actions could not have been convincingly played on stage. It would have been too difficult to make it realistic, and too messy as well. Moreover, the events described don't sound particularly funny. One could almost say that they sound like a muted version of the blinding of Gloucester by Cornwall in *King Lear*. Such a claim would, however, be badly mistaken. The description *is* funny, and is so for several reasons.

◇ *The Comedy of Errors* is a comedy. We know that because of the title and the action thus far in the play. So, we know that Doctor Pinch won't be killed; indeed, we are sure that he won't even be seriously injured.

◇ We know a great deal about Pinch himself before and after the escape of Antipholus and Dromio of Ephesus, and what we know means that we don't feel sympathy for him. Before, we know he's a quack physician and charlatan conjuror (or exorcist). After, we know that he is (in the words of Antipholus of Ephesus):

> a hungry, lean-faced villain,
> A mere anatomy, a mountebank,
> A threadbare juggler and a fortune-teller,
> A needy, hollow-eyed, sharp-looking wretch,
> A living dead man . . . [a] pernicious slave (5.1.238–42).

In essence, he is someone safe to laugh at.

◇ We never see Pinch again in the play, so his humiliation (including his terrible haircut) remains only in our mind's eye.

◇ No one is hurt on stage. If the actions of Antipholus and Dromio of Ephesus were performed on stage, it wouldn't be funny at all.

For all these reasons, Shakespeare's comedy of *reported* slapstick in *The Comedy of Errors* works. Again, as so often, Shakespeare has worked within the limits of his medium to great effect by choosing with remarkable deftness what to show and what to tell.

Let's move on to the cases of Shakespearean slapstick performed on stage.

◇ In *A Midsummer Night's Dream*, there are two examples: first, Titania's falling in love with Bottom even though the latter has grown ass's ears (3.1); and, second, the rude mechanicals' marvelously incompetent performance at the end of the play of "A tedious brief scene of young Pyramus/And his love Thisbe; very tragical mirth" (5.1.56–57).

◇ In *Twelfth Night*, there are three: first, Malvolio's discovery of the letter (purportedly from Olivia) declaring her love for him (2.5); second, Malvolio's decision to wear crossed garters over yellow stockings in accordance with the letter; and, third, the mock swordfight between Viola/Cesario and Sir Andrew Aguecheek for the love of Olivia (3.4).

◇ In *I Henry IV*, there is the botched robbery at Gad's Hill (2.2) as well as Prince Hal's revealing of Falstaff as a boaster and a coward (2.4).

◇ In *Henry V*, there's Fluellen's forcing Pistol to eat a leek after the latter has insulted the national symbol of Wales (5.1).

◇ In *The Taming of the Shrew*, there's the two-scene Induction in which Christopher Sly is duped by a Lord into thinking he's a gentleman, with the deception involving a change in clothes and a page dressed as a woman.

◇ In *The Merry Wives of Windsor*, there are three examples of performed slapstick involving Falstaff. In 3.3, he is persuaded to get into a laundry basket full of dirty laundry to escape from a jealous husband. In 4.2 he dresses in women's clothes to escape detection. In 5.5 he appears as a mythological creature, Herne the Hunter, replete with antlers.

◊ In *Antony and Cleopatra*, Cleopatra strikes the messenger twice and drags him up and down the stage because he refuses to tell her what she wants to hear: that Antony isn't married to Octavia (2.5).

◊ In *The Tempest*, Caliban and Trinculo become a two-headed, four-legged monster when Trinculo, frightened by thunder, hides under Caliban's cloak (2.2).

It is reasonable to say that there are only a little over a dozen instances of slapstick in all 38 of Shakespeare's plays. Given my emphasis thus far on language, it's important to see that sometimes Shakespeare emphasizes the physical over the verbal in his effort to secure laughter from his audience. It's also clear that he relies on certain tried and true formulas when he does want to make his audience laugh at the action on stage. These formulas include:

◊ The unexpected: Titania falling in love with Bottom in *A Midsummer Night's Dream*, and Cleopatra abusing the messenger in *Antony and Cleopatra*.

◊ The metadramatic: that is, Shakespeare using drama to talk about the nature of drama itself. In *A Midsummer Night's Dream*, the rude mechanicals present a truly awful version of the tragic story of Pyramis and Thisbe. They do so in honor of the marriage of Duke Theseus and Hippolyta, and their audience includes not only Duke Theseus and Hippolyta but also the other two just-married couples: Hermia and Lysander; and Helena and Demetrius. In *Twelfth Night*, Viola/Cesario and Sir Andrew Aguecheek duel while watched by Sir Toby Belch, Fabian, Antonio, and Officers. In *The Taming of the Shrew*, Christopher Sly along with the page, attendants, three servingmen, and the Lord form an audience watching the play within a play—in this case the taming of the shrew, Kate.

◊ The ludicrous: Falstaff as Herne the Hunter; Trinculo and Caliban as a two-headed monster; and Bottom as an ass.

◊ The ingenuous: no one in these comic scenes has any sense of irony; no one understands until afterwards how foolish he or she appears. This innocence is crucial; without it, the audience would be much less likely to laugh because it would see that the target of their laughter is "in" on the joke as well.

◊ The sexually disruptive: again and again Shakespeare "bends" gender to comic effect. It's as if he's asking his audience to consider the nature of identity even as they laugh at the action on stage. So, Falstaff in *The Merry Wives of Windsor* dresses as a woman to escape a jealous husband, even though he doesn't make a convincing woman. As Evans says in a

Welsh accent when Falstaff is escaping: "By Jeshu, I think the 'oman is a witch indeed. I/like not when a 'oman has a great peard. I spy a great/ peard under his muffler" (4.2.180–82). And so, a drunken Sly with his new identity as a rich Lord in *The Taming of the Shrew* is sexually tempted by the sight of a male page dressed up as his wife. "Madam," he says to him/her, "undress you and come now to bed" (Induction.2.114). The page/wife seems equally eager, for she complains about the length of time she has been "abandoned from [his] bed" (Induction.2.112). In the end, of course, she begs off with a pro forma excuse, but the comic threat of the sexually disruptive remains in *The Taming of the Shrew*, to which Sly's story is merely an introduction. It remains particularly potent on the Renaissance stage, of course, where all the female parts were played by boys. So, in the case of *Twelfth Night*'s Viola/Cesario, for example, a boy plays a young woman who plays a young man.

Shakespeare's Cosmic Humor

Let's take it for granted that everyone who reads or watches Shakespeare will find something to laugh at. For some, it will be the sexual humor; for others, the involved wordplay; for some, the reported buffoonery; for others, the slapstick enacted on stage. Yet, the more I've read, seen, and taught Shakespeare, the more I have become convinced that his greatness as a humorist lies not in the intensity of the laughter he produces but in the nature of the laughter itself. Shakespeare's humor is, in fact, cosmic. By that I mean that his central insight is life's absurdity. Long before the rise of the absurd in theatre (of which Beckett's *Waiting for Godot* is a prime example), Shakespeare was saying again and again in his comedies and the humorous moments in his other plays (histories, tragedies, and romances) that even the funniest moments in life are tinged with sorrow because we know they will not last.

In essence, Shakespeare's cosmic humor forces us to assess ourselves as human beings, a species with enough self-consciousness to know that we are born, live, and die with no empirical understanding whatsoever of the meaning of life. The human condition is surely much more a state of frustration at unfulfilled desires, needs, wants, and dreams than it is of satisfaction, fulfillment, and happiness. Shakespeare understood this extraordinarily clearly in his plays, and it shows in his verbal and physical humor alike.

To focus the discussion, let's look back at those dozen or so examples of slapstick that were listed earlier, to see this cosmic dimension in his humor.

◈ *A Midsummer Night's Dream*. Titania's falling in love with Bottom raises the whole question of the nature of love. As we would all surely acknowledge, love is blind. What is it about an individual that attracts us? The rude mechanicals' marvelously incompetent performance of "Pyramus and Thisbe" brings up the whole question of illusion in representation. Why is it ludicrous for someone to play a wall (as Snout does) or moonshine (as Starveling does) when what the audience sees is clearly artificial and convention-ridden anyway? More broadly, of course, it brings up bigger questions: How do we know what reality is, and how do we see through the roles that we all play for each other?

◈ *Twelfth Night*. Malvolio's unrequited love for Olivia surely speaks to all of us and the foolish things we have done in the name of desire. None of us may have gone as far as to wear crossed garters over yellow stockings because our lover supposedly asks us to, but getting down on one knee to propose is pretty ludicrous when you think about it, as are some of the conventional clothes worn at weddings (the bride's dress with its massive train; the groom's tuxedo or morning clothes; and the large—sometimes very large—hats). Similarly, Malvolio's misrepresentation of what Maria's fraudulent letter says about Olivia's desire for him is funny, but haven't we all foolishly misrepresented (at least to ourselves) events in our lives in the hope of achieving a particular end? And then there's the mock swordfight between Viola/Cesario and Sir Andrew Aguecheek for the love of Olivia. Again, it's really funny to see two reluctant duelers doing everything they can to avoid a conflict. As always, however, the comedy has a cosmic edge. It could easily end in tragedy (the swordfight between Mercutio and Tybalt does in *Romeo and Juliet*), and even when it doesn't it still resonates for the audience. Have you never found yourself doing something stupid and desperately wishing you could have changed your mind long ago?

◈ *1 Henry IV*. The botched robbery at Gad's Hill is comical, but Falstaff's exaggerated retelling of the event is funnier still because of the ways in which he exaggerates the strength of the "enemy" and the desperate ways in which he tries to explain away what happened after he discovers that Prince Hal tricked him. (See Fig. 4.1.) Once more, the comic appeal of the scene is not simply to our love of Falstaff's larger-than-life presence, but more profoundly to our realization that he is just a caricature of us all with our love of exaggeration and our capacity to rationalize what we do. "I knew that," we say after someone comments on something foolish that we've said or done—even when it's clear we didn't.

◈ *Henry V*. Fluellen's forcing Pistol to eat a leek after Pistol has insulted the national symbol of Wales is funny largely because force-feeding anyone vegetables is so ludicrous. The added dimension to the joke is there, nonetheless, and it comes from the way in which the humor zeroes in

Figure 4.1
Thomas Stothard's *Falstaff Describing the Fight at Gadshill* (c. 1827). Note his exaggerated gestures.

on the whole question of patriotism. Why should we feel loyalty to an abstraction or a construct such as country or nation? Why do we seem at our most blind when our love of country is challenged? Samuel Johnson once remarked that "patriotism is the last refuge of a scoundrel" (Boswell 2:158). The history of wars suggests as much.

◊ *The Taming of the Shrew.* The two-scene Induction in which Christopher Sly is duped raises the question of class in a very direct way. Why do we give authority to some based on wealth? on manners? on blood? Why do we seem unable to treat each other as individuals? as equals? Sly decides he's a lord because he smells "sweet savors" and feels "soft things" (Induction.2.71). How superficial, then, is the idea of class, but how profound its influence throughout history.

◊ *The Merry Wives of Windsor.* Falstaff in this play (as in *1 Henry IV* and *2 Henry IV*) is the emblem of humanity's undying hope and unending desire. Only Falstaff, we feel, would—out of lust for Mistress Ford and her money—get into a laundry basket full of dirty laundry, be thrown into the Thames, dress in women's clothes, and appear, finally, as a mythological creature, Herne the Hunter, replete with antlers. Once we stop laughing at what happens to him, however, it surely dawns on us that we are as much at the mercy of instinctual drives as Falstaff is. For some of us, it may be lust or love; for others, food or survival; for still others, power. *The Merry Wives of Windsor* is a very funny play, but it is also a profound one. "What humiliations," it asks, "are you prepared to go through to get what you want?" Former President Clinton and Monica Lewinsky are surely names enough to prove my point.

◊ *Antony and Cleopatra.* Cleopatra's abuse of the messenger is humorous because it is so unexpected and so little like the behavior expected of a queen. Yet, it underlines the intensity of her desire for Antony *not* to be married. So, Shakespeare asks us to think as we are laughing: What are we prepared to do to try to make reality fit with our vision of reality? Perhaps, of all things, Cleopatra is another Falstaff in this scene.

◊ *The Tempest.* Trinculo's creation of a two-headed, four-legged monster by his creeping under Caliban's cloak gives Shakespeare the opportunity for a gross joke. Stephano's reaction to the monster is to remark, "Four legs and two voices—a most delicate/ monster! His forward voice now is to speak well of his/ friend; his backward voice is to utter foul speeches and/ to detract" (2.2.90–93). From one end, then, fine speeches; from the other, the equivalent of flatulence. It also gives Shakespeare the opportunity to focus on another of humanity's greatest drives: the need for shelter. Why does Trinculo hide under Caliban's cloak? As he himself puts it, "Alas, the storm is come again!/ My best way is to creep under his gaberdine. There is/ no other shelter hereabout. Misery acquaints a man/ with strange bedfellows. I will here

shroud till the/ dregs of the storm be past" (37–41). "What are you prepared to do to find shelter?" asks Shakespeare of his audience.

There remains one scene left to examine in our discussion of
Shakespeare's humor. It's one that crystallizes beautifully the cosmic
quality of Shakespeare's humor, for it sits almost on the dividing line
between comedy and tragedy and works on several different levels. The
scene, *Twelfth Night* 4.2, dramatizes Feste's visit—first in the guise of Sir
Topas (the curate) and later as himself—to Malvolio, who is being held
on Sir Toby Belch's orders in a dark room because he (Malvolio) is supposedly insane.

◇ On the most superficial level, the scene is genuinely funny. Feste as Sir
   Topas begins by pointing out to the audience that he isn't the first religious official to hide behind the sanctity of a clerical gown. He then
   encounters Malvolio directly. Malvolio insists that the room in which he
   is being held is dark; Sir Topas counters with a couple of paradoxes
   which make it seem as if he is contradicting Malvolio when in fact he's
   agreeing with him. The "bay windows" are transparent as "barricadoes"
   (i.e. you can't see through them at all), and the "clerestories" (or upper
   windows) are "lustrous as ebony" (37–39). Malvolio is so bemused at
   this point that he doesn't notice how nonsensical are Sir Topas's words.
   Then Sir Topas uses philosophy to judge Malvolio's sanity. He asks him
   a question from Pythagoras's doctrine of the transmigration of souls.
   Malvolio has a good response, but Sir Topas says he's incorrect anyway.
   For a modern audience, the scene has the absurdity of a sketch from
   Monty Python's Flying Circus.

   Then Feste as Feste rather than Sir Topas addresses Malvolio. By
   clever wordplay, he manages to trap Malvolio into insisting that he is as
   sane as he (Feste) is. However, since Feste is a Fool, that's not saying
   much. Then Feste stages a mock argument between himself and his
   alter ego, Sir Topas, which ends with Sir Topas rebuking Feste for
   speaking with the madman. Malvolio, who can see none of this, is completely taken in. Again, he insists that he's as sane as "any man in/
   Illyria" (107–08). Given the absurdity of much of the action in the play,
   that's not saying much either.

◇ On a deeper level, the scene is genuinely sad and rather disturbing. The
   comedy works because the audience has earlier lost patience with
   Malvolio's officious high-handedness towards Sir Toby Belch, Sir Andrew
   Aguecheek, Maria, and Fabian. However, Malvolio's punishment does
   seem out of proportion to his sins. It would be awful to suffer Malvolio's
   experience of being locked up in a dark room for a long period of time
   with no idea when release might come. Yet, Shakespeare diminishes the
   sympathy we feel (in a sense, he ensures that the humor works) by hav-

ing Malvolio indulge in exaggeration. It's hard to judge an individual's pain when so much of his time is spent in complaints that are manifestly false. "Sir Topas," says Malvolio, "never was man thus wronged" (29). And then he goes on: "I say there/ was never man thus abused" (47–48) and "Fool, there was never man so notoriously/ abused" (87–88). Oh, really? What of the innocent men and women tortured by the Inquisition (to name but one group from Shakespeare's age)? I do think that the appropriate response to Malvolio's punishment is Fabian's, when he says the motivation was "sportful malice" and should "rather pluck on laughter than revenge" (5.1.365, 366).

◊ On a yet deeper level, Shakespeare is raising the question of what defines sanity. Given that there is no absolute standard or test, the term (which is crucial to human identity) is ultimately definable only by its contrary, insanity. Here, Shakespeare points out the difficulty of any definition even with reference to contrastive terms. On the one hand, we have a man locked in a dark room who is so distraught that he doesn't recognize when Sir Topas is spouting nonsense. On the other, we have a Fool (Feste) who indulges in a dialogue with his alter ego (Sir Topas), and then has the temerity to tell Malvolio that he must give up spouting nonsense: "leave thy vain bibble-babble," he insists (97).

◊ On the deepest level, Shakespeare is dramatizing the situation in Plato's famous "Allegory of the Cave." In this dialogue, Socrates equates the human condition to people chained in a cave for whom reality is merely a series of shadows projected onto the wall of the cave by objects illuminated by a fire. Most people see only the shadows; a few may glimpse the objects; very few may even be able to unchain themselves and get out of the cave to see the sun. So, most of us, Shakespeare is suggesting, are like Malvolio: literally and metaphorically in the dark about what is going on. The powers that control the universe, Shakespeare is suggesting too, can be at times like Feste/Sir Topas: malicious, absurd, almost schizophrenic.

And, just in case the audience should arrogantly think that it, *of course*, is like Plato's true enlightened, Shakespeare points out through his love of stage metaphors that all we ever see on stage are shadows of reality. Sir Toby Belch praises Feste for his acting job ("The knave counterfeits well" [20]), and the audience hopes, too, that the actor does indeed act well. If he doesn't, the scene won't work. In truth, we are not much better off as modern theatergoers than Malvolio is as prisoner. We sit in a darkened room (the auditorium) and watch reality imitated in the hope that it will help us understand life better. And this imitation of reality is particularly complicated, of course, when we have characters such as Feste, a human being who as an actor plays a role (Feste) who plays a role (Sir Topas). In a sense, we are worse off than Malvolio. He will be released from the dark room and will come to understand how and why the trick was played on him. We will be "released" from the theater without understanding the magic of how drama works to transform fiction into reality, and without understanding the "why" of existence. In a sense, we may leave any Shakespeare play sadder and wiser, but we are only exchanging one dark room (the theater) for another (our own minds). Nonetheless, that hard-won knowledge of our own ignorance is surely priceless.

Writing and Discussion Assignments

1. Given its setting, the scene between Hamlet, Horatio, and the gravediggers (*Hamlet* 5.1.1–216) should be sad. How does Shakespeare manage to create humor from something so serious as digging graves? How does the scene affect the rest of the action in 5.1 and 5.2?

2. In the Induction to *The Taming of the Shrew*, Christopher Sly is tricked. What is your reaction to the trickery? Laughter? Annoyance? Disbelief? What would be the effect on the play if the Induction (all 276 lines) were omitted?

3. Study the relation between *1 Henry IV* 2.2 and 2.4. How funny is 2.2 (the Gad's Hill robbery), and what does 2.4 (Falstaff's explanation of what happened at the robbery) add to the humor? Pay attention in this question to both performed and reported slapstick.

4. Take a careful look at what happens in *Antony and Cleopatra* 2.5 and 3.3. In what ways is Cleopatra's interaction with the messenger funny? In what ways does it add to our understanding of her personality and her relation with Antony? Pay attention in this question to verbal humor as well as to performed slapstick.

5. What is the basis of Lucio's humor in *Measure for Measure* at the expense of the Duke, and how fair do you consider his final punishment in 5.1?

6. Why is the behavior of the rude mechanicals (Quince, Bottom, Flute, Snout, Snug, and Starveling) in *A Midsummer Night's Dream* so funny? Explain the humor of their actions with reference to the terms discussed in this chapter.

7. The Fool in *King Lear* is supposed to be a comic character. Is he? If he is, to what degree is his humor *cosmic*? Look carefully at my definition of the term in the preceding pages and try to find examples of this sort of humor in the role he plays.

8. Imagine that you've been assigned the role of the Porter in *Macbeth* 2.3. What is humorous about the role, and how would you play the part in order to bring out all of its comedy?

Further Reading

Colman, E.A.M. *The Dramatic Use of Bawdy in Shakespeare*. London: Longman, 1974.

Elam, Keir. *Shakespeare's Universe of Discourse: Language-Games in the Comedies.* Cambridge: Cambridge UP, 1989.

Huston, J. Denis. *Shakespeare's Comedies of Play.* New York: Columbia UP, 1981.

Partridge, Eric. *Shakespeare's Bawdy.* New York: Routledge, 1991.

Richmond, Hugh M. *Shakespeare's Sexual Comedy: A Mirror for Lovers.* Indianapolis: Bobbs-Merrill, 1971.

Swinden, Patrick. *An Introduction to Shakespeare's Comedies.* New York: Barnes & Noble Books, 1973.

Part 2

Staging

Chapter 5

Marry, our play is "The most lamentable comedy, and most cruel death of Pyramus and Thisbe"

A Midsummer Night's Dream
1.2.11–12

Shakespeare's Genres

Chapter Overview

◇ Understanding the meaning of genre to Shakespeare and to us.
◇ Understanding the origins and characteristics of Shakespeare's four major genres: comedy; history; romance; and tragedy.
◇ Understanding the meaning of three other key terms: problem play; Roman play; and tragicomedy.

In this chapter, we examine the kinds, or genres, of plays Shakespeare wrote. We will look at the four major genres of comedy, history, romance, and tragedy as well as some more recent and useful scholarly categories: problem play, Roman play, and tragicomedy. Given the purpose of this book (to make Shakespeare more understandable to students and the general reader alike), genre criticism is a wonderful way of analyzing the plays. It gives us valuable insight into how Shakespeare's plays are constructed.

Shakespeare was keenly aware of genre as he wrote his plays. In *Hamlet*, Polonius tells the young prince that the traveling troupe of actors has arrived, and praises their ability in terms of their experience in numerous genres. According to Polonius, they are "[t]he best actors in the world, either for/ tragedy, comedy, history, pastoral, pastoral-comical,/ historical-pastoral, tragical-historical, tragical-comical-/historical-pastoral, scene individable, or poem unlim-/ited" (2.2.396–400). Clearly Shakespeare is poking gentle fun, through Polonius as pedant, at two tendencies of the era: for critics to be too schematic in the application of dramatic theory, and for playwrights to attempt to create impossibly "mixed" forms in the pursuit of newness. Just as clearly, however, he is someone who, as a practicing playwright, knew the genres then in vogue, and he knew his sources, too, for Polonius continues his commendatory speech to Hamlet by naming two of the major Classical sources for Renaissance tragedy and comedy: "Seneca cannot be too heavy, nor Plautus too/ light" (400–01).

There are, indeed, several advantages to examining the Shakespeare canon for its uses of comedy, history, and tragedy. Such an examination

◇ allows for useful comparisons and contrasts to be made among plays

◇ allows for Shakespeare's work to be compared with that of other Renaissance dramatists

◇ allows for a reader to assess the development of Shakespeare's technique over time

◇ allows for a reader to see how much Shakespeare's technique was built on the creation of "mixed" forms: tragedies that contain crucial moments of comedy; comedies that include an acceptance of the tragic in life; histories that revolve around the buffoonery of Falstaff and the death of kings

◇ allows for a reader to see Shakespeare as the acme of a dramatic tradition rather than as a uniquely original artist.

Genre and the Folio of 1623

It makes sense to begin the discussion of Shakespeare's understanding of genre in his plays with their first collected printing in the Folio of 1623 (the book usually referred to simply as the First Folio). With the organization of the First Folio, we have a picture of how two of Shakespeare's fellow actors—the editors of the book, John Heminges and Henry Condell—defined genre only seven years after the playwright's death. At first glance, the picture looks very much in focus, with the contents page organizing the canon into three categories: comedies; histories; and tragedies. These categories, moreover, are set apart from each other by ruled horizontal lines above and below the generic labels, and by vertical ruled lines on either side of the two columns. It is as if each genre is seen as incontrovertibly distinct from the other two. (See Fig. 5.1.)

Nothing, it would seem, could be simpler than to go with the First Folio's arrangement in any discussion of the content of the plays. On closer inspection, however, the categories start to look rather suspect.

◇ The listing is incomplete, for it fails to mention *Troilus and Cressida* among the "Catalogue of the severall Comedies, Histories, and Tragedies contained in this Volume." The play *is* printed in the First Folio, but it is labeled *The Tragedy of Troilus and Cressida* and appears right before the first of the plays in the category of "Tragedies": *Coriolanus*. It exists in a

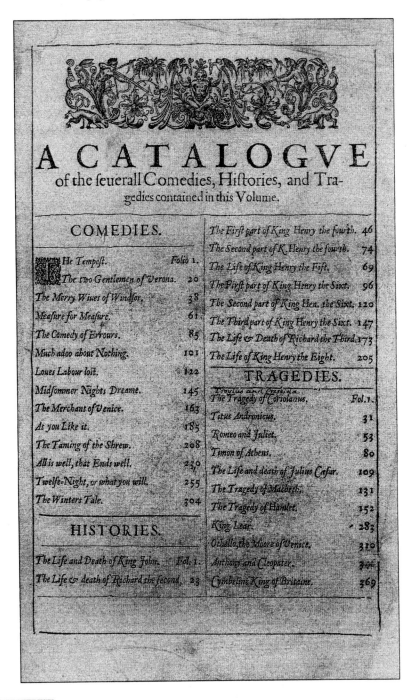

A CATALOGVE

of the feuerall Comedies, Hiftories, and Tragedies contained in this Volume.

COMEDIES.

He Tempeſt.	Folio 1.
The two Gentlemen of Verona.	20
The Merry Wiues of Windſor.	38
Meaſure for Meaſure.	61
The Comedy of Errours.	85
Much adoo about Nothing.	101
Loues Labour loſt.	122
Midſommer Nights Dreame.	145
The Merchant of Venice.	163
As you Like it.	185
The Taming of the Shrew.	208
All is well, that Ends well.	230
Twelfe-Night, or what you will.	255
The Winters Tale.	304

HISTORIES.

The Life and Death of King John.	Fol. 1.
The Life & death of Richard the ſecond.	23

The Firſt part of King Henry the fourth.	46
The Second part of K. Henry the fourth.	74
The Life of King Henry the Fift.	69
The Firſt part of King Henry the Sixt.	96
The Second part of King Hen. the Sixt.	120
The Third part of King Henry the Sixt.	147
The Life & Death of Richard the Third.	173
The Life of King Henry the Eight.	205

TRAGEDIES.

Troylus and Creſſida.	
The Tragedy of Coriolanus.	Fol. 1.
Titus Andronicus.	31
Romeo and Juliet.	53
Timon of Athens.	80
The Life and death of Julius Cæſar.	109
The Tragedy of Macbeth.	131
The Tragedy of Hamlet.	152
King Lear.	283
Othello, the Moore of Venice.	310
Anthony and Cleopater.	346
Cymbeline King of Britaine.	369

Figure 5.1
The 1623 Folio's Contents page. Note how the genres are separated from each other within boxes.

sort of undefined space. Some modern editors (Bevington and Evans, for example) have placed it in the comedy grouping while trying at the same time by sleight of hand to locate it in more than one category: Bevington by labeling it a satire in his introduction to the play; Evans by giving the title of the play as *The History of Troilus and Cressida*. Shakespeare and his contemporaries seem to have been equally at a loss about what sort of play Shakespeare had created. The title page of an early printing of the 1609 Quarto of the play calls it *The Historie of Troylus and Cresseida;* a later printing of the same Quarto, *The Famous Historie of Troylus and Cresseid*. That later printing also includes an advertisement which talks at length *not* about the play's tragic or historical aspects, but about its comic elements: "the palme comicall"; "Commedies [by Shakespeare], that are so fram'd to the life"; "such savored salte of witte is in his [Shakespeare's] Commedies"; and so on (Allen and Muir 705–06).

◇ The listing is illogical. The histories are organized chronologically according to the timetable of English history from *The Life and Death of King John* (who reigned from 1199 to 1216) to *The Life of King Henry the Eight* (who reigned from 1509 to 1547). By contrast, the plays in the other two categories seem to follow no apparent order. The comedies category begins with *The Tempest* and ends with *The Winter's Tale*. Yet, these are two of Shakespeare's last plays. The tragedies category begins with *The Tragedy of Coriolanus* (which is generally dated about 1608) and finishes with *Cymbeline King of Britaine* (the first recorded performance of which was in 1611). Yet, Shakespeare began writing tragedies in the late 1580's or early 1590's.

◇ The titles of the plays themselves conflict with the way they are listed in the First Folio's Table of Contents. *Richard III* is grouped under the history plays, but the title page of its folio printing labels it a tragedy, *The Tragedy of Richard the Third: with the Landing of Earle Richmond, and the Battell at Bosworth Field*.

◇ Earlier quarto printings of the histories support the transgeneric tendencies of the First Folio. The 1595 Quarto of *3 Henry VI* is titled: *The true Tragedie of Richard Duke of Yorke, and the death of good King Henrie the Sixt*. The 1597 Quarto of *Richard III* has a title page that reads: *The Tragedy of King Richard the third*. The Quarto of *Richard II* (which also dates from 1597) is similarly called a "Tragedie." The same transgeneric leanings show up in the quarto versions of the comedies, too. The title page of the 1600 Quarto of *The Merchant of Venice*, for example, reads: *The most excellent Historie of the Merchant of Venice*. The Quarto's running head compounds the confusion: *The comicall Historie of the Merchant of Venice*.

◇ The First Folio and the Quartos are not alone in treating history as tragedy or as finding history in comedy. Francis Meres in his *Palladis Tamia* (1598) cites no less than four of Shakespeare's *history* plays as proof of his brilliant work in *tragedy: King John, Richard II, Henry IV,* and *Richard III.*

So, where does all this intermingling of genres leave the reader or audience? Several insights can be drawn from theatrical theory and practice in Shakespeare's time.

◇ Genre mattered. It was a means by which playwrights could map out the development of plot and character. It was a means by which audiences could know ahead of time the sort of action that would be presented.

◇ Genre was fluid. Shakespeare clearly knew about genre theory when he constructed his plays. His plays, however, show that the importance of genre to the period is evident much less in the observance of its guidelines than in its breaching of them. Indeed, it was against the Elizabethan tendency to mix genres that Sir Philip Sidney ineffectively rails in his *Defence of Poetry* (1583; 1595) when he complains about the "gross absurdities" arising from the playwrights' failure to follow the rules for "right tragedies" and "right comedies." From Sidney's purist perspective, tragicomedy is a "mongrel" that lacks the hallmark of both: "Honest civility" (67, 75).

◇ Genre theory was subordinated to theatrical practice. Put simply, playwrights were far more interested in producing plays than in theorizing about their practices. Shakespeare, it is useful to remember, has left us no theoretical statement (outside the plays themselves) underpinning his dramaturgic practice. Indeed, the major statement about drama in the English theatre during the Renaissance—Sidney's *Defence of Poetry*— only deals with the topic as a sidelight to poetry in general, and *it was written by someone with no experience as a playwright.*

◇ Genre guidelines were profoundly affected by the frequent collaboration that took place in the creation of plays during the Renaissance. Shakespeare himself collaborated with John Fletcher in *The Two Noble Kinsmen,* for example, and wrote part of *Sir Thomas More,* a play that was in all likelihood the work of many hands. Collaboration is likely to lead by its very nature to the blurring of the distinctions among genres since the understanding of how to apply a particular genre to the needs of a particular play is bound to vary among playwrights, as will the overall vision of how to translate story into action.

◇ Genre was not nearly as fixed as the First Folio suggests. The editorial work on the First Folio by Shakespeare's colleagues Heminges and Condell succeeded in dovetailing Shakespeare's oeuvre into three slots (comedy, history, and tragedy), but it did so by ignoring the numerous elements in all his plays that undermine such a rigid distinction. To see how profound has been the effect of their decision on later generations consider how different the nature of Shakespeare scholarship would have been had the ordering of the plays in the First Folio been alphabetical or chronological. The first is neutral; the second might have largely solved the continuous disputes about the dating of the plays. Either would have altered the terms of all subsequent discussion. *King Lear*, for example, which is universally considered one of Shakespeare's greatest tragedies, might have been viewed far more frequently as a history play. After all, the 1608 Quarto of the play does title it, *[The] True Chronicle Historie of the life and death of King LEAR and his three Daughters.*

Genre and the Modern Critic

Partly in response to the realization that a tripartite structure for Shakespeare's plays hinders almost as much as it helps to understand his drama and partly from a serious wish to appreciate Shakespeare's quicksilver genius, critics nowadays generally subdivide the Shakespeare canon into several genres and subgenres. Indeed, at times the labeling can be rather confusing because there is little consensus about the validity of particular labels. So, to the old stalwarts (comedy, history, and tragedy), critics have added one other major category (romance) and three lesser categories (problem play, Roman play, and tragicomedy). It's my intent, now, in an effort to make Shakespeare's plays more understandable, to define these categories both in terms of their theatrical origins and their characteristics. As always with Shakespeare, however, there is a sobering truth: while analysis may help to make experiencing his plays more meaningful, it can never entirely explain the depth of his insights into the human condition.

The Major Genres

Comedy

The First Folio lists fourteen Shakespeare comedies: *The Tempest; The Two Gentlemen of Verona; The Merry Wives of Windsor; Measure for Measure; The Comedy of Errors; Much Ado about Nothing; Love's Labor's Lost; A Midsummer Night's Dream; The Merchant of Venice; As You Like It; The Taming of the Shrew; All's Well That Ends Well; Twelfth Night;* and *The Winter's Tale.* Scholars these days generally remove *The Tempest* and *The Winter's Tale* to the genre of romance but add *Troilus and Cressida* to the comedies, so that we are left with a genre that comprises thirteen plays. The earliest comedies date from the late 1580's (*Love's Labor's Lost, The Two Gentlemen of Verona,* and *The Comedy of Errors*); the latest from 1604 to 1605 (*All's Well That Ends Well* and *Measure for Measure*).

Origins. The origins of Shakespearean comedy can be traced back to two Roman playwrights, Plautus (ca. 254–184 BC) and Terence (ca. 190–159 BC), who were themselves indebted to the work of the Greek comic playwrights Aristophanes (ca. 448–ca. 388 BC) of the Old Comedy and Menander (ca. 343–291 BC) of the New Comedy. *The Comedy of Errors* and *Twelfth Night* are based, in part, on Plautus's *Menaechmi*. *The Taming of the Shrew* derives one of its plots from Terence's *Eunuchus* and Plautus's *Captivi*. Much later sources for Shakespeare's comic technique include crude early Tudor interludes such as Nicholas Udall's *Ralph Roister Doister* (1550–1553) and *Gammer Gurton's Needle* (probably by William Stevenson, 1552–1563) as well as more sophisticated comedies by his contemporaries such as John Lyly (with his *Gallathea* [1592] and *Endymion* [1588]) and Robert Greene (with his *Friar Bacon and Friar Bungay* [1589–1592]). Regardless of the sources Shakespeare consulted in constructing his comedies, they always undergo radical transformation in his plays. So much for practice. When it comes to theory, Shakespeare would almost certainly have been familiar with the treatise on comedy by the Roman author Donatus (fourth century AD), a work which rehashes Aristotle and Horace as well as constructing a history for the origins of comedy in Classical times.

Characteristics. It is hard to come up with a list of the defining characteristics for Shakespeare's comedy, in part because generalization always involves a significant degree of distortion, and in part because Shakespeare was fond of hybrid, transgeneric drama and was always experimenting with new ways of entertaining audiences and readers. Shakespeare's comedies span a wide affective and thematic spectrum, so what I offer here can only be the starting point for vigorous discussion. In such a spirit, at least three examples are provided after each characteristic: two plays that support the definition, and one that subverts it.

The Comedies

Major Characteristics

They trace the course of young love that ultimately triumphs despite obstacles.

They begin in trouble and end in peace.

They depict romance and end in marriage or the promise of marriage.

In comparison to the tragedies, they employ character types rather than fully individualized characters.

They are thematically concerned with the nature of identity.

In comparison to the tragedies, they emphasize female experience.

They exclude death.

(continued)

They reward virtue and punish vice.

They revolve around a contrast of "worlds," often youth vs. age or country vs. court or city.

They bring renewal to particular characters as well as to society.

They are fundamentally light-hearted and verbally exuberant.

They are meant to make us laugh at ourselves as human beings in all our absurdity.

◊ **The comedies trace the course of young love that ultimately triumphs despite obstacles.**

Such a claim is true for *A Midsummer Night's Dream* (with its pairing of Lysander and Hermia and Demetrius and Helena after their night of tribulation in the woods outside Athens). It is true also in *Much Ado about Nothing,* where Claudio and Hero's love survives Don John's efforts to ruin it. The lovers in *Troilus and Cressida,* however, manifestly do not triumph. Cressida plays false with Diomedes; Troilus distracts himself from his sorrow at the end of his love affair by resolving to continue to fight the Greeks even after the death of Hector.

◊ **The comedies, as Shakespeare's fellow playwright Thomas Heywood put it when describing Renaissance comedy in general, "begin in trouble and end in peace."**

Such a claim (quoted in Barnet 31) is true in *The Taming of the Shrew* (where Katharina's initial shrewishness becomes submission, by the end of the play, to Petruchio's rule in marriage). It is true also for *The Comedy of Errors,* where Antipholus and Dromio of Syracuse begin the action in fear of their lives because of an Ephesean proclamation against all citizens of Syracuse. Yet, the play ends in peace with the reunion of the Antipholus twins, their parents (Egeon and Emilia), and the family's servants (the Dromio twins). *Twelfth Night,* however, ends far less peacefully, with Malvolio's anger against Sir Toby Belch, Sir Andrew Aguecheek, and Maria unassuaged.

◊ **The comedies depict romance and end in marriage or the promise of marriage.**

Such a claim is true for *As You Like It,* for much of the play is taken up with the burgeoning love of Rosalind/Ganymede and Orlando. The play ends with three marriages: Rosalind/Ganymede and Orlando; Celia and Oliver; and Phebe and Silvius. Similarly, *Love's Labor's Lost* is all about courtship and ends with the prospect of marriages between the Princess of France and the King of Navarre, Katharine and Dumaine, Maria and Longaville, and Rosaline and Berowne. *Measure for Measure* is altogether different, however. Every example of romance in the play is tainted. Claudio's love for Juliet is damned by the authorities because Juliet becomes pregnant; Mariana's love for Angelo is not mutual at all; Isabella fails to answer the Duke when he asks her to marry him. As to marriage in the play, given the lack of romance it is not hard to hypothesize what happens even if you have never read the play. Marriage is anything but the voluntary culmination of love. The Duke insists on the marriage between Claudio and Juliet; Angelo marries Mariana on the Duke's orders; Isabella is noncommittal about the Duke's proposal; and Lucio—at the Duke's command—is forced to marry the pregnant woman he has abandoned.

◇ **The comedies (in comparison to the tragedies) employ character types rather than fully individualized characters.**

Such an assertion holds true in *Love's Labor's Lost* and *A Midsummer Night's Dream*. In both, it is difficult to keep the pairs of lovers straight. In some measure that is the result of the complexities of plot. To a significant degree, however, it is the consequence of the lovers being interchangeable representatives of youthful passion. We find it hard to remember who pairs with whom among the likes of Maria, Katharine, Rosaline, Longaville, Dumaine, and Berowne (in *Love's Labor's Lost*) or Helena, Hermia, Demetrius, and Lysander (in *A Midsummer Night's Dream*). The characters themselves get thoroughly confused, too. And that is precisely Shakespeare's point about the changeable nature of desire. Because he is blind, Cupid fires off his quiver of arrows in all sorts of directions.

Such an assertion about Shakespeare's tendency toward type finds support, too, in the very titles of his comedies, for they do not bear the individualized names of people (as the tragedies do) but focus instead on occasions (*Twelfth Night* or *A Midsummer Night's Dream*), on catch phrases (*As You Like It* or *All's Well That Ends Well*), or on groups (*The Merry Wives of Windsor*).

Yet, as always, Shakespeare goes beyond the effort to categorize. Falstaff may be a buffoon in *The Merry Wives of Windsor*, but he is also clearly individualized. Malvolio may be the type of the foolish official, but his suffering at the hands of Feste, Sir Toby Belch, Maria, and Fabian is very real and clearly personalized. It is because of precisely these qualities that Malvolio's last words are so memorable: "I'll be revenged on the whole pack of you!" (5.1.378).

◇ **The comedies are thematically concerned with the nature of identity.**

Such an assertion is supported by the confusion that results from the pairs of twins in *The Comedy of Errors*, by the cross-dressing that takes place in the comedies (Viola as Cesario in *Twelfth Night*, for example), and by the sort of gender-bending that occurs in the courtship of Rosalind/Ganymede and Orlando in *As You Like It*. It is supported, too, by the ease with which characters can be fooled about the identity of others, whether by the "bed trick" (Mariana for Isabella) or the "head trick" (Ragozine's for Claudio's) in *Measure for Measure*. Indeed, I can think of no comedy (with the possible exception of *The Two Gentlemen of Verona*) in which the question of identity is peripheral.

◇ **The comedies (in comparison to the tragedies) emphasize female experience.**

Such an assertion has considerable textual support, for it is in the comedies that women control some of the action. The Merry Wives' hoodwinking of Falstaff (*The Merry Wives of Windsor*), Portia's successful defense of Antonio against Shylock's claim (*The Merchant of Venice*), and Julia's reachievement of Proteus's love (*The Two Gentlemen of Verona*) are but three instances among many of a pattern of women taking control of the action. That control, however, is by no means universal. At the end of *The Taming of the Shrew*, for instance, Katharina's subservience in marriage to Petruchio is complete, for it is, she argues, "love, fair looks, and true obedience" that a wife owes to her husband (5.2.157).

Even where women have control, it is frequently limited or ceded at the end of the action to men. In *The Merry Wives of Windsor*, Mistresses Ford and Page have no trouble making Falstaff look foolish several times over, but both are blindsided by the elopement of Anne Page and Fenton. In *The Merchant of Venice*, Portia goes from saving Antonio from death at the edge of Shylock's knife (in 4.1) to apologizing to her husband, Bassanio (in 5.1), for the trickery she employed to do so and promising to answer all his questions under oath.

◇ **The comedies exclude death.**

Such a claim is accurate for all the comedies except one, *Troilus and Cressida*. In this play, Hector is killed onstage in Act Five Scene Four by Achilles and the Myrmidons. However, *Troilus and Cressida*—as pointed out earlier—is an anomaly. The First Folio was clearly puzzled by the play's genre, but seems (based on placement and title) to have considered the play more of a tragedy than anything else. Its status as a comedy is a twentieth-century categorization.

Above all, perhaps, it needs to be realized how close the comedies come to fatal action. The comedies may exclude death from the stage, but it is always waiting in the wings. I'll cite just four examples. Antonio almost dies at Shylock's hand in *The Merchant of Venice*. Egeus's demand for the death of his disobedient daughter in *A Midsummer Night's Dream* is countermanded only at the end of the play by Duke Theseus. Hero in *Much*

Ado about Nothing "dies" only to be resurrected as her veiled cousin in order to marry Claudio. Duke Vincentio in *Measure for Measure* sentences Lucio to death for abandoning Mistress Kate Keepdown (whom he makes pregnant), but rescinds the order before dispatching him to prison.

◇ The comedies reward virtue and punish vice.

Such a claim is accurate with regard to most of the comedies. Portia, in *The Merchant of Venice*, is rewarded for virtuously following her father's Will with regard to her marriage by finding true love with Bassanio. Mistress Page in *The Merry Wives of Windsor* is rewarded for her faithfulness in marriage, with the opportunity to poke fun at Falstaff not once or twice, but three times. However, the comedies sometimes postpone the punishment of vice so that it occurs outside the confines of the drama. Don John, who plays the villain in *Much Ado about Nothing*, is caught, but his punishment is explicitly postponed until after the conclusion of the play's action. Benedick may have some "brave punishments for him," but he advises the assembled company: "Think not on him till tomorrow" (5.4.126, 125).

As with their treatment of death, the comedies' handling of virtue and vice is complicated. Much depends on how the two key terms are defined. With regard to virtue, let's look briefly at *Measure for Measure*. In that play, Isabella—for whom virtue is everything—receives a rather dubious reward at the end of the play: an offer of marriage from the Duke. Whether such a proposal is a reward is a matter of argument. Indeed, Isabella seems so uncertain whether it is that she says nothing whatsoever in reply to the Duke's offer. As for vice, let's look briefly at *Twelfth Night*. In that play, Malvolio is punished by being locked in a dark room and treated as insane. His vices? He criticized Sir Toby Belch and Sir Andrew Aguecheek for partying late at night and he was foolish enough to have fallen for the "letter trick" devised by Maria. In this case, is the correction in proportion to the vice?

◇ The comedies revolve around a contrast of "worlds," often youth vs. age or country vs. court or city.

Such a claim is true for *A Midsummer Night's Dream* and *The Merry Wives of Windsor*. In the former, there is the maturity of Theseus and Hippolyta contrasting with the youthfulness of Lysander, Hermia, Demetrius and Helena. There is also the world of the Duke's court in Athens contrasting with the world of the magical wood close by the city. In the latter, the Fords, the Pages, and Falstaff (representing age) contrast to Anne Page and Fenton (representing youth), and Windsor contrasts to the woods of Windsor Park. Such paired contrasts do not, however, work well in elucidating *The Merchant of Venice*. Youth and age are not contrasted in the play, and although the urban (Venice) and the pastoral (Portia's country estate at Belmont) do contrast, the distinction is muted by the presence of a much more significant and serious religious distinction: Jew and Gentile.

◇ The comedies bring renewal to particular characters as well as to society.

Such a claim is true for *Much Ado about Nothing*. Beatrice, Benedick, and Claudio learn much about themselves from the twists and turns of the plot, and society (as defined by the authority figure, Don Pedro) deals with the threat represented by Don John's misanthropic evil. The same could be said for *The Merry Wives of Windsor*. Master Ford learns the foolishness of unbridled suspicion; Falstaff learns the absurdity of aged lust. Society is renewed by the marriage of Anne Page and Fenton as well as by Falstaff's inclusion in a festive celebration of the Page-Fenton marriage at the end of the play. "Good husband," says Mistress Page, "let us every one go home/And laugh this sport o'er by a country fire—/ Sir John and all" (5.5.235–37).

Yet this characteristic of comedy obviously does not apply to the central characters of *The Two Gentlemen of Verona*. It is hard to see how Proteus, Julia, Valentine, and Sylvia are renewed by their adventures. It is hard to see how society is renewed either. The Duke and Thurio are released at the end of the play, but it is hard to see how they or the outlaws are renewed. In truth, their actions are almost wholly masked by the oddity and nastiness of the stage action involving Proteus, Valentine, and Silvia. First, Proteus attempts to rape Silvia, whom he professes to love. He is prevented by his friend, Valentine, only to be offered Silvia once again when he (Proteus) shows contrition. Then, when Julia (who truly loves Proteus) faints, revives, and reveals her identity, Proteus falls in love with *her* once more.

◇ The comedies are fundamentally light-hearted and verbally exuberant.

Verbal exuberance is undeniably present in all of Shakespeare's comedies: ubiquitously in *A Midsummer Night's Dream*, *As You Like It*, and *Twelfth Night*; limited to Launce the Clown and his dog, Crab, in *The Two Gentlemen of Verona*. Lightheartedness is the dominant tone of most of Shakespeare's comedies, with *A Midsummer Night's Dream* and *The Merry Wives of Windsor* remarkable in this regard, but *Measure for Measure*, *All's Well That Ends Well*, and even *Twelfth Night*, do not fit the mold at all. The tone of the first two in particular is somber, even bitter at times.

◇ The comedies are meant to make us laugh at ourselves as human beings in all our absurdity.

There is surely no doubt that all of us, women as well as men, can see something of ourselves in Shakespeare's wonderfully rich characterization of Falstaff. Not by accident did he bring him back from the dead to star again in *The Merry Wives of Windsor*. It is hard, too, not to laugh at ourselves as lovers when we witness the absurd behavior of the foursome in an Athenian wood (*A Midsummer Night's Dream*) or the pairs of lovers in the Forest of Arden (*As You Like It*). The effect of a comedy such as *Measure for*

Measure or, in most respects, *The Merchant of Venice* is, however, very different. Whatever laughter there is comes from nervousness at our realization of how sharp and unforgiving is Shakespeare's investigation of the seamiest side of human motivation. Chagrin rather than laughter characterizes the audience's reaction to Shakespeare's darkly comic vision in these two plays.

Subgenres. To the broad genre of Shakespearean comedy, critics have added the **subgenres** (or subcategories) of *aristocratic lyric, bourgeois* (or *city*), *dark, festive, forgiveness, golden, Italianate, love-game, mature, philosophical, romantic,* and *satiric.* Another schema that enjoys some popularity among critics is the chronological division into *early* or *apprentice* (1589–1598), *middle* (1599–1600), and *late* (1601–1605). To define so many different subgenres would be counterproductive and dull, so I will restrict myself to just a couple of observations about them. First, these labels do, of course, overlap. (Only some thirteen comedies, it should be remembered, need to bear the weight of so much categorizing.) Second, the attempt at labeling constitutes a careful, clever, reflective effort to describe the bewildering variety of Shakespearean comedy so that the meaning of individual plays is clarified and the connections among the plays made more evident.

History

The First Folio lists ten history plays, all of them dealing with English history between the late twelfth century and the mid-sixteenth century. These ten consist of two single plays and two tetralogies (one usually labeled "minor" and the other "major"). The sequence of plays in the two tetralogies can sometimes confuse students because the historical and compositional chronologies are different. The minor tetralogy was written *first* but deals with an historical period *later* than the major tetralogy. So, the minor tetralogy was written between about 1589 and 1594 but covers the historical period from 1455 to 1485. The major tetralogy was written between about 1595 and 1599 but covers the historical period from 1398 to 1455, with the years between 1422 and 1455 being covered in an Epilogue to *Henry V.*

◇ The two singleton history plays cover the reigns of King John (1199–1216) and Henry VIII (1509–1547). They will not be dealt with in this chapter. The first (*King John*) is different on content grounds from the rest of the history plays, for it covers the reign of a king who (from the Tudor or Shakespearean perspective) reigned in an almost mythic past. The second (*Henry VIII*) is different on formal grounds, for it consists of a series of tableaux rather than the sort of dramatic action that characterizes the rest of the Shakespeare canon.

◇ The "minor" tetralogy (so-called because it dates from early in Shakespeare's career) covers English history from the last years of the Hundred Years War to the bloody conclusion of the Wars of the Roses (1455–1485), the period of civil war in which two powerful groups of nobles, the Houses of York and Lancaster, fought over the kingship. It comprises the three Henry VI plays (now called *1 Henry VI, 2 Henry VI*, and *3 Henry VI*) and *Richard III*.

◇ The "major" tetralogy (so-called because it dates from Shakespeare's maturity as a playwright) covers the reigns of the three kings who came before Henry VI: Richard II (who reigned from 1377 to 1399), Henry IV (1399–1413, about whom Shakespeare wrote two plays, *1 Henry IV* and *2 Henry IV*), and Henry V (1413–1422).

One might think the genre of the history play would be more stable than that of the comedy since it is anchored in the lives of a particular sequence of English kings. Appearances in Shakespeare, however, are always deceptive. As I indicated earlier in this chapter when I discussed the First Folio's interpretation of genre, Shakespeare's plays about English history merge in places with tragedy. Indeed, no less than three of the eight English history plays were titled "tragedies" in their quarto publication. When one includes plays about Britain's legendary history (*Macbeth, Cymbeline*, and *King Lear*, which was labeled a "history" in quarto), plays about the history of Rome (*Titus Andronicus, Julius Caesar, Antony and Cleopatra*, and *Coriolanus*), and the comedy about Antonio, the merchant of Venice (which was titled in quarto, *The most excellent Historie of the Merchant of Venice*), then the genre of the history plays looks almost as fluid as that of the comedies.

Origins.   The history play as a genre was in its infancy when Shakespeare began to create his version of English history before the time of the Tudors. It is not too much of an exaggeration to say that Shakespeare virtually invented the form, for although Shakespeare's fellow playwrights wrote history plays (Greene's *The Scottish History of James the Fourth* [1590] comes to mind) it is only Marlowe's *Edward II* (1591–1593) that has some of the qualities of Shakespearean history: the tragic but sometimes contemptible central figure set against a backdrop of inexorable historical events; the complex relation between the public and the private man.

From the history plays written by other dramatists a generation or two before Shakespeare wrote his two tetralogies, one can trace the origins of the form to the morality plays of the late medieval period (such as *Mankind* [ca. 1470] and *Everyman* [ca. 1500]) and their preoccupation with the social effects of sin. Shakespeare, however, moved the genre forward and succeeded (as he so often did during his career) in making gold from dross, in revivifying the moribund. For example, John Bale's *King John* (1539), an early Tudor play, is primitive in comparison to Shakespeare's play of the same name in its treatment of character and history. Morality, as Bale presents it, is a dramatic concept that exists in an uneasy middle ground between universal type and individuated character.

By contrast, Shakespeare presents us with characters whose motivations are explicable solely in human terms. History for Bale means the didactic presentation of events by characters as unrealistic as their names (such as Sedition, Nobility, and England) suggest. For Shakespeare, history is an altogether more human and murky experience, one where the rules of academic history writing outlined in Thomas Blundeville's *True Order and Methode of Wryting and Reading Hystories* (1574) have no place.

Then, there are the nondramatic sources on which Shakespeare relied for the "facts" in his two historical tetralogies. He used two very extensively: Edward Hall's *Union of the Two Noble and Illustre Families of York and Lancaster* (1548), and Raphael Holinshed's *Chronicles of England, Scotland, and Ireland* (1577; second edition, 1587). Hall sees history as part of a divine plan; Holinshed, by contrast, foregrounds historical uncertainty and relegates God's role in English history to the background. It would be completely wrong, however, to say that Shakespeare simply presented some hybrid of Hall's and Holinshed's versions of English history. In dramatizing the story of a nation, he transformed his sources to a remarkable degree. He selected incidents that he knew would work well on stage; he compressed chronology; he altered geography. Whenever he needed to, he invented characters and events. The end result is a set of dramas so carefully constructed that to this day the meaning of the plays (in a broad sense, what Shakespeare's view of history was) has elicited more radical disagreement among critics than any other single aspect of Shakespeare's work.

Characteristics. In light of the continuing disagreement among scholars about how to interpret the overarching meaning of the tetralogies, the following characteristics are in no sense definitive. They are offered as a starting point for further discussion, analysis, and research.

The History Plays

Major Characteristics

They seek to answer a fundamentally political question: "What are the qualities of the perfect king"?

They portray a country's transformation from medieval to early modern.

They depict the lives of the common people in deliberate contrast to those of their rulers.

They show the dangers in having a nation disunited.

They show the role of providence in England's history.

They require what Lawrence Danson has referred to as "a double consciousness in the audience—of the individual play and of the longer historical narrative to which it refers" (90).

> *(continued)*
>
> They use radical contrast as a means of highlighting the psychological effect of events on the central characters as well as rendering events more dramatically for the audience.

◇ **The history plays seek to answer a fundamentally political question: "What are the qualities of the perfect king"?**

In light of the absence of a direct heir to Queen Elizabeth I as well as the tenuous position Protestant England held in relation to Catholic Europe (principally Spain and France), the question was a pressing and very real one to Shakespeare and his audience. When we look at Shakespeare's gallery of pre-Tudor kings, the sight is unimpressive. Richard II cannot be that perfect king, for he is unable to wield power effectively. Yet, he does have the disarming quality of a poetic self-consciousness. Henry IV is handicapped as a ruler by having usurped the crown from the legitimate king, Richard II. Few will trust him because the act that secured the throne is damningly traitorous. For him, the experience of kingship is more than anything else, weariness. For the audience, indeed, he is not even the major character in the two plays that bear his name. Prince Hal and Falstaff vie for that honor. Henry VI is pious, virtuous, and utterly unable to rule his kingdom's many powerful factions. His weakness even more than the ambitions of his nobles causes the civil war that engulfs England. Richard III is ruthless and eloquent, but absolutely devoid of the human feeling that any monarch needs to have.

Whom, then, does that leave? Only Henry V. On the surface, he looks like an ideal king: Godly; brilliant in battle; successful as a diplomat (by securing the continuation of his line through marriage to the French king's daughter, Katharine of Valois). Yet, Shakespeare—as he always does—complicates the picture; he won't let the audience or reader off that easily. Henry V's rejection of Falstaff at the end of *2 Henry IV* ("I banish thee, on pain of death . . . Not to come near our person by ten mile" [5.5.63, 65]) seems extraordinarily harsh. His piety, too, is at times unconvincing and priggish. On the one hand, he is quite capable in *Henry V* 2.2 of staging a political arrest (of Cambridge, Scroop, and Grey) and of murdering prisoners during the battle of Agincourt because they will hinder the English defense against a possible French counterattack (4.6.35–37). On the other, he can say without a trace of irony at being told of the English victory: "Praisèd be God, and not our strength, for it!" (4.7.86).

◇ **The history plays portray a country's transformation from medieval to early modern.**

Perhaps the easiest way to illustrate this development is to offer two snapshots: one from the beginning of Richard II's reign (the year is 1398) and the other from the end of Richard III's reign in 1485. The first (*Richard II* 1.3) is a highly formalized event in which Thomas Mowbray, Duke of Norfolk, and Henry Bolingbroke, Duke of Hereford, appear before their king at Coventry each to accuse the other of high treason, with the argument to be settled by combat. The scene has all the qualities of a pageant. By contrast, the final three scenes (5.3–5.5) in *Richard III*, which dramatize the battle of Bosworth Field, are all rapid action.

The effect of the two scenes is markedly different, too. *Richard II* 1.3 moves history into the realm of myth. It is static and historically distant, for the banishment of Norfolk and Mowbray, which the scene depicts, occurred almost two hundred years before Shakespeare's audience would have witnessed his dramatization of the moment. By contrast, *Richard III* 5.3–5.5 gives history an immediacy which all of Shakespeare's audience would have felt. The events occurred only a little more than 100 years before Shakespeare's play was produced, and they led directly to the founding of the Tudor dynasty. Who, after all, was the Earl of Richmond, who defeated Richard III at the end of the play? None other than Henry VII, Elizabeth I's grandfather.

Richard II 1.3

History as Mythic Pageant

The Lord Marshal stage manages the event in the proper fashion. His duties interrupt the proceedings no less than half a dozen times (31–34, 42–45, 52–53, 100–01, 103, and 117).

The Heralds announce the combatants as required by heraldic custom (104–16).

Richard halts the proceedings when he throws down his baton, so the combatants never actually fight (117).

Richard declares their doom: first Bolingbroke's and then Norfolk's (123–43, 148–53).

The combatants swear to abide by the sentence (178–92).

Bolingbroke and his father, John of Gaunt, reflect on the familial sorrow that will result from Richard's sentence of banishment for six years (253–309).

Richard III 5.3–5.5

History as Immediate Action

The opening part of 5.3 switches between Richard III's camp (1–18, 47–78) and Richmond's (19–46, 79–117).

The ghosts of those whom Richard has killed serially appear both to Richard III and to Richmond, and we see the reactions of the two men (118–222).

> *(continued)*
>
> The two men as leaders of their armies get their men psyched up for battle: Richmond at 223–70; Richard III at 271–351.
>
> Act 5 scene 4 (only 13 lines long) reenacts part of the battle, and the stage direction to 5.5 shows the death of Richard III at Richmond's hand.
>
> The rest of 5.5 (a scene of only 41 lines) is given over to counting the dead and to Richmond's predicting the end of civil war: "Now civil wounds are stopped, peace lives again./ That she may long live here, God say amen! (40–41).

◇ **The history plays depict the lives of the common people in deliberate contrast to those of their rulers.**

As I suggested earlier, one of the qualities that distinguishes Shakespeare's version of history is the way in which he mixes the genres of history and comedy. It is precisely this mixing which enables him to spend so much time in his history plays on the lives of common people. *Richard II* includes the wonderful scene in which the gardener delivers a lecture on politics to his assistant by drawing an extended analogy between maintaining a garden and maintaining a state (3.4). (See Chapter 6, pages 176–177 for my discussion of the staging of this scene.) *1 Henry IV* and *2 Henry IV* are as much about the antics of Falstaff and his retinue (Bardolph, Francis, Gadshill, Mistress Quickly, Ned Poins, Peto, and Pistol) as they are about Henry IV's travails as king. Six scenes in *1 Henry IV* (excluding Falstaff's antics at the battle of Shrewsbury) and nine scenes in *2 Henry IV* (excluding the battle in Gaultree Forest) are dominated by the comedy caused by Falstaff and his friends and hangers-on, not to mention the tomfoolery of the likes of Justices Shallow and Silence as well as assorted hopeless soldiers (Fang, Snare, Moldy, Shadow, Wart, Feeble, and Bullcalf).

One might expect *Henry V* to be a little different since that monarch may represent, for Shakespeare, the nearest to an ideal monarch in English history (before Elizabeth I, at least). Yet, the common people crop up again to act as a wonderful counterweight to the burdensome affairs of the kingdom. Many of the same cast of ne'er-do-wells show up from the previous pair of plays about Henry V's father: Pistol, Bardolph, and Mistress Quickly. Gone is Falstaff (although his death is reported in 2.3), but added is Corporal Nym as well as a group of common soldiers (John Bates, Alexander Court, and Michael Williams) who debate very shrewdly with Henry V about his wisdom in invading France (4.1). To this cast of common folk are added representatives of all four regions of Britain: from Scotland, Captain Jamy; Ireland, Captain MacMorris; Wales, Captain Fluellen; and England, Captain Gower. Indeed, Shakespeare seems at least as interested in giving the views of the commoners about Henry's decision to invade France as he is in presenting the royal perspective.

Two out of the three *Henry VI* plays, however, are remarkably free of the lowlife comedy that characterizes Shakespeare's later Falstaffian histories (the two *Henry IV* plays and *Henry V*). *1 Henry VI* offers no perspective from the common people, and *3 Henry VI* includes only one brief but telling scene in which the effect of the civil war on the lives of the common soldiers is emphasized (2.5). *2 Henry VI* is the odd one out of the trio, for it devotes almost all of Act 4 to Jack Cade's rebellion and presents it in a way that emphasizes Cade's vicious buffoonery (at one point he executes people for being literate!). Here, the purpose is to offer some macabre comic relief after the murder of Gloucester in 3.1 as well as to point out the dangers of civil war.

Richard III, like the three plays devoted to Henry VI's reign, has none of the comic relief we associate with *1* and *2 Henry IV* and *Henry V*. Yet, like *2 Henry VI*, *Richard III* does depict the common people pointedly. Gone may be an event as cataclysmic as Cade's rebellion, but the citizens of London do correctly predict trouble ahead after the death of Edward IV (2.3) only to show themselves easily fooled by Richard's protestations of reluctance to rule (3.7). Shakespeare's point seems to be that folk wisdom has merit but is no match for the wiles of a monarch as hungry for power as Richard, Duke of Gloucester.

◇ **The history plays show the dangers in having a nation disunited.**

Richard II ends in usurpation of the crown by Henry Bolingbroke. *1* and *2 Henry IV* involve the effort by Harry Hotspur and others to overthrow Henry IV as well as serious dissension between the king and his son, Prince Hal. *1*, *2*, and *3 Henry VI* focus on the Wars of the Roses, a civil war between the two most powerful noble families in England: The Houses of Lancaster and of York. This trio of plays ends with the usurpation of the crown by Edward IV. *Richard III* has as its main theme the bloody seizure of power by Edward IV's brother, Richard, Duke of Gloucester. The play ends with another usurpation, this time by Henry, Earl of Richmond. Even *Henry V* alludes to disunity in the effort by Scroop, Cambridge, and Grey to assassinate the king before he embarks for France.

And why should Shakespeare emphasize disunity? As a message to Elizabethan theatergoers, asking them to reflect on the instability of the Tudor dynasty itself. English society may have achieved a golden age under Elizabeth, but that achievement occurred only after the break with Rome by Henry VIII in 1534, the brief minority kingship of Edward VI (1547–1553), the ten-day monarchy of Lady Jane Grey (1553), and "Bloody Mary"'s six-year reign (1553–1558), in which the kingdom allied itself with Spain through her marriage to Philip II and lurched back to Catholicism.

◇ **The history plays show the role of providence in England's history.**

This idea was central to Edward Hall's retelling of history in his *Union of the Two Noble and Illustre Families of York and Lancaster* (1548) and was first propounded in modern times by E.M.W. Tillyard in his *Shakespeare's History Plays* (1944). What Hall and Tillyard argue is that Henry Bolingbroke (later Henry IV) committed a crime against God when he usurped the throne from God's lawfully appointed representative, Richard II. That crime was punished during Henry VI's reign with the internecine Wars of the Roses. God's providence appears in the form of Henry Tudor, Earl of Richmond and later Henry VII, the founder of the Tudor dynasty and Elizabeth I's grandfather. He was himself a usurper, but he usurped the throne from its bloodiest occupant, Richard III, who had himself unlawfully wrested the throne from Edward V. Henry VII, moreover, succeeded in "solving" the conflict between the Houses of York and Lancaster by uniting the two families. Himself a Lancastrian, he married Elizabeth of York, the eldest daughter of Edward IV. God's plan is thus fulfilled by the Tudor dynasty.

As the previous paragraph probably suggests, the devil is very much in the details when it comes to English history. However, the key point is this: from Shakespeare's perspective in the history plays, the succession of Henry VII and the founding of the Tudor dynasty was a heaven-sent solution to a century of bloody conflict on English soil.

◇ **The history plays require what Lawrence Danson has referred to as "a double consciousness in the audience—of the individual play and of the longer historical narrative to which it refers" (90).**

Shakespeare's audience would, of course, have had that understanding of English history, and it is the purpose of this part of the chapter to provide a contemporary audience with some of that same understanding. Whether Shakespeare himself intended from the beginning to construct a one hundred-year narrative of this sort is unclear. Certainly he didn't compose the story in its natural chronology since the earlier (minor) tetralogy deals with the two kings nearest to the Tudor dynasty (Henry VI and Richard III) while the later (major) tetralogy goes back to the three earlier kings in the sequence (Richard II, Henry IV, and Henry V). What is obvious from the plays we have is that Shakespeare ends each tetralogy climactically with plays that offer resolution: *Henry V* with the victory at Agincourt and marriage to Katharine of Valois; *Richard III* with the victory at Bosworth field and the promise of marriage to Elizabeth of York.

◇ **The history plays use radical contrast as a means of highlighting the psychological effect of events on the central characters as well as rendering events more dramatically for the audience.**

Such a technique is extraordinarily persistent in the history plays. Richard II contrasts with Henry Bolingbroke, so his sorrow in loss of kingship is shown. Henry IV contrasts with his son, Prince Hal, and so the heaviness of the burden of kingship is displayed. Prince Hal in his Falstaff days contrasts with Prince Hal as the king, so right kingship is demonstrated.

Henry VI contrasts with Talbot and, later, the Duke of York, so weak kingship is exposed. Richard III contrasts with Henry Tudor, Earl of Richmond,
so evil kingship is shown. To emphasize such a contrast further
Shakespeare uses a number of devices available to the dramatist, most
notably symbolism. When Richard II is deposed, for example, two symbols
reinforce the tension in the event: a crown and a mirror. The first is held by
both Richard and Bolingbroke as the former says:

> Now is this golden crown like a deep well
> That owes two buckets, filling one another,
> The emptier ever dancing in the air,
> The other down, unseen, and full of water.
> That bucket down and full of tears am I,
> Drinking my griefs, whilst you mount up on high
> (4.1.185–90).

The second, the mirror, is used by Richard immediately after the deposition to see if the event has fundamentally changed him:

> Was this face the face
> That every day under his household roof
> Did keep ten thousand men? Was this the face
> That, like the sun, did make beholders wink? (4.1.282–85).

So, when Richard shatters the mirror he is acknowledging the profound
shock of the change from king to commoner: "[h]ow soon my sorrow hath
destroyed my face" (4.1.292).

Tragedy

The 1623 Folio lists eleven tragedies, but scholars pare this list down to
only ten since the Folio's inclusion of *Cymbeline* among the tragedies is
thought to be an editorial error. The Folio lists the ten as *Coriolanus, Titus
Andronicus, Romeo and Juliet, Timon of Athens, Julius Caesar, Macbeth, Hamlet,
King Lear, Othello,* and *Antony and Cleopatra.* The apparent generic stability
of this group is, however, misleading for a couple of reasons. First, as
pointed out earlier in this chapter, the term *tragedy* was included in the
titles of three of Shakespeare's history plays, either in quarto, folio or both.
There is, then, something about these three histories that smacked of the
tragic to Shakespeare's contemporaries. Second, Shakespeare wrote
tragedies for much of his career, beginning with *Titus Andronicus* (perhaps
as early as 1589) and ending with *Coriolanus* (perhaps as late as 1609).
Because he was writing tragedies for as long as twenty years, it is notoriously difficult to generalize about them. It is possible to see development

in the ten plays; it is possible to characterize overlapping groups of them; but overarching characteristics are few.

Origins. As with the histories and comedies, the origins of Shakespearean tragedy are many. The greatest immediate influences were two: Christopher Marlowe's *Tamburlaine* (1587) and Thomas Kyd's *The Spanish Tragedy* (1587). In the first, Shakespeare will have found elevated language, a dramatic effect of terror and pity, and, above all, powerful, dignified characters who struggle against their fate. In the second, he will have come across the themes of madness and revenge set in a complex plot featuring self-referential characters. The most distant influence? Aristotle. It's hard to know exactly how much of Aristotle's theory of tragedy Shakespeare may have known. It does seem, as Lawrence Danson suggests on the evidence of *King Lear* 5.3.235–36 (26), that he knew about katharsis (or the purgation of pity and fear). It seems, too, on the basis of *Hamlet* 1.4.23–36 that he knew something about hamartia (or, as it is often termed, "tragic flaw"). It is certainly clear that *if* he knew about the Aristotelian Unities (of time, place, and action), he wisely gave them a wide berth, for only in the magic of *The Tempest* does he find any virtue in them.

If we count forward from Aristotle to Marlowe, there lies a wide range of influences on Shakespearean tragedy:

◇ Greek tragedy, in particular Euripides' *Hecuba*. It may have had some small influence.

◇ The Roman tragedies of Seneca with all their bloody horror. These had an influence, on *Titus Andronicus* particularly, although that influence did not manifest itself in Shakespeare's direct use of particular plays as sources. Rather, it was their philosophy and tone that attracted. Seneca's tragedies are preoccupied with tyranny and revenge (as are Shakespeare's). Seneca's tragedies blend passion and stoicism (as do Shakespeare's). Seneca's tragedies push the limits of what can be enacted (as do Shakespeare's).

◇ The "de casibus" poetry of the medieval era, which dwelled on the fall of princes from prosperity through suffering to despair. Chaucer's "Monk's Tale" in the *Canterbury Tales* parodies such poetry; John Lydgate's *The Fall of Princes* (a 36,000 line translation of a French version of Boccaccio's *De Casibus Illustrium Virorum*) embraces the theme unreservedly.

◇ English medieval miracle and morality plays. These were important in the development of Elizabethan tragedy. The former sometimes focused on the downfall of tyrants; the latter on the struggle between virtue and vice. Both types of plots, despite their simplicity, inform the much more sophisticated tragedies of Shakespeare and his contemporaries.

◇ *The Mirror for Magistrates* (1559), a collection of first-person narratives about the lives of famous people. It was well known to Shakespeare, and went through multiple editions during his lifetime. Its influence was widespread in his work and not just in his tragedies. *3 Henry VI* alludes to the *Mirror*; *Richard II*, *Richard III*, and *1 Henry IV* used it as a source. The story of *King Lear* would have been available to Shakespeare in *The Mirror* as would that of *Cymbeline*. In a more general way, the decline and fall of the famous and what can be learned from their downfall (which is the main subject of *The Mirror for Magistrates*) is one of the major themes of Shakespearean tragedy.

◇ Earlier English tragedies such as Thomas Preston's *The Life of Cambises* (1561?), Sackville and Norton's *Gorboduc* (1562), and John Pickering's *A Newe Enterlude of Vice, Conteyninge the Histoyre of Horestes* (1567). These are crude plays long on declamation and didacticism, but they show a definite family relation to Shakespeare's work.

Characteristics. Even more than in my discussion of the characteristics of Shakespearean comedy and history, there are dangers of oversimplification. With those generalizations that can be applied to all ten tragedies, there are always exceptions. There is, however, real value in making such generalizations, because they help us to make comparisons among the plays, they emphasize for us the uniqueness of each tragedy, and they show us the remarkable range of Shakespeare's art.

The Tragedies
Major Characteristics

They are multigeneric.

They develop through carefully interwoven multiple plots.

They trace the lives of important people from a state of comfort and security to despair and dissolution.

They each focus on the trials of one extraordinary man against a backdrop of society.

They dramatize the struggle between full self-realization and the acquiescence to social norms.

They dramatize the abuse of women, and portray that abuse as reprehensible, evil, or pathological.

They present a vision of stoicism in the face of suffering and failure.

They show humanity's weaknesses as inevitable. The best anyone can do is to learn from them.

They repeatedly dramatize moral ambiguity.

They require of the principal characters an eloquence to match the horror they witness or experience.

They produce in an audience a state of psychic exhaustion akin to Aristotelian katharsis.

◇ **The tragedies are multigeneric.**

Romeo and Juliet blends comedy and tragedy. *Timon of Athens* blends satire and tragedy. *Julius Caesar* and *Coriolanus* blend history and tragedy. *Hamlet, King Lear, Macbeth,* and *Antony and Cleopatra* blend comedy, history, and tragedy. Only *Titus Andronicus* presents an unleavened tragic vision. Shakespeare is interested in hybrid plays that work, not in plays whose greatest virtue is purity.

◇ **The tragedies develop through carefully interwoven multiple plots.**

The best example of this technique is *Hamlet.* Here, Shakespeare develops three revenge plots: Hamlet/Claudius (the main plot); Laertes/Hamlet (a subplot); and Fortinbras/Old Hamlet (a second subplot). In each case, the motive for revenge is the desire on a son's part to avenge a dead father (and in Laertes' case, a dead sister, too). Each plot reflects upon the action in, and meaning of, the other two. Shakespeare wants us to draw parallels between them in order for us to understand the complexities of human relationships more fully. The comedies are also very sophisticated in their structure, but plot twists in that genre depend more on such devices as mistaken identity than on multiple interconnected plots.

◇ **The tragedies trace the lives of important people from a state of comfort and security to despair and dissolution.**

Othello, for example, begins as a man who has both reputation and love, but ends as a murderer scorned by the very authorities who had once thought so highly of him. The exception to this generalization is *Hamlet,* since the prince is anything but secure after the untimely death of his father.

◇ **The tragedies each focus on the trials of one extraordinary man against a backdrop of society.**

Of the ten tragedies, seven support this generalization well; three do not. *Romeo and Juliet, Macbeth* (*The Macbeths* would be a more accurate title), and *Antony and Cleopatra* focus on paired protagonists. It is true, however, that no Shakespeare tragedy (indeed, no play by Shakespeare) features the trials of one extraordinary woman in isolation.

◇ **The tragedies dramatize the struggle between full self-realization and the acquiescence to social norms.**

Antony and Cleopatra presents a good example of this struggle. In the case of Antony, the tragedy unfolds between two poles: Cleopatra (as self-realization), whose love represents all that is forbidden; and Octavia (as social norm), who represents all that is expected of a member of the Triumvirate. Shakespeare asks the audience to see the play in such terms.

On the one hand, the first speech in the play (by Philo) ends with this invitation: "Take but good note, and you [Demetrius] shall see in him/The triple pillar of the world transformed/Into a strumpet's fool. Behold and see" (1.1.11–13). On the other, Antony's first speech of any length is an extraordinarily powerful and moving statement of what matters to him in life: Cleopatra's love.

> Let Rome in Tiber melt and the wide arch
> Of the ranged empire fall! Here is my space.
> Kingdoms are clay; our dungy earth alike
> Feeds beast as man. The nobleness of life
> Is to do thus; when such a mutual pair
> And such a twain can do 't, in which I bind,
> On pain of punishment, the world to weet
> We stand up peerless (1.1.35–42).

In the case of Cleopatra, the tragedy unfolds between two poles as well: Antony (as self-realization), whose love is an ever-present proof of her value; and Octavius (as social norm), whose political cunning and military authority might guarantee her survival and the continuation of Egypt as a powerful kingdom. At the end of the play, the choice has been made with Antony and Cleopatra both the victims of suicide. The cost of the choice, however, has been immense in terms of death and suffering and the audience remains uncertain about how to judge the decision they made: Were they foolish to lose everything for their love, or was the world worth less or even worthless? When Antony says to Cleopatra after the disastrous battle of Actium:

> Fall not a tear, I say; one of them rates
> All that is won and lost. Give me a kiss.
> Even this repays me (3.11.68–70),

how are we to react? Do we deride such romanticism or see it as the fullest expression of human experience?

◇ **The tragedies dramatize the abuse of women, and portray that abuse as reprehensible, evil, or pathological.**

In Shakespeare's first tragedy, *Titus Andronicus*, Lavinia, Titus's daughter, is raped and mutilated by Tamora's sons, Demetrius and Chiron. And how is Lavinia comforted by her family after being the victim of such horrible brutality? By her father, Titus, killing her because she has been shamed by the acts committed by Demetrius and Chiron. In one of Shakespeare's last tragedies, *Antony and Cleopatra*, Octavius Caesar tries to trick Cleopatra into becoming part of the triumphal parade in Rome to celebrate his victory over Antony. He leaves her little option in response but suicide.

Between these two plays we have Ophelia driven to madness and suicide by Hamlet's cruel, calculated indifference. We have Gertrude, in *Hamlet*, who accidentally dies from poison administered by her husband, Claudius, but meant for Hamlet. Claudius makes no effort to save her. We have Lady Macduff and her children, in *Macbeth*, slaughtered on Macbeth's orders as punishment for Macduff's fleeing to England. We have Cordelia, in *King Lear*, exiled by her father because she will not flatter him and subsequently murdered in prison on Edmund's orders. And in *Othello*, we have Bianca, framed by Iago for the attempted murder of Cassio; Emilia, murdered by her husband, Iago; and Desdemona, murdered by her husband, Othello.

There is clearly a pattern here to the action and, just as clearly, retribution for such action. Titus serves Demetrius and Chiron to Tamora, their mother, in a pie, an act for which he is shortly afterwards killed. Hamlet is grief stricken by Ophelia's death and subsequently dies with a "wounded name" (5.2.346). Macbeth is killed by Macduff despite the auguries which appear to make him invulnerable. Edmund is killed by his brother, Edgar, and realizes the sinfulness of his behavior ("Some good I mean to do/Despite of mine own nature" [5.3.248-49]). Othello kills himself out of grief for murdering his own wife. Iago will be tortured at Lodovico's orders in an effort to have him explain his actions and save his soul. Only Octavius escapes retribution for his abuse of women, and he is, unlike the others, an historical figure who went on to greatness (as the Emperor Augustus). Nevertheless, he is upstaged by Cleopatra's death speech ("Give me my robe" [5.2.280-313]), and has to make do with some final words (5.2.353-66) in which he pays tribute to Antony and Cleopatra ("No grave upon the earth shall clip in it/A pair so famous"). He even admits that they have been as important as he has been in recent events ("their story is/No less in pity than his glory which/Brought them to be lamented"). Such an admission is, in itself, a sort of retribution for one as single minded as Octavius.

◇ **The tragedies present a vision of stoicism in the face of suffering and failure.**

Shakespeare's tragic view of life depicts the world as made up of people who are doomed to suffer and to fail, whether by fate, misfortune, error, or *even* virtue. The best that one can do under such conditions is to endure with courage, determination, and self-knowledge. By such means, transcendence can be achieved.

Macbeth, for example, is brought to ruin in part by the Weird Sisters' prophecies, in part by the misfortune of meeting them, and in part by his own ambition. He makes a fatal error by attempting to change what is predicted for him (he will be king, but not found a dynasty). Even though he is a pitiless murderer (of King Duncan and his guards, and of Lady Macduff and her children), he shows courage at the end when he faces Macduff knowing full well that he will die. He also shows throughout an awareness of the cost of such ambition to himself and to his wife. So, the audience comes to sympathize with him for the trauma he goes through even as it condemns what he does. In a sense, too, the audience is asked to put itself in Macbeth's position and answer a simple but unnerving question: "How would you have acted?"

Macbeth illustrates all the important elements of this tragic vision— even, paradoxically, that which emphasizes virtue's role in the downfall of the **protagonist** (or lead character). Macbeth is certainly the bloodiest of Shakespeare's heroes, yet he has two virtues—love of his wife and bravery—and both play a role in his downfall. The first leads him, in part, to kill Duncan. The second leads him to fight on rather than to sue for peace, even after the Weird Sisters' prophecies are shown to be false.

And this pattern of virtue as a cause of disaster occurs elsewhere in Shakespeare's tragedies. Hamlet, for example, is brought down by two virtues: loyalty and honesty. The first shows in his faithful efforts to avenge his murdered father; the second in his refusal to believe that Laertes would descend to trickery in the fatal fencing match. In the same way, Brutus (in *Julius Caesar*) is brought down by his virtuous pursuit of a misguided solution to the dangers of dictatorship while Timon (in *Timon of Athens*) suffers disaster because of an unyielding sense of virtue. Of all of Shakespeare's many insights in his tragedies this is, surely, his most disturbing.

◇ **The tragedies show humanity's weaknesses as inevitable. The best anyone can do is to learn from them.**

King Lear is a good example of these two insights. King Lear acts stupidly at the beginning of the play in giving up the authority of his kingship while trying to maintain his status, but his stupidity is completely understandable. Because of his power, he has become used to sycophancy and has lost the ability to tell genuine emotion from flattery. By the end of the play, he has learned how foolish he has been, but only after dreadful suffering. As he says to his one true daughter, Cordelia, after their capture by Albany's forces: "Come, let's away to prison./ We two alone will sing like birds i' the cage./ When thou dost ask me blessing, I'll kneel down/ And ask of thee forgiveness" (5.3.8–11).

In a similar way, Gloucester suffers horribly for an initial error in judgment when he believes the story of his illegitimate son (Edmund) that his legitimate son (Edgar) is plotting against his (Gloucester's) life. Like Lear, then, he cannot distinguish the false from the true. Also like Lear, he comes to realize his error when it is too late: after he has been blinded, he says to Edgar (disguised as poor Tom) "I stumbled when I saw" (4.1.19). Like Lear, too, his error is seen as completely understandable, arising as it does from the human wish to avoid the consequences of one's actions: Gloucester does his best to hide the fact that he is the illegitimate Edmund's father. As he says to Kent at the beginning of the play: Edmund has been abroad for a long time, and is going abroad again ("He hath been out nine years, and away/ he shall again" [1.1.32–33]). Out of sight, out of mind.

◇ **The tragedies repeatedly dramatize moral ambiguity.**

This moral ambiguity has the value of a universal generalization, for Shakespeare presents us again and again with a world in which every important action is seen from radically different perspectives.

In *King Lear*, for example, it is easy to condemn the king for his naïve acceptance of Goneril and Regan's flattery, but it should not be forgotten that Cordelia's refusal to elaborate upon her love beyond the plain statement "I love Your Majesty/ According to my bond, no more nor less" (1.1.92–93) is stubborn and unkind. It is easy to blame Goneril and Regan for their heartless ambition, but it should not be overlooked that King Lear presented them with the opportunity and that in asking why King Lear needs any of his old followers around him ("What need you five-and-twenty, ten, or five,/To follow in a house where twice so many/Have a command to tend you?" [2.4.263–65]), Goneril has logic on her side. In *King Lear*, too, it is easy to see Edmund as the villain, but to do so is to ignore the trenchant arguments he has against the social stigma of illegitimacy. In his "gods, stand up for bastards!" soliloquy (1.2.1–22), he reasons well against just this stigma:

> Why bastard? Wherefore base?
> When my dimensions are as well compact,
> My mind as generous, and my shape as true,
> As honest madam's issue? Why brand they us
> With base? With baseness? Bastardy? Base, base?
> Who in the lusty stealth of nature take
> More composition and fierce quality
> Than doth within a dull, stale, tirèd bed
> Go to th' creating a whole tribe of fops
> Got 'tween asleep and wake? (6–15).

It is important to remember, too, that Edmund's anger derives from years of scant regard from his father except as the butt of jokes such as those with which the play itself begins. Similarly, it is easy to condemn Gloucester for the speed with which he listens to Edmund's lies about Edgar, but it should be noted that he is in a state of profound shock when he first listens to Edmund's lies. He has just come from Lear's disastrous division of the kingdom as he encounters his son. He cannot believe what he has seen—"Kent banished thus? And France in choler parted?/And the King gone tonight?" (1.2.23–24)—but he is ready to believe anything.

Multiple perspectives on events are offered in all the tragedies, whether the focus be on Antony and Cleopatra's or Romeo and Juliet's love, Macbeth's ambition, Othello's jealousy, Hamlet's madness, Coriolanus's pride, Caesar's arrogance, or Titus's revenge. Shakespeare skillfully sidesteps didacticism, and the consequence is ambiguity everywhere—just as in life.

◊ **The tragedies require of the principal characters an eloquence to match the horror they witness or experience.**

The clearest examples of such eloquence are the soliloquies that occur with great frequency in many of the tragedies. A development of sorts can be seen from the early self-consciousness of Aaron's grandiloquent "Now climbeth Tamora Olympus' top" (2.1.1–25) in *Titus Andronicus*, through the self-revelation of Hamlet's "To be, or not to be" (3.1.57–90), to the surreal edginess of Macbeth's "Is this a dagger which I see before me [?]" (2.1.34–65). Nor is such eloquence offered to the protagonists alone. Claudius, in *Hamlet*, soliloquizes his wish for salvation despite his murderous usurpation of the throne ("O, my offense is rank! It smells to heaven" [3.3.36–72]). Iago, in *Othello*, explains his motivation ("That Cassius loves her [Desdemona], I do well believe 't" [2.1.287–313]). And Edmund, in *King Lear*, argues against the stigmatizing of bastardy ("Thou, Nature, art my goddess" [1.2.1–22]).

◊ **The tragedies produce in an audience a state of psychic exhaustion akin to Aristotelian katharsis.**

Such an affective statement is impossible to support except anecdotally, but it is certainly the case from my own experience as well as that of others with whom I have talked that the effect of a well-acted Shakespearean tragedy (especially the major tragedies: *Hamlet, Othello, King Lear, Macbeth,* and *Antony and Cleopatra*) is a paradoxical feeling made up of horror, pity, elation, and fear. There is horror at what we witness; pity for those who suffer; elation that it has not happened to us; and fear that it may. A convenient label for such a feeling is **katharsis**.

Subgenres. Within the broad category of tragedy, Shakespeare scholars often speak of particular groupings: "love tragedies" (*Romeo and Juliet, Othello, Antony and Cleopatra*); "major (or "great") tragedies" (*Hamlet, Othello, King Lear,* and *Macbeth*); "revenge tragedies" (*Titus Andronicus* and *Hamlet*); "Roman tragedies" (*Julius Caesar, Antony and Cleopatra,* and *Coriolanus*); and "satiric tragedies" (*Timon of Athens* and *Troilus and Cressida*).

Romance

The First Folio recognizes only three principal genres: Comedy; History; and Tragedy. To that trio, critics since the nineteenth century have added a fourth: romance. The term *romance* refers to Shakespeare's last plays: *Pericles, Cymbeline, The Winter's Tale, The Tempest,* and the play on which he collaborated with John Fletcher, *The Two Noble Kinsmen*. In these plays (written between 1607 and 1613), Shakespeare reverted to comedy, but to a form of comedy manifestly different from that which he wrote in the first dozen years of his career. It is not a term without referential problems since the word *romance* has been used so frequently over the years in literary criticism to describe many different sorts of works, but it has the great merit for Shakespearean studies of referring to an agreed-upon group of plays.

A generation or so ago the term **tragicomedy** began to be used to describe what is more commonly known as the romances. Joan Hartwig, for example, in *Shakespeare's Tragicomic Vision* (1972) sees the quartet of plays as distinctive in two particular respects: its treatment of the gap between illusion and reality; and its foregrounding of audience perception. The term, then, does not simply describe a blending of tragedy and comedy, but refers to the way in which it is presented to the audience or reader. The term *tragicomedy* has an advantage, too, over the more popular term *romance:* it was understood as a mixed genre in Shakespeare's time. However, it has not proved a popular term.

Origins.   The ultimate source for Shakespeare's romances is the Greek and Roman romance tradition (*Pericles,* for example, is derived from the ancient Greek tale of Apollonius of Tyre), but Shakespeare uses later interpreters or variants of that tradition. So, for instance, *Cymbeline* is based in part on Boccaccio's medieval *Decameron* (Second Day, Ninth Tale), and *The Winter's Tale* on Greene's *Pandosto: The Triumph of Time* (1588).

A more significant influence on Shakespeare's romances is the masque, a form of courtly entertainment in which playwrights such as Beaumont and Jonson excelled. It is characterized by allegory, spectacle, and the direct appearance of mythological figures. Perhaps the greatest influence, however, in pushing Shakespeare to create his romances, was his acting company's use from 1608 onwards of the Blackfriars Theatre. This theatre was much smaller than the Globe and enclosed rather than open. Admission prices were much higher, too, so the audience was different from that which went to Shakespeare's earlier plays. It was here that the King's Men acted during the winter, so it was here too that Shakespeare experimented in his final plays with the dramatic possibilities presented by the new acting space.

Characteristics.   Any definition of Shakespearean romance would probably include most of these qualities:

The Romances

Major Characteristics

Events occur over a long period of time.

The plots involve restoration and renewal after loss, suffering, and repentance. Joy comes only after the profoundest despair.

(continued)

The tone is serene and elegiac.

Providence has a more obvious role than in the earlier plays.

Characterization is less substantial than in the earlier plays, particularly the tragedies.

The family rather than the individual becomes the center of Shakespeare's attention, and in particular the relation between fathers and daughters.

Spectacle is used as a means to emphasize the fact of artistic illusion.

◇ **Events in the romances occur over a long period of time.**

Pericles includes Pericles' daughter, Mariana, abandoned in Tharsus for 14 years. *Cymbeline* begins by looking back 20 years to the kidnap of two of King Cymbeline's children. *The Winter's Tale* requires a gap of 16 years between the first three Acts and the last two, as Time himself announces at 4.1.4–9. *The Tempest* refers to events that happened 25 or more years earlier, when the witch Sycorax was abandoned on the island by sailors.

◇ **The plot of the romances involves restoration and renewal after loss, suffering, and repentance. Joy comes only after the profoundest despair.**

Pericles offers a good example of this romance pattern. Pericles loses loved ones three times in the play: first, Antiochus's daughter because of her incestuous relation with her father; second, Thaisa, whom he marries but believes to have died subsequently in childbirth; third, Marina, his daughter, whom he also supposes has died after he leaves her with Cleon and Dionyza. From the depths of despair, he achieves joy when he meets Marina once again and is reunited with Thaisa through the ministrations of the goddess Diana.

◇ **The tone of the romances is serene and elegiac.**

At the end of *The Tempest*, for instance, Prospero has achieved all that he planned. What remains? Smooth sailing for the King of Naples ("calm seas, auspicious gales,/ And sail so expeditious that shall catch/ Your royal fleet far off" [5.1.318–20]), and an acceptance of death ("Every third thought shall be my grave," says Prospero [5.1.315]). Nor is this tone merely grafted on to the end of the play. Throughout the play, Prospero is utterly in control of events and is surprised by nothing that happens. At the same time, however, there is a clear sense that Prospero and Miranda's life on the island will be irrevocably altered by those events. It surely comes as no surprise that Prospero gives up the enforced life of a recluse for a life of retirement without the benefit of his "rough magic" (5.1.50). Prospero knows that he can never get back the years he has lost through his brother's treachery, but he also truly believes that "The rarer action is/ In virtue than in vengeance" (5.1.27–28).

As always, however, there are exceptions to generalizations about Shakespeare's work. The tone of the second half of *The Winter's Tale* (from 4.1 onwards) is light (centered as it is on the young lovers, Florizel and Perdita) and elegiac in mood (with the reunion of Leontes and Hermione). The first half of the play is, however, a throwback to the tragedies, with the plot being driven by the jealous madness of Leontes. That first half is grim and disturbing, for it includes accusations of adultery, an attempt at poisoning, an order to commit infanticide, and the supposed death of Hermione.

◇ **Providence has a more obvious role in the romances than in the earlier plays.**

In *The Tempest*, Prospero himself acts as Providence, for he has virtually unlimited magical powers with which he controls events, and three goddesses (Iris, Ceres, and Juno) enact a bridal masque to show their solicitude for Miranda and Ferdinand's happiness. In *Pericles*, the goddess Diana appears to Pericles as in a vision in order to guide him to a reunion with Thaisa, his supposedly dead wife and the goddess's high priestess. In response to such providence, Pericles can only say to Diana: "Your present kindness/ Makes my past miseries sports" (5.3.41–42). In *Cymbeline*, Jupiter appears to Posthumus in a vision, and tells his assembled family that Posthumus "shall be lord of Lady Imogen,/ And happier much by his affliction made" (5.4.107–08). In *The Winter's Tale*, the oracle of Apollo at Delphos delivers Apollo's judgment on Hermione's supposed adultery, and that judgment is "ear-defeaning" and "Kin to Jove's thunder" (3.1.9, 10).

◇ **Characterization in the romances is less substantial than in the earlier plays, particularly the tragedies.**

In the tragedies, the major characters reveal their thoughts to us in soliloquies. We feel as if we know them and understand their suffering, for they appear to be fully realized beings. In the romances, the major characters are types, for Shakespeare's focus is on their symbolic value and their place within a larger spectacle. So, if we look for a moment at kingship in these plays, we find these stock characters: Prospero (in *The Tempest*), the wronged ruler who goes about revenge in the right way; Leontes (in *The Winter's Tale*), the jealous husband and misguided king; Pericles, the image of unmerited suffering stoically born; and Cymbeline, the fairy-tale king misled by evil advisors. And if we look at the depiction of female innocence, we find the same reliance on type: Imogen (in *Cymbeline*), the epitome of triumphant virtue; Hermione (in *The Winter's*

Tale), the wronged but patient and faithful wife; Miranda (in *The Tempest*), the idealized vision of natural girlhood; and, most remarkable of all, Marina (in *Pericles*), unsullied despite being sold into prostitution.

These are all wonderful characters and they work perfectly within the romance genre, but they have neither the inner life of the major characters in Shakespeare's tragedies, nor the factual depth of historical figures, nor the spontaneous foolishness of the characters in his comedies.

◊ **The family rather than the individual becomes the center of Shakespeare's attention, and in particular the relation between fathers and daughters.**

In many ways, this characteristic of the romances is the most intriguing because it does not appear with anything like the same persistence in his other plays, *A Midsummer Night's Dream* and *King Lear* notwithstanding. Again and again in the romances, parents are reunited—often very improbably—with their children. In *The Tempest*, Ferdinand is reunited with Alonso despite his having "beheld/ The King my father wrecked" (1.2.439–40). In *Cymbeline*, the title character has a daughter (Imogen/Fidele) and two sons (Guiderius/Polydore and Arviragus/Cadwal) restored to him against all odds. In *The Winter's Tale*, Perdita is restored to Leontes after sixteen years. In *Pericles*, the title character has his daughter, Marina, and his wife, Thaisa, restored to him in a very unlikely way.

Again and again in the romances, these reunions take place after those who are apparently dead are, as it were, restored to life. The list in the romances of those who are reunited after being thought dead is a long one: almost all the occupants of an entire ship in *The Tempest*, along with Prospero and his daughter, Miranda; Pericles (who recovers from a catatonic state) as well as Marina and Thaisa; Imogen, Posthumus, Guiderius, and Arviragus in *Cymbeline*; Perdita and Hermione in *The Winter's Tale*. It seems as if the magic of the romances can even cheat death at will.

◊ **Spectacle is used in the romances as a means to emphasize the fact of artistic illusion.**

Pericles, according to its title page in the 1609 Quarto, includes "strange, and worthy accidents" (Allen and Muir 751), some of which are compressed into dumb shows (or mimes) at 2.Chorus.16, 3.Chorus.14, and 4.4.22. *Cymbeline* includes the appearance of a literal deus ex machina (or "god from the machine") when Jupiter riding an eagle is winched down onto the stage in 5.4. *The Winter's Tale* features the most famous of all the stage directions in Shakespeare's plays (*Exit, pursued by a bear* [3.3.57]) as well as the sudden revivification of Hermione's statue at 5.3.103. It is, however, in *The Tempest* that spectacle most obviously reinforces artistic illusion. In this play Prospero himself takes on the role of playwright and works as a master of illusion. We see a ship-wreck at the beginning of the play, only to discover at the end that the ship and all its crew is unharmed. We see the antics of Prospero's sprite, Ariel, who wears a cloak that renders him invisible. We see men fall asleep and awaken at the whim of this sprite. We see a magical banquet appear and disappear in an instant. We see a bridal masque involving Iris, Ceres, and Juno. We see Caliban, Stephano, and Trinculo chased by spirits in the shape of hunting dogs. And, finally, against all odds, we see everyone reunited at the play's conclusion: unharmed, wiser, and, in some cases, penitent. After seeing such wonderful theatrical spectacle, it truly seems a shame that Prospero decides to give up his role as magician.

The Minor Genres

Problem Play

This term was first used by Frederick S. Boas in his *Shakespeare and His Predecessors* (1896) to define that group of Shakespeare's plays which dealt with social problems. He had adopted it from scholars of the social realism of Ibsen and Shaw. Boas included *Hamlet, All's Well That Ends Well, Measure for Measure,* and *Troilus and Cressida* among the problem plays, a choice echoed by Tillyard in his *Shakespeare's Problem Plays* (1950). Ernest Schanzer, in *The Problem Plays of Shakespeare* (1963), opts for a rather different set of texts: *Julius Caesar, Measure for Measure,* and *Antony and Cleopatra.* Other critics have suggested yet more plays, among them *The Merchant of Venice,* and *The Taming of the Shrew.*

This disagreement among scholars about what constitutes the problem plays suggests why the term itself has fallen into disuse: instability. For some, the term "problem play" means a play that deals with a social issue. But don't nearly all of his plays (except perhaps the frothiest comedies) do so? For some, the term means a play that seems to be neither comedy nor tragedy nor history, but to sit rather uncomfortably on those imaginary lines that separate the genres. In this sense, the "problem" in "problem play" is definitional. But since Shakespeare is never a respecter of genre, almost all of his plays can qualify in one way or another as "problem plays." The term is no longer useful because of its ambiguity and inclusiveness, although the idea that Shakespeare seems more concerned in some of his plays with moral dilemmas can be helpful in the analysis of the range of meaning in the Shakespeare canon. It is also the case that most of the plays critics have included under the "problem play" banner go rather more neatly under another one: **dark comedies,** that is, comedies where the sense of resolution that comes from the plot-driven marriages is undercut by an atmosphere of disquiet.

Roman Play

This term is used to describe the three Shakespeare plays that are set in Ancient Rome and use Plutarch's *Lives* as their primary source: *Julius Caesar; Antony and Cleopatra;* and *Coriolanus. Titus Andronicus* is excluded from this group because, although it is set in Ancient Rome, it is mythic rather than historical and belongs emphatically in a subgenre of Tragedy: **Senecan revenge** (see page 135 in this chapter). The term *Roman play* would not be particularly useful were it not that all three plays share some common attributes: a fascination with politics and right conduct; an emphasis on the pre-Christian moral code; a confusion over the nature of good and evil; a concern over the loyalty an individual owes to the state; and a belief that anything outside Roman control is essentially barbaric.

Writing and Discussion Assignments

1. One of the characteristics shared by Shakespeare's comedies and tragedies is the use of complicated plots. Examine *Twelfth Night* and *Hamlet* for the ways in which Shakespeare's plotting techniques vary in the two plays.
2. Select any one characteristic of Shakespearean tragedy and examine the way in which it manifests itself in *Hamlet, Othello, King Lear,* or *Macbeth.*
3. Look at *Richard III* carefully as a tragedy rather than as a history play. How many of the characteristics of Shakespearean tragedy does it display?
4. With the exception of *The Tempest,* Shakespeare's plays routinely ignore the dramatic unities of time, place, and action. In the absence of these ways of unifying dramatic action, how does Shakespeare hold his plays together? Choose any one play by means of which to examine this issue.
5. Discuss Shakespeare's treatment of the common people in one or more of Shakespeare's history plays. Which social group, if any, does he seem to favor: the upper classes, the middle classes, or the lower classes?
6. Imagine that you are an editor of a collection of Shakespeare's plays. How would you organize those plays, and why? You could, for example, choose to follow the 1623 Folio. You could choose, instead, to opt for a chronological organization, a thematic sequence, or some other approach. Whichever strategy you choose, you need to defend you choice.

Further Reading

Colie, Rosalie. *The Resources of Kind: Genre Theory in the Renaissance.* Berkeley: U of California P, 1973.

Danson, Lawrence. *Shakespeare's Dramatic Genres.* Oxford: Oxford UP, 2000.

Doran, Madeleine. *Endeavors of Art: A Study of Form in Elizabethan Drama.* Madison: U of Wisconsin P, 1954.

Fowler, Alastair. *Kinds of Literature: An Introduction to the Theory of Genre and Modes.* Cambridge: Harvard UP, 1982.

Howard, Jean E. "Shakespeare and Genre." *A Companion to Shakespeare.* Ed. David Scott Kastan. Oxford, Eng.: Blackwell Publishers, 1999. 297–310.

Tennenhouse, Leonard. *Power on Display: The Politics of Shakespeare's Genres.* New York: Methuen, 1986.

Chapter  6

*And as imagination bodies forth
The forms of things unknown, the
poet's pen
Turns them to shapes and gives to
airy nothing
A local habitation and a name*

A Midsummer Night's Dream
(5.1.14–17)

Shakespeare's Stagecraft

Chapter Overview

◇ Understanding the importance of rapid exposition in Shakespeare's plays.
◇ Understanding how Shakespeare lets us know who his characters are.
◇ Understanding how Shakespeare handles entrances and exits.
◇ Appreciating how Shakespeare makes the most of the limitations of the Elizabethan/Jacobean stage.
◇ Appreciating how Shakespeare takes advantage of the peculiarities of the Elizabethan/Jacobean stage.
◇ Appreciating how Shakespeare sews together the action, varies the tempo, combines comedy with tragedy, and mixes the profound with the mundane.
◇ Appreciating how Shakespeare uses stage metaphors and metadrama.

In these days of extraordinarily sophisticated special effects and the louder-than-life sound of THX® or Dolby Digital®, it is hard sometimes for a contemporary reader or watcher of Shakespeare's plays to imagine the worlds he creates in his plays. Much of contemporary culture demands only passivity from its "consumers"; Shakespeare, by contrast, demands above all, an energetic commitment of the imagination. Indeed, Shakespeare's greatest achievement is his transformation of an apparent liability, the bare Elizabethan/Jacobean stage, into his greatest strength as a dramatist. Through the power of stagecraft and language, and with the intensely active involvement of the audience, Shakespeare's world comes alive in extraordinary ways.

However, because the contemporary reader or watcher is unused to such simplicity of setting combined with such density of language, the initial reaction of many students is confusion and frustration: confusion at the speed with which so many ideas develop; frustration at being unable to understand Shakespeare's compressed figurative language. It is with the first of these common reactions—confusion about how Shakespeare is handling the stage action—that I am concerned in this chapter.

At first, the reaction of anyone when reading or watching a Shakespeare play is at the very least an almost visceral uneasiness as the mind tries to catch up with what's happening. It makes no difference whether the person is an expert, an amateur, or a neophyte. Shakespeare presents us with a new world, one devoid of the kinds of physical markers of time and place we have grown used to. Questions such as "Who are these people?" and "Where is the action taking place?" form a major part of the initial reaction. These questions can be answered, however; the blizzard of information that the play surrounds us with can clear very quickly. How? If the reader understands two essential qualities of Shakespearean drama:

1. Despite all his wonderful language and memorable characterization, Shakespeare knew instinctively that action is the lifeblood of drama. Again and again, Shakespeare uses action as the antidote to dullness. He relegates what he can't show on stage to narrative and off-stage event; he reserves for spectacle what he instinctively knows will work.
2. For all his brilliance and apparently inexhaustible invention, the playwright actually uses a limited set of devices, or tricks of the trade. He does so, however, with inspired variation to create his magical world from a bare stage. Once you see these devices at work, a pattern emerges, and when you comprehend that pattern, the bewilderment disappears. Knowing this pattern makes the experience of understanding Shakespeare much more pleasurable.

Getting up to Speed

The central problem facing Shakespeare as a dramatist was the need to begin his plays with exposition. It didn't matter whether the play was a history, a comedy, a tragedy, or a romance; it didn't even matter whether the stories were well known (*Richard III* or *Henry V,* say) or new (*Love's Labor's Lost* or *The Tempest*). The audience in Shakespeare's time needed to be brought up to speed quickly. In that respect, the *modern* audience is no different. The problem from the dramatist's point of view is that exposition is essentially dull, and the last thing any dramatist would want to do— especially at the beginning of a play—is bore the audience. Shakespeare's solution? To get the essential background filled in as soon as possible, and to get it done in as sensational a way as the story would allow. In every one of Shakespeare's plays, the first act is devoted to that task; in some— A Midsummer Night's Dream, for example—the exposition spills over into the next act; however, there is always a good reason for such anomalies. And, of course, on the Elizabethan stage, where there were no pauses between acts, such a distinction would not be evident at all. Again and again in Shakespeare's plays, you can see that clever combination at work: exposition; brevity; and excitement. Give the background. Make it short. Try for sensation.

In Shakespeare's early work, the bloody revenge tragedy *Titus Andronicus* (1589?), it takes him only 496 lines out of 2708 to lay out the plots and themes of the play. As far as plots in *Titus Andronicus* are concerned, there are several: the struggle for the position of Emperor of Rome, the conflict between the Goths and the Romans, the tangled lust relation among several characters, the struggle between father and sons, the struggle between father and daughter, and the struggle between the civilian authority and the military. As for the themes or issues, again Shakespeare opts for complexity over simplicity: the dangers of power, the temptation of lust, the ubiquity of violence, the prevalence of racism, the cruelty of patriarchy, the existence of pure evil, the desire for revenge. Almost all of these plots and themes are brought to center stage by the end of Act 1 (pure evil doesn't actually appear until Aaron's wonderful soliloquy—"Now climbeth Tamora Olympus' top"—which begins Act 2), and it takes the remainder of the play to see them worked out in the arena of human affairs.

How does Shakespeare make such condensed exposition exciting? As I indicated earlier, with action. In the course of Act 1 and, so, in fewer than 500 lines, Shakespeare gives us two brothers battling for the supreme position in the world: Emperor of Rome. He also gives us two murders: one off stage (of Tamora's son, Alarbus, at 1.1.141); the other very much on stage (of Titus Andronicus's son, Mutius, at 1.1.293). He spices it up further by having the first murder defended as just and the second murder be that of a son by a father. So much for blood.

Then, there's that other topic that seems to fascinate human beings almost as much: lust. No sooner has Saturninus decided to marry the dull but virtuous Lavinia ("Lavinia will I make my empress,/Rome's royal mistress, mistress of my heart" [1.1.241–42]) than he can't help but notice that Tamora is gorgeous ("A goodly lady, trust me, of the hue/That I would choose, were I to choose anew" [1.1.262–63]). And, *of course*, during the first act he does, indeed, choose anew. From all this action, chaos comes, and it's a chaos that any audience can understand once it sees that the groundwork has been laid.

If we look at a late Shakespeare play, his greatest romance, *The Tempest* (ca. 1611), the same pattern of exposition, brevity, excitement recurs.

Another Shakespearean characteristic appears as well: an intense dislike of doing exactly the same thing twice.

◊ **Exposition:** The major exposition occurs in 1.2.1–377, for it gives the essential background on how Prospero and Miranda became marooned on an uninhabited island and what they have been doing since they first arrived there twelve years before.

◊ **Brevity:** Shakespeare keeps it as short as he can. The exposition is almost 400 lines in length, but then it does cover a considerable amount of background and time.

◊ **Excitement:** To keep everyone entertained during the exposition, Shakespeare includes the magic of Ariel, Prospero's airy spirit. He also brackets the exposition with a shipwreck (1.1) and with the beginning of the love affair between Miranda and Ferdinand (1.2.391–505). On both sides, excitement. As in his other plays, the material does double duty: enticing the audience to become involved in the drama and explaining to it what *has* happened and what, in all likelihood, *will*. By the end of the play, Miranda and Ferdinand will become engaged, and Prospero will be avenged for his mistreatment at the hands of Alonso (the King of Naples), Sebastian (Alonso's brother), and Antonio (Prospero's brother), who has usurped his position as Duke of Milan.

◊ **Newness:** Shakespeare never liked to do the same thing twice. *The Tempest* shows this aversion well. A dozen or so years before *The Tempest*, the Chorus in *Henry V* had begged off from depicting on stage the two armies, of England and France, battling each other. He had done so because having horses on the stage would be a logistical nightmare as well as—in all likelihood—unintentionally funny. Instead, he had opted for wonderful word painting to substitute for the real thing. With *The Tempest*, Shakespeare now tries a different approach and stages something impossible—not horses on stage, true, but something even more spectacular: a shipwreck.

Handling the Introductions

Just as Shakespeare faced the task as a dramatist of getting his audience up to speed as quickly and imaginatively as possible, so he had to deal with another problem that occurs to some degree in almost any play but which occurs particularly and acutely in Shakespeare's, that is, in plays with very large casts. His first comedy, *The Comedy of Errors* (ca. 1588), has 18 characters. His first tragedy, *Titus Andronicus* (ca. 1589), has 27. His first history play, *Henry VI Part 1* (ca. 1589), has 48 named parts, and that count doesn't include the assorted heralds, soldiers, servingmen, jailers, attendants, ambassadors, and fiends that people the landscape. His first romance, *Pericles*

(1606?), has at least 54. If the characters can't wear name tags ("Hello, I'm . . ."), how is the reader or audience to know quickly and *remember* who is who? The answer is obvious, but adroitly handled by Shakespeare: the play has to name the characters as often and as unobtrusively as possible.

Of course, some of the broader distinctions in class or profession are clear from costumes: it's not by accident that the one indulgence of the Elizabethan stage was, as William Ingram has pointed out in "The Economics of Playing," the cost of the finery the characters wore. Stage directions, too, can reveal the emotional state of characters. For example, in *Richard III* when Queen Elizabeth enters at 2.2.33 *"with her hair about her ears,"* the audience knows that she is distraught at the death of her husband, Edward IV. However, as far as identification is concerned, for Shakespeare it's up to each character to name the new ones who come on stage. Once you realize how much of this sort of naming goes on, you can appreciate its value. You would, I think, be very nearly lost without so simple a device. Once you see, too, what Shakespeare is doing, you have to be impressed with how many different ways he can fulfill essentially the same purpose: providing an aural cast list with some editorial bias.

One of Shakespeare's favorite devices, which you can see working in *2 Henry IV, 1 Henry VI,* and *Hamlet* among others, is the guard or porter scene. What better way to stage drama than to have an episode in which one character is duty bound to demand the identity of another? So, in *2 Henry IV* 1.1, Shakespeare has the Porter at Northumberland's castle ask the man at the gate: "What [i.e., who] shall I say you are?" (2). The man replies: "Tell thou the Earl/That the Lord Bardolph doth attend him here" (2–3).

In *1 Henry VI* 1.3, the First Warder asks someone who knocks to identify himself, but provides a clue as to his rank by the way he asks the question: "Who's there that knocks so *imperiously?*" (5; emphasis added). The response: "It is the noble Duke of Gloucester" (6).

In *Hamlet* 1.1, Shakespeare goes one better than in these two history plays by having the scene take place on a cold night. So, even people who should be able to recognize each other can't because of the dark and because of the cloaks that enshroud them. In quick succession and in response to the repeated question "Who's there?" the audience is able to identify Bernardo, Francisco, Horatio, and Marcellus. And just in case some members of the audience don't remember names well, they are repeated: Marcellus's name is mentioned three times before the ghost enters between lines 129 and 130, and Bernardo's four times. Horatio's name (perhaps in deference to his importance in the play) is mentioned no less than eight times. Francisco may seem the odd man out with a paltry count of only one, but then he does exit at line 20. He does not exit, however, before Shakespeare makes a little extra mileage out of the business of his naming. Marcellus simply addresses Francisco as "honest soldier" (19).

Perhaps he does so because they do not know each other well, or perhaps the playwright is taking an early opportunity to show the audience which side it should support as the conflict between Hamlet and Claudius develops.

Shakespeare's more workaday, but nonetheless effective, method of naming is to involve his cast in something rather like a baton exchange in a track-and-field relay race, with one character announcing who is about to enter. So, in *2 Henry IV*, in the same scene I referred to on the previous page (1.1), we have the following "hand-offs":

> LORD BARDOLPH
>> Here comes the Earl [of Northumberland] (6)
> NORTHUMBERLAND
>> Here comes my servant Travers ... (28)
> LORD BARDOLPH
>> Look, here comes more news (59)

Similar examples could be provided from the beginning scenes of every Shakespeare play. Once the naming has been done, however, the practice is redundant and drops out of the later scenes entirely. In dramatic terms, the device has served its purpose because the audience or reader now knows who's who.

Comings and Goings

In addition to the problems of exposition and naming, Shakespeare had another, equally difficult, problem to solve: how to get his characters on and off stage frequently, rapidly, *and* naturally. He needed to do this to advance the action and to allow different groups of characters to talk about particular concerns. Just as in real life, conversations in drama change depending on who is in the room. Obviously such methods as those adopted by Samuel Beckett in his absurdist masterpiece, *Waiting for Godot*, would not work. Beckett can have a character exit to pee offstage, but that wouldn't fit well with the decorum of the Elizabethan stage.

In many ways, Shakespeare's successful handling of this problem is among his greatest achievements precisely because, while he never draws attention to the entrances and exits, they are essential to the rapid development of plot and become more difficult as the pieces of the action come together toward the close of each play. If we look at what the playwright does at the end of his most skillfully plotted comedy, *Twelfth Night*, then we can observe the master at work.

The final scene (5.1) of 408 lines has ten entrances and seven exits. These are organized as follows; I've added after each a brief explanation for why they happen when they do.

Entrance 1 (before line 1): *Enter Clown [Feste] and Fabian.*

Feste and Fabian enter with Feste carrying a letter from Malvolio to Olivia. Their entrance picks up the plot from the end of 4.2 (two scenes earlier).

Entrance 2 (between lines 6 and 7): *Enter Duke [Orsino], Viola, Curio, and Lords*

It's about time Orsino showed up. We haven't seen him since the end of 2.4 when he sent Viola/Cesario off as a go-between on her/his second mission to Olivia to plead his undying love for her. Orsino must be wondering what's going on.

Entrance 3 (between lines 45 and 46): *Enter Antonio and Officers*

Antonio had been arrested in 3.4 "at the suit/Of Count Orsino" (328–29). What more natural than that those who had arrested him should bring him before Count Orsino?

Entrance 4 (between lines 93 and 94): *Enter Olivia and attendants*

Olivia enters as a result of Feste's being sent (at line 45) to get her. She explicitly acknowledges Orsino's request to see her: "What would my lord?" (98).

Entrance 5 (between lines 148 and 149): *Enter Priest*

The priest enters and delivers proof of the marriage of Olivia and Sebastian.

Entrance 6 (between lines 169 and 170): *Enter Sir Andrew*

This entrance and the one following are a continuation of the fight between Sir Andrew Aguecheek, Sir Toby Belch, and Sebastian in 4.1.

Entrance 7 (between lines 190 and 191): *Enter [Sir] Toby and Clown [Feste]*

Entrance 8 (between lines 207 and 208): *Enter Sebastian*

This entrance sets up the essential moment in the play when Viola/Cesario and Sebastian are, for the first time, both on stage at once.

Entrance 9 (between lines 280 and 281): *Enter Clown [Feste] with a letter, and Fabian*

Feste and Fabian enter after having seen to the tending of Sir Toby Belch's and Sir Andrew Aguecheek's wounds offstage. Feste also carries the letter from Malvolio to Olivia. Coincidentally, Viola brings up Malvolio's name shortly before they return. Shakespeare manages to make dramatic foreshadowing look natural.

Entrance 10 (between lines 326 and 327): *Enter [Fabian, with] Malvolio*

Fabian enters with Malvolio, but does so only after Shakespeare has explored the implications of the Viola-Orsino-Olivia-Sebastian relation.

Exit 1 (after line 45): *Exit Feste*

Orsino naturally asks the first of Olivia's servants whom he talks with, Feste, to go and tell Olivia he's waiting to talk with her.

Exit 2 (after line 140): *Exit an attendant*

The attendant is sent off to fetch the priest who married Olivia and Sebastian (although Olivia thought she was marrying Viola/Cesario).

Exit 3 (after line 207): *Exeunt Feste, Fabian, Sir Toby, and Sir Andrew*

Feste and Fabian leave the stage helping the injured Sir Andrew Aguecheek and Sir Toby Belch to their beds. Shakespeare needs to have Feste and Fabian leave the stage because their presence would be unnecessary and even inappropriate for the recognition scene that follows between Viola/Cesario and Sebastian.

Exit 4 (after line 315): *Exit Fabian*

Fabian exits to fetch Malvolio from his confinement by Sir Toby Belch.

Exit 5 (after line 378): *Exit Malvolio*

Malvolio exits swearing that he'll "be revenged on the whole pack of you!" (378). His presence would spoil the festivities: a double marriage.

Exit 6 (after line 388): *Exeunt [all, except Feste]*

Only Feste remains on stage to deliver his final song, a bittersweet ballad about time passing.

Exit 7 (after line 408): *Feste*

The stage is at last bare.

What then can the reader or audience learn from Shakespeare's handling of the entrances and exits of his characters?

◆ He does both with great skill.

◆ He masks the dramatic reason with a realistic gloss.

◆ He ensures that conversations naturally ebb and flow according to the particular set of characters assembled.

Unless you see the skill, it all looks rather random. It is anything but. *Indeed, the entrances and exits, far more than the individual scenes and acts, form the essential units of any Shakespearean play: the building blocks that create the structure of his drama.*

There are—as one might expect—occasional lapses in Shakespeare's 38 plays, places where the exits and entrances are less well managed. Nearly always, however, Shakespeare handles the stage business of entrances and exits with great skill. It's hard to imagine, for example, a smoother way of clearing the stage than his strategy in *Antony and Cleopatra* 4.3. In this scene, he has an entire company of soldiers leave the stage searching for the source of mysterious oboe music beneath the stage, music which symbolizes Antony's favorite god, Hercules, abandoning him. It's hard to imagine, too, a more exciting exit than the one in *The Winter's Tale*: "*Exit, pursued by a bear*" (3.3.57). Seeing what Shakespeare is doing helps to remove one more roadblock in the way of getting at his simple message: deftly presented action lies at the heart of drama.

Placing Yourself in the Action

Even with the exposition, the naming, and the understanding of how Shakespeare moves his characters around the stage, the audience still lacks one piece of information by means of which to orient itself: place. Shakespeare as a Renaissance dramatist seems initially to be yet again in a difficult position: without all the paraphernalia of realistic drama, how can he provide those he wants to entertain with a sense of where they are? His simple answer: much of the time, it doesn't matter. Action is what matters and, very often, that can occur without being anchored to a specific place. This is particularly true when the staging itself, so simple in English Renaissance drama, would have given little clue.

Students frequently ask about the specific location of the action, and although editorial notes frequently cite particular places, such specificity is unnecessary. Indeed, too much concern with it distracts from understanding Shakespeare's intent in his plays: to throw the action against a neutral backdrop in which language (and also costume) can illuminate everything more effectively. How does one know, then, where the characters are at all? Because they drop hints, and because they wear clothes appropriate to a given occasion.

When Menas, in *Antony and Cleopatra*, offers to kill Antony, Lepidus, and Octavius Caesar in order to make his master, Sextus Pompeius, ruler of the world, we know exactly where the action is taking place because of what he says:

> These three world-sharers, these competitors,
> Are in thy vessel. Let me cut the cable,
> And, when we are put off, fall to their throats.
> All there is thine (2.7.71–74).

They are on a boat tied up to the shore. They don't need to be in a boat for you to visualize the scene. The boat doesn't need a name. You don't need to wonder what sort of boat it is.

Court scenes (one end of the social scale) would be splendidly costumed; scenes in prison (the other end of the scale) would be performed in ragged clothes; a shipwreck survivor (Pericles, for example, in *Pericles* 2.1) would come on stage in wet clothes. Clothes as a language are surely well-enough understood by everyone so that it would be obvious to all that the second scene in *Hamlet* is a formal royal occasion even though no one says it is. The sound of trumpets with which it would begin is part of that message about place, as is the particular set of characters assembled, but on a bare stage clothes definitely make the man or woman. Similarly, in *Measure for Measure* 4.3, a scene which takes place in a prison, the executioner, Abhorson, would have been dressed for the task (he might even have carried the requisite axe) while the drunken prisoner, Barnardine, would have been dressed in filthy rags.

The proof that Shakespeare is right in his sense of how drama works, that a fixation with specificity of place comes at a cost and distracts from what is essential, is nicely laid out in two of his plays: *Coriolanus*, and *A Midsummer Night's Dream*.

In *Coriolanus*, the final scene (5.6) begins in Antium (Aufidius's "native town" [49]); at line 94, it moves to Corioles, Coriolanus's hometown. Shakespeare does so to make a parallel between Coriolanus's triumph in Rome at the beginning of the play and his death at the end. He sacrifices realism for dramatic effect. At least one critic, Alan Dessen, in "Shakespeare and the Theatrical Conventions of his Time" has found the sudden—logically impossible—shift in location to be "most perplexing" (93). But to the audience, it wouldn't have been, and it needn't be to the reader. Action, Shakespeare understood, can take place very successfully in an indeterminate space.

In fact, so certain is Shakespeare that specificity of place can be harmful to drama that at the end of *A Midsummer Night's Dream* he has the working-class acting troupe (Quince, Bottom, Flute, Snout, Snug, and Starveling) perform a wonderfully, albeit unintentionally, funny version of the story of Pyramus and Thisbe ("a tedious brief scene of young Pyramus/ And his love Thisbe" [5.1.56–57]). A significant element in the humor lies in the cast's insistence on achieving as much realism as it can. Instead of the audience's imagining a wall and moonshine, the actors have to represent them. The Prologue announces as much:

> This man with lime and roughcast doth present
> Wall, that vile wall which did these lovers sunder;
> And through Wall's chink, poor souls, they are content
> To whisper. At the which let no man wonder.

> This man, with lantern, dog, and bush of thorn,
> Presenteth Moonshine; for, if you will know,
> By moonshine did these lovers think no scorn
> To meet at Ninus' tomb, there, there to woo
> (5.1.130–37).

Worse still, both actors when they come on stage give their real names and announce again what they represent. Wall goes even further. Once his part in the play is done, he announces it's time to go: "Thus have I, Wall, my part dischargèd so;/And, being done, thus Wall away doth go" (5.1.203–04). Shakespeare is taking a risk here. If he's wrong about the unimportance of place, then the audience will not find the scene amusing. He risks being laughed *at* not *with*.

My advice when encountering Shakespeare's unusual attitude to place? Don't worry too much about logic and realism; such a concern is unnecessary and distracting. Spatial freedom allows audience and reader to collaborate directly in the creation of meaning. Shakespeare only asks us to listen carefully and watch observantly.

Making Lemonade (from Lemons)

At the beginning of the previous section, I suggested that Shakespeare's handling of place turned to great advantage what might seem to be highly damaging. The same can be said of a broader set of the theatrical conventions of the time. Again and again, as Alan Dessen has observed in his essay on Elizabethan and Jacobean theatrical conventions, Shakespeare turns what a modern audience or reader would see as weaknesses into strengths. Seeing how he does so helps anyone new to Shakespeare's stagecraft make sense of the world he presents us with in his plays. Let's look at just one of the examples cited by Dessen—battle scenes—and an additional one: boys playing the women's roles.

Battle Scenes

The Globe stage was only about 25 feet in depth and 44 feet in width, with two massive pillars, which held up the ornate roof above the stage, obstructing the openness of that area of about 1100 square feet. (See Fig. 6.1.) That's more than *forty* times smaller than a football field. Under those circumstances, realistic battle scenes—the sort of thing that has become passé since the movie *Braveheart* was released—were not an option for Shakespeare. He knew that, and he also knew that he ran the risk of having some of the most dramatic moments in his plays rendered ludicrous because of the limitations of the stage with which he had to work.

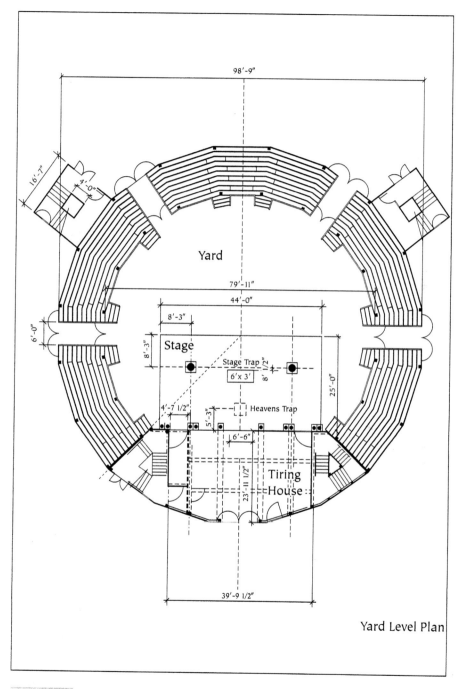

98'-9"

16'-7"

4'-0"

Yard

79'-11"

44'-0"

8'-3"

8'-3"

6'-0"

Stage

Stage Trap

8' 1/2"

6'x 3'

25'-0"

4'-7 1/2"

5'-3"

Heavens Trap

6'-6"

Tiring House

23'-11 1/2"

39'-9 1/2"

Yard Level Plan

Figure 6.1
Architectural plan of the New Globe in Southwark, London (1996). The design is
based on the best research about the design of the original Globe.

His solution, as so often with his stagecraft, was to work within the limitations: to make lemonade from lemons; to use the device of synecdoche and have the part stand for the whole. If he couldn't depict a battle on stage, then what he could do was to dramatize skirmishes by enacting small battles between just a few soldiers. In so doing, he also managed to show his audience the reality of warfare at that time. Any battle in Europe from the medieval to the late Renaissance broke down into a long and confused series of individual conflicts at close range. Archery, cavalry, and—eventually—munitions did their part to change the nature of warfare, but the fundamentals remained the same for a long time. So, when Henry V says to the Frenchman Mountjoy at the battle of Agincourt: "I tell thee truly, herald,/I know not if the day be ours or no" (4.7.82–83), he is expressing a truth about war that his audience would have understood. A contemporary audience or reader, brought up on the Vietnam War, the troubles in Northern Ireland, the conflicts in Bosnia and Kosovo, and the violence in the Middle East, would understand, too. War even in this age of "smart" bombs, sophisticated warplanes, and long-range rifles is hell—quite often at close range.

Just how few soldiers Shakespeare needs is evident in *Henry V*. The well-done film versions by Laurence Olivier and Kenneth Branagh show a significant amount of conflict between quite large groups. The play, however, does something rather different. The battle of Agincourt occupies part of Act Three and most of Act Four (3.6–4.7), yet only one scene actually depicts fighting: 4.4. And that scene, which involves Pistol, a boy, and a French soldier, is really more an excuse for some groundling comedy than it is an actual struggle. Sometimes, Shakespeare adopted a slightly different strategy: using skirmishes as a means to represent the ebb and flow of battle. In *Antony and Cleopatra*, for instance, Shakespeare depicts the battle of Alexandria (4.3–4.8) in six short scenes, none of them longer than 39 lines. The battle is shown as a series of movements by both sides across the stage, with the common man represented by one of Antony's veteran soldiers, the appropriately named Scarus, and by one of Caesar's labeled simply "Soldier."

Either way (whether by individual soldiers or by skirmishes), Shakespeare gains some very valuable effects through such stagecraft. In the case of *Henry V*, for example, he undercuts the unity of the intensely patriotic message presented by the Chorus and so gives his audience a range of possible responses: from war as a wonderful pursuit carried out by, as the king himself puts it, "We few, we happy few, we band of brothers" (4.3.60), to war as "brawl ridiculous" (4.0.51) in which the main intent—if the low-life characters in the play are representative—is to get as much booty as possible and then get home alive. With *Antony and Cleopatra*, the message is a little different: war can be a last chance to save reputation and power (in both cases, Antony's), but it can also be an activity characterized by repeated betrayal—in this instance by Cleopatra, that "foul Egyptian" as Antony calls her (4.12.10).

In either case, just as with his use of an indeterminate space, Shakespeare was not above showing how close he could come to disaster. In *Henry V*, the Chorus at the beginning of the Act in which the battle of Agincourt is shown apologizes for the inadequacy of the "special effects":

> And so our scene must to the battle fly;
> Where—O, for pity!—we shall much disgrace
> With four or five most vile and ragged foils,
> Right ill-disposed in brawl ridiculous
> The name of Agincourt (4.0.48–52).

The Chorus concludes, however, with an appeal to exactly that power in the audience or reader over which Shakespeare was wonderfully adroit at gaining control, the imagination. He asks the audience to "sit and see,/ Minding true things by what their mockeries be" (52–53).

If you understand what Shakespeare is trying to do with his staging of battles, if you see how successful he is with the options available to him, if you appreciate how much more meaning derives from such a technique than from war depicted on a larger canvas, then the small scale of Shakespeare's wars becomes more understandable, and another, apparently odd, aspect of his craft becomes comprehensible. Above all, Shakespeare was a dramatist of the imagination not of spectacle.

Boys as Women

As a matter of convention, boys played the women's roles in English Renaissance drama. It was not until after the Restoration in 1660 that women began to act on the stage. This transvestism is, of course, hidden from modern audiences because all of the performances on film and stage—except those which undertake the experiment of being carefully authentic—assign the roles according to gender. It is, nevertheless, important to come to terms with the effect of this Renaissance convention, for while it is almost completely absent from theatrical practice today it significantly affected Shakespeare's stagecraft. At the very least, two aspects of Shakespearean drama will be lost to you without such an understanding: Shakespeare's delight in jokes at the expense of the convention, and his exploitation of dramatic irony.

The first can be seen in the frequent references in Shakespeare to the practical difficulties and dramatic possibilities of having boys play the women's roles. In *A Midsummer Night's Dream*, Francis Flute is chosen by Peter Quince to play the part of Thisbe, the woman whom Pyramus loves, in the dramatic scene that the rude mechanicals want to stage at the celebration of Theseus's marriage to Hippolyta. Flute objects ("Nay, faith, let not me play a woman") and for a very practical reason: "I have a beard coming" (1.2.42).

In *Twelfth Night*, Shakespeare emphasizes the possibilities. Viola is shipwrecked on Illyria's shore, and goes on to dress herself as a young man, and become Orsino's companion and Olivia's love interest. Along the way, she also falls in love with Orsino. So, we have a he playing a she disguised as a he. Shakespeare delighted in the complexities of such a situation so much so that in another comedy, *As You Like It*, he goes one step further when the central female character, Rosalind, disguises herself as a boy named Ganymede (after the androgynous servant of Jove). Thus far, we have a situation that in terms of gender is only a little more complex than in *Twelfth Night*. The plot thickens, however, when he/she/it is courted by Orlando, one of the sons of Sir Rowland de Boys, even though Orlando knows that Rosalind/Ganymede is ostensibly male. His reason? Because Rosalind/Ganymede has promised that by such means Orlando will be cured of the insanity of love. Of course, no such thing happens.

Finally, in *Antony and Cleopatra*, Shakespeare delivers perhaps his most condensed moment of dramatic irony. Towards the end of the play, Cleopatra decides to kill herself because she is not reassured by Caesar's deceitful promises. She is convinced that he intends public humiliation for her. That humiliation could take several forms, but one which preys on her mind is the idea that her love affair with Antony will become the stuff of Roman comedy:

> The quick comedians
> Extemporally will stage us and present
> Our Alexandrian revels; Antony
> Shall be brought drunken forth, and I shall see
> Some squeaking Cleopatra boy my greatness
> I' the posture of a whore (5.2.216–21).

This nightmare is a powerful one because of Shakespeare's straightforward language, but when stagecraft is considered, it becomes a fascinating statement. It is, after all, a nightmare about a boy playing Cleopatra. And who's giving voice to that nightmare? A boy playing Cleopatra. As before, when Shakespeare drew attention to his own stagecraft in the Agincourt battle scenes in *Henry V*, so here he does the same with one of his two central characters. Clearly, he enjoyed sailing close to the wind, for he could only hope that in *Antony and Cleopatra* his depiction of the Egyptian queen wouldn't remind his audience of "the posture of a whore."

Taking Advantage

So far I have emphasized the adaptive in my picture of Shakespeare's stagecraft: this is what Shakespeare can do *despite* the limitations of the stage during the English Renaissance. Briefly, we will look at several examples of the way in which the fluidity of Shakespeare's stage held tremendous *advantages* for him. The first three examples, from *Twelfth Night, A Midsummer Night's Dream,* and *Macbeth* show the power of symbolism. The fourth, from *Hamlet,* shows the value of the special effects available to Shakespeare. The remainder, from *The Merchant of Venice, Henry V, Titus Andronicus,* and *Cymbeline,* show the value of props on a bare stage.

The Power of Symbolism

Malvolio's punishment for self-love and officiousness is to be tied up and thrown into a dark room in Olivia's house by Sir Toby Belch. As part of the prank, Maria, a gentlewoman in Olivia's house, has Feste, Olivia's Fool, visit Malvolio in the guise of a priest, Sir Topas. In this scene (4.2), Malvolio insists that he is in a dark room; Feste declares that it is actually broad daylight. (See Chapter 4, pages 109–11, for a discussion of the humor in this scene.)

Shakespeare's staging of the episode emphasizes how right Feste is and how wrong Malvolio *appears* to be. At the Globe, the scene would have been staged in broad daylight with Feste on the stage in full view and Malvolio probably behind the central doors at the back of the stage in the "discovery" space. (See Fig. 6.2.) From the point of view of the audience, then, when Malvolio says he is in "hideous darkness" (31), he is surely wrong. The audience cannot see him, but has no reason to believe his statement accurate.

What the audience does, I think, come to see is that Shakespeare is asking it to see the scene as symbolic. When Feste says to Malvolio, "Madman, thou errest. I say there is no darkness/but ignorance, in which thou are more puzzled than/the Egyptians in their fog" (43–45), the spectators or readers are being asked to "read" Malvolio's behavior up to that time in terms of the darkness of ignorance, a mental darkness reinforced by the simple fact that the scene takes place in daylight. And his behavior *has* been extraordinarily ignorant. He thinks he has a chance of wooing Olivia even though he is merely her steward (2.5; 3.4). He thinks it acceptable to be rude to Orsino's messenger, Cesario, and throw down the ring in the dirt at his feet, a ring which Cesario supposedly gave to Olivia as a token of Orsino's affection for her (2.2). He thinks it acceptable to chastise Sir Toby Belch, Sir Andrew Aguecheek, and Maria for partying late at night, even though Belch and Aguecheek are his social betters, his "masters" as he calls them (2.3.86), and Maria at least his equal. However, Shakespeare as usual asks the reader to see both sides of the issue. Yes, Malvolio has been ignorant, but in the end Olivia does admit (albeit not to his face but to his departing back), "He hath been most notoriously abused" (5.1.379).

Again and again in his plays Shakespeare exploits the symbolic power of his staging techniques, techniques which tend to be obscured in modern versions of his work where a greater realism holds sway. In *A Midsummer Night's Dream,* all of the confusion among the lovers in the wood in Acts 2

Figure 6.2
The double doors and balcony at the back of the New Globe's stage. The doors hide a "discovery" space.

and 3, which according to the language of the play occurs in darkness, would in fact have been staged in daylight. The symbolic value: love blinds even more powerfully than a realistic modern version of the play would suggest. In *Macbeth*, the stage direction that opens the play reads: *Thunder and lightning. Enter three Witches* (1.1). The Witches' words that end the short scene read: "Fair is foul, and foul is fair./Hover through the fog and filthy air" (11–12). Unless Shakespeare happened to be extraordinarily lucky, these effects (except for the sound of thunder) would have had to be provided by the minds of the audience and not by Mother Nature or by theatrical special effects. If the audience succeeds in imagining such effects, then so has it effectively acknowledged the power of the three Witches.

Hamlet and the Hell beneath the Stage

One of the key concerns Hamlet has early in the tragedy is to discover whether the ghost of his father is actually a devil sent to trick him to his damnation. The hero addresses the Ghost:

> Be thou a spirit of health or goblin damned,
> Bring with thee airs from heaven or blasts from hell,
> Be thy intents wicked or charitable,
> Thou com'st in such a questionable shape
> That I will speak to thee (1.4.40–44).

Even as late as the end of Act 2, Hamlet remains in some doubt:

> The spirit that I have seen
> May be the devil, and the devil hath power
> T' assume a pleasing shape; yea, and perhaps,
> Out of my weakness and my melancholy,
> As he is very potent with such spirits,
> Abuses me to damn me (2.2.599–604).

It's not hard to *hear* why Hamlet doubts, given the way in which Shakespeare sets up the end of 1.5. In that scene, Hamlet has Horatio and Marcellus swear to keep secret the appearance of the Ghost on the battlements that night. They hesitate. How are they encouraged? By the Ghost crying to them from beneath the stage: "Swear," "Swear," "Swear by his [Hamlet's] sword" (158; 164; 170). And as they move about the stage, so the Ghost follows them from below. Nothing would have been easier given the fact that the Globe stage was raised above the level of the floor by some five feet. What's the symbolism of such a device? Considered spatially, the Ghost's orders come from below, from that space which existed as the exact opposite to that space above the roof of the stage, which was known as the Heavens and from where the **deus ex machina** (or god in some sort of conveyance such as a chariot) could be winched down when necessary. (See Fig. 6.3.) From the symbolism of 1.5, it's not hard to understand why Hamlet hesitates over the authenticity of the Ghost's account of his own death. The voice of the Ghost seems to come from Hell.

Props and the Value of Minimalism

One of the benefits of simple staging that is often overlooked is the value of whatever props are actually used. On a stage full of the devices of realism, one prop more or less scarcely matters. Does one really need another piece of furniture in Ibsen's *A Doll's House* or another artefact of suburban living in Miller's *Death of a Salesman?* In contrast, on Shakespeare's stage, props stand out.

So, for example, in *Henry V* 1.2, the chest containing the Dauphin's insult of a gift of tennis balls to the English king is an extraordinarily powerful image that rivets the attention of the audience, particularly when Shakespeare teasingly hides its contents: "What treasure, uncle?" asks the king; "Tennis balls, my liege," replies Exeter (258). And so, in *The Merchant of Venice*, Portia's marriage to Bassanio takes center stage in 2.1, 2.7, 2.9, and 3.2 because of the three caskets (of gold, silver, and lead), one of which contains Portia's picture. By the time Bassanio tries for Portia's hand, the audience already knows which chest contains her picture because the Prince of Morocco and the Prince of Aragon have already opened two of them and have failed in their quest. Will Bassanio guess the correct chest (the one made of lead)? If he fails, then he must leave immediately and never marry anyone. Surely, this is high stakes gambling, brought directly to the audience's notice by the three chests on stage.

Then there are those instances of gore that Shakespeare occasionally indulged in to keep his audience guessing. In his romance, *Cymbeline* (which dates from late in his career), Shakespeare has Guiderius, one of the sons of Cymbeline, King of Britain, decapitate—off stage—Cloten, one of the Queen's sons by an earlier husband, and then enter on stage with the severed head. The head is finally left next to the headless corpse at the end of 4.2. However, Shakespeare never outdid the shock effect of his early revenge tragedy, *Titus Andronicus*. It's hard to see how he could have. In 3.1, the mutilated Lavinia (without a tongue and with her hands chopped off) exits carrying Titus Andronicus's severed hand in her mouth while Marcus (Titus Andronicus's brother) and Lucius (Titus Andronicus' son) leave the stage carrying the severed heads of two of Titus Andronicus's other sons, Martius and Quintus.

And what are the lessons to be learned from Shakespeare's exploitation of the resources available to him? Always to interpret (whether as reader or watcher) what is said and done on more than one level. Always to ask the question: "How does the staging add to the meaning of the words?"

Figure 6.3
The ornate "Heavens" in the New Globe's ceiling above the stage. The deus ex machina is lowered through a door in the middle panel of the design.

Threading the Needle

Earlier in this chapter, we looked at the skill with which Shakespeare handled the entrances and exits of his characters, with the final scene from *Twelfth Night* being used to illustrate the argument. Now, we will move for the remainder of the chapter from the microcosm to the macrocosm, from particular instances of stagecraft to Shakespeare's handling of the overall structure (what is sometimes termed the **architectonics**) of his plays. The intention is to get you to look at a Shakespeare drama in such a way that you can see both the wood *and* the trees.

Let's return to *Twelfth Night* to look at the way in which Shakespeare handles the large-scale version of the entrances and exits of his characters, that is, how he weaves his various plot lines together. As a playwright who avoided the plot simplicity argued for by Aristotle in his *Poetics* under the label of the three unities of time, place, and action, Shakespeare faced a difficult problem: if he introduced so many plots, how could he keep the audience aware of what was going on? His solution was simple in theory and tremendously difficult to accomplish in fact: each plot needed to be interwoven with the others; each needed to be brought to center stage with enough frequency that the audience would remember what was happening and be able to reflect on the ways in which the various plot lines functioned as a commentary on each other. Like an expert juggler, Shakespeare had to keep several objects in the air; it would be nice, too, if he could do it without appearing to break into a sweat. He does keep up that illusion; he makes it look easy.

In *Twelfth Night*, there are no fewer than five plots, each one providing a commentary on the nature of love:

1. The Orsino-Olivia pairing shows the theatricality of love.
2. The Viola/Cesario-Orsino-Olivia-Sebastian foursome, the parameters of love.
3. The Belch-Aguecheek pairing, the vanity of love.
4. The Belch-Aguecheek-Maria-Malvolio grouping, self-love.
5. The Antonio-Sebastian duo, male love as friendship.

Each is interwoven with the others; a particular plot strand is dropped only to be picked up seamlessly in a later part of the play. Table 6.1 illustrates how Shakespeare interweaves his material.

Table 6.1
Textual Interweaving in **Twelfth Night**

Scene and Line Numbers	Textual Connection to Earlier Scene	Scene and Line Numbers	Textual Connection to Earlier Scene
1.3	1.1.33	4.1.1-22	3.4.219
1.5.96	end of 1.4	4.1.23-43	3.4.397
2.2	end of 1.5	4.1.44-64	4.1.22
2.5	2.3.175	4.2	3.4.127
3.1	end of 2.4	4.3	end of 4.1
3.2.1-52	end of 2.3	5.1.1-6	end of 4.2
3.2.64-82	end of 2.5	5.1.7-45	end of 2.4
3.3	end of 2.1	5.1.46-93	3.4.386
3.4.1-13	end of 3.1	5.1.84-148	5.1.45
3.4.14-143	end of 3.2	5.1.149-69	end of 4.3
3.4.144-98	3.2.63	5.1.170-207	4.1.49
3.4.199-219	3.4.13	5.1.209-77	end of 4.3
3.4.220-312	3.4.198	5.1.278-379	5.1.6
3.4.313-97	end of 3.3		

What observations does the data yield?

1. The textual connections become more complex as the play goes on. Act 1, for instance, has only two connections; Act 2 has two; Act 3 has 10; the short fourth Act has five; and the *only* scene in Act 5, an extraordinary number: eight.

2. Shakespeare has two scenes which account for the majority of the connections: 14 out of a total of 27. Those are 3.4 and 5.1.

3. Scene 3.4 uses one technique for connecting plots, that of close interweaving. All of the connections within 3.4 are to other parts of Act 3, from the end of 3.1 to 3.4.198.

4. Scene 5.1 uses another technique which is absolutely appropriate for a resolution scene in Shakespearean comedy: it connects to numerous earlier scenes (from as early as the end of 2.4 to as late as the end of 4.3).

5. Shakespeare was extraordinarily adept at weaving the separate pieces of his story together. So adept, indeed, that the audience or readers are scarcely aware of how their continued involvement in the story is assured by such means. Without such a method, Shakespeare would have been reduced to one of two inferior options: either to tell a much simpler, single-stranded story, or to tell a series of stories one after the other. The first worked for the Greeks, but that was 2000 years before Shakespeare came on the scene; the second could never work as drama because there would be no way in which the tension on which drama depends could be generated.

Table 6.1 represents a schematic analysis. It has tremendous value and can be carried out with any Shakespeare play. Without such an analysis, you cannot as easily see which plots truly matter to Shakespeare and which are less significant. Subjectively, you might feel, for example, that the Antonio-Sebastian plot is not crucial to *Twelfth Night* in the way the Viola/Cesario-Orsino-Sebastian-Olivia plot is. By looking at how interwoven each plot is, you can find *objective* confirmation for a *subjective* feeling.

Varying the Tempo

Some of Shakespeare's plays are very long indeed, with *Hamlet* taking 3906 lines from beginning to end. Even a short play, such as *A Midsummer Night's Dream* is 2222 lines long. Given the fact that it usually takes anywhere from two-and-a-half to four hours to present a full version of a Shakespeare play, it was critical for the playwright to change the tempo of the action frequently. The worst thing that could happen as far as stagecraft is concerned would be for the playwright to use his whole range of devices only to forget that if the pace doesn't change then monotony sets in. You can see this happen in an early English Renaissance play: Sackville and Norton's *Gorboduc*. It's not a very good play anyway, but its manifest failure lies in the unchanging pace of events. All that anyone really remembers from that play is the long speeches, which give to the play a deadness that no amount of audience interest can revive.

Shakespeare knew Sackville and Norton's *Gorboduc*, and he learned its lesson well: change the pace frequently. If we look at *Hamlet*, we can see

Shakespeare's technique put to its ultimate test: can he hold an audience's attention for more than four hours and almost 4000 lines? The answer is a resounding "yes," for the play is probably the greatest in Western literature. It is successful for many reasons, but one of them is the way in which Shakespeare applies his stagecraft (or dramaturgy, as it is sometimes called) to the play's pacing.

If we look only at the play's first five scenes from the point of view of a spectator at a performance, the emphasis is manifestly on varying the pace.

1.1 This scene is fast paced. It occupies only 147 lines and has frequent entrances (of Horatio and Marcellus once, and the Ghost twice) and exits (of Francisco once and the Ghost twice).

1.2 This scene is altogether different, with a lengthy court subscene occupying the initial 128 lines. This subscene is broken only by the exit of Voltimand and Cornelius after line 41. It's followed at line 129 by Hamlet's opening soliloquy (129-59), a speech which—of course—stops the action completely. Then Shakespeare concludes 1.2 with another subscene: a discussion among Horatio, Marcellus, and Bernardo. The pace differs here, too. This time we're back with something closer to the slowness of 1.2.1-128.

1.3 This scene adopts a different strategy to pacing by allotting approximately equal time to the subscenes involving Laertes and Ophelia (1-51), Laertes and Polonius (51-88), and Polonius and Ophelia (89-137).

1.4 This scene adopts the same balanced strategy as 1.3, with the first 38 lines before the Ghost appears being balanced by the final 53 (39-91) in which Horatio, Marcellus and Hamlet react to the Ghost's appearance.

1.5 This scene adopts yet another attitude to pacing. The slowness of the opening dialogue (including the Ghost's long set speech of no less than 50 lines [43-92] and Hamlet's response of 21 lines [93-113]) stands in sharp relief to what follows: rapid-fire dialogue between Horatio, Marcellus, and Hamlet. There are 13 speeches in 13 lines (114-26). Overall, the dialogue after Horatio and Marcellus enter at 1.5.114 comprises 43 speeches in only 86 lines (114-99). Contrast that with the first 113 lines of 1.5, a subscene which comprises only 19 speeches. The message is clear: Shakespeare *never* wants the audience to settle into a fixed, monotonous rhythm.

If we turn briefly to another of Shakespeare's sublime tragedies, *Antony and Cleopatra*, and examine it from the point of view which most students adopt to Shakespeare's plays (that of a reader rather than of a spectator), we can see another example of pacing. In this case, the remarkable pacing is designed to give as vivid a sense as possible of global warfare: Egypt vs. Rome. The act and scene divisions were not in the 1623 Folio, but later scholars have added their own divisions. If we go with the typical division, then the Act we are interested in—Act 4—has no less than *fifteen* scenes. The Act takes the plot from the beginning of the battles around Alexandria to Cleopatra's decision in her monument to give Antony a proper "Roman" burial. The overall effect is consistent, sustained motion. The shortest scene in Act 4, 4.11, is only four lines long. The longest, 4.14, occupies just 145 lines. The average length of scenes: a mere 40 lines. Indeed, the entire Act occupies only 596 lines—ten lines *less* than a single scene (2.2) in *Hamlet*.

And where does all this analysis of *Hamlet* and *Antony and Cleopatra* leave us? With a much better sense of what Shakespeare is trying to do. Without paying enough attention to how the play is constructed, the reader or viewer will lack an informed sense of the subtlety of Shakespeare's achievement. On the one hand, he was acutely aware of the need to vary the pace of the action in order to avoid monotony; on the other, he deliberately tailored the length of scenes and acts to the particular requirements of a given play. What was happening in *Hamlet* and *Antony and Cleopatra* can be seen at work in every one of Shakespeare's 38 plays. It is simply one more aspect of his tremendously rich stagecraft.

Easing up on the Rack

In addition to varying the tempo of his scenes, Shakespeare was determined to intensify as much as possible the intended effect of the action, whether the play was a history, comedy, tragedy, or romance. It is, however, a mark of Shakespeare's greatness that he doesn't go the obvious route in his search for intensity of effect. The obvious means in tragedy, for example, would be to pile tragic episode on tragic episode. Shakespeare tried that in *Titus Andronicus*, but with limited effect. Too much killing leads to satiety. The counter-intuitive method would be to combine the tragic with carefully placed comic scenes. Shakespeare used this counter-intuitive method in almost all of his tragedies, doing so with great success. The effect of such a mixing of the tragic and the comic as occurs in Shakespeare's tragedies is complex. On the one hand, from the point of view of the audience or reader it is the psychological equivalent of a torturer easing up on the rack only to tighten it immediately afterwards. The result? More intense pain. On the other, the effect of such a mixing produces disorientation: the psychological equivalent of traveling in unexplored territory. Each scene is new and unexpected. Each grows in intensity as a result.

Let's look at two examples to analyze Shakespeare's technique at close hand.

The Porter in *Macbeth* (2.3)

Immediately after Macbeth and Lady Macbeth have killed Duncan (who was a guest at their castle) and framed his guards for the murder, Macduff enters to speak with the murdered king. His entrance, however, is no simple matter, for Shakespeare cares enough about the intensity of the emotional effect of his tragedy to create in less than 50 lines a wonderfully comic character: the Porter.

The Porter begins by complaining about being woken up so early to answer Macduff's insistent knocking at the gate. He imagines that he's the porter of Hell's gate (which is, of course, ironically true given the very recent murder of Duncan) and runs through a list of people who deserve to be in Hell: a farmer who commits suicide because of financial ruin; a man who equivocates about his crime and refuses to admit his guilt; a tailor who shortchanges his customers by skimping on the amount of cloth he uses. Suddenly, he realizes he can't be the porter at Hell's gate: it's too cold in Macbeth's castle. Then, Macduff acts as the Porter's straight man in a comedy routine. The Porter states, "drink, sir, is a great provoker of three things" (24). Right on cue, Macduff responds, "What three things does drink especially provoke?" (25). The Porter's speech in reply is full of the sort of sexual innuendo and word play that his audience would have loved and which contemporary audiences find funny, too:

> Marry, sir, nose-painting, sleep, and urine.
> Lechery, sir, it provokes and unprovokes: it provokes
> the desire but it takes away the performance. There-
> fore much drink may be said to be an equivocator
> with lechery: it makes him and it mars him; it sets him
> on and it takes him off; it persuades him and dis-
> heartens him, makes him stand to and not stand to;
> in conclusion, equivocates him in a sleep and, giving
> him the lie, leaves him (27–35).

Within 30 lines of this stand-up comedian's joke, Macduff has entered, gone to find Duncan, and returned with the awful cry: "O, horror, horror, horror!" (63). The effect is extraordinary precisely because a little earlier and just for a moment the audience had let its guard down: perhaps everything would be all right.

The Clown in *Antony and Cleopatra* (5.2)

The Porter scene in *Macbeth* is unusual in that it occurs early in the play. A more frequent placement for the use of comedy intended to lull the audience into a false sense of optimism is late in a tragedy. The humorous exchanges among Hamlet, Horatio, and Osric over Laertes' challenge to a fencing match are well known (*Hamlet* 5.2.81–193). Less well known is the exchange in *Antony and Cleopatra* between a "rural fellow" (or Clown) who brings Cleopatra the means for her suicide and the Egyptian queen herself (5.2.233). The subscene is short—less than forty lines—yet it accomplishes Shakespeare's intent: to make Cleopatra's death the more heart-wrenching for the audience by apparently trivializing it. The Clown brings Cleopatra the asps hidden in a basket of figs, and she quizzes him about what it feels like to be bitten by that poisonous snake. The Clown's response uses malapropisms. (This is one of Shakespeare's favorite comic devices in which a character uses the wrong word to humorous effect; see pages 99–101 for a detailed analysis of the device.) According to him, the snake's "biting is/immortal [sic]" (246–47); he knows that it is because he was told so by a woman just yesterday. She told him "how she/died of the biting of it" (253–54). He continues to give Cleopatra advice even as she asks him to leave, for he seems naïvely to assume that she wants the snake as a pet: "Give it nothing, I pray you, for it is not worth the feeding" (269).

It's in light of such comedy that Cleopatra's suicide less than 40 lines later needs to be assessed. The impact is what Shakespeare surely intended: to make her death seem all the more unexpected and pitiable. That intensity of effect characteristic of Shakespeare's tragedies (sometimes referred to as katharsis) is far more likely to occur because Shakespeare temporarily eases up on the emotional rack that all of his best tragedies set up and deftly employ.

Painting in Chiaroscuro

The effect of Shakespeare's use of comedy in the midst of tragedy is to intensify the experience *and to keep the audience off balance.* No sooner has an audience come to terms with the emotional effect of a series of events than the playwright forces it to reassess its response. In a similar way, Shakespeare frequently mixes profound philosophical musings with mundane stage business in all of his plays, regardless of genre. I term this device "painting in **chiaroscuro**" after a style of painting that highlights whatever is depicted on the canvas by the careful use of light and dark shading. To illustrate what I mean let's take a closer look at this particular instance of stagecraft in *Hamlet* and in *Richard II*.

The Gravediggers in *Hamlet* (5.1)

It is hard to imagine a more mundane job than gravedigging—digging earth to receive human remains. Indeed, the gravediggers themselves in this scene are so used to the job that they pass the time as they dig telling riddles and singing songs. Against this backdrop of two people utterly unmoved by what they do, Hamlet uses the opportunity to speculate on the permanence of death. Dark shading against a light background. He examines the skull of the court jester, Yorick, and finds in that examination, too, a reason to see all human beings as fundamentally equal:

> Alas, poor
> Yorick! I knew him, Horatio, a fellow of infinite jest,
> of most excellent fancy. He hath borne me on his
> back a thousand times, and now how abhorred in my
> imagination it [the skull] is! My gorge rises at it. Here
> hung those
> lips that I have kissed I know not how oft. Where be
> your gibes now? Your gambols, your songs, your
> flashes of merriment that were wont to set the table on
> a roar? Not one now, to mock your own grinning?
> Quite chopfallen? Now get you to my lady's chamber
> and tell her, let her paint an inch thick, to this favor
> she must come. Make her laugh at that (183–94).

Nothing that had come before in this scene prepares the audience for Hamlet's reminiscence; nothing, I think, could contrast better with it than the gravediggers' complacent attitude to their work.

The Gardener in *Richard II*

Act 3, Scene 4 of this history play opens with King Richard's Queen wondering how to distract herself from the sorrow she feels at being separated from her husband, who has gone to war against the usurper Bolingbroke. A master gardener and two assistants enter. What follows is a wonderful and totally unexpected blending of horticultural advice and political opinion, for which the reader is prepared by the Queen's comment: "They will talk of state, for everyone doth so/Against a change; woe is forerun with woe" (27–28). On the one hand, there is mention of "young dangling apricots," "bending twigs," "too-fast-growing sprays," "noisome weeds," and the "fall of leaf." On the other, there is talk of state affairs, with all of the gardening references symbolizing what is wrong with England as Richard II is deposed by Henry Bolingbroke, the future Henry IV. The series of speeches is here quoted in full to give you an indication of the intricacy with which Shakespeare mixes the mundane and the profound:

GARDENER   *[to one man]*
            Go bind thou up young dangling apricots
            Which, like unruly children, make their sire
            Stoop with oppression of their prodigal weight.
            Give some supportance to the bending twigs.
            [To the other.] Go thou, and like an executioner
            Cut off the heads of too-fast-growing sprays
            That look too lofty in our commonwealth.
            All must be even in our government.

	You thus employed, I will go root away
	The noisome weeds which without profit suck
	The soil's fertility from wholesome flowers.
MAN	
	Why should we in the compass of a pale
	Keep law and form and due proportion,
	Showing as in a model our firm estate,
	When our sea-wallèd garden, the whole land,
	Is full of weeds, her fairest flowers choked up,
	Her fruit trees all unpruned, her hedges ruined,
	Her knots disordered, and her wholesome herbs
	Swarming with caterpillars?
GARDENER	Hold thy peace.
	He that hath suffered this disordered spring
	Hath now himself met with the fall of leaf.
	The weeds which his broad-spreading leaves did shelter,
	That seemed in eating him to hold him up,
	Are plucked up root and all by Bolingbroke:
	I mean the Earl of Wiltshire, Bushy, Green (29–53).

How much more interesting a statement Shakespeare provides us with here than the simple comment: Richard II's "yes men" are dead. Above all, the way in which he mixes the mundane and the profound asks the reader to think of modern political parallels to the situation in England at the end of the fourteenth century as well as to speculate on whether the overall analogy between gardening and politics is a fair one. Shakespeare is opening up the play and its meaning rather than narrowing it down to a particular set of long-ago events.

Shakespeare's Stagecraft

11 Major Devices

"Getting up to Speed": how the playwright handles all the necessary exposition of background

"Handling the Introductions": how he tells the audience who is who on the stage

"Comings and Goings": how he handles exits and entrances

"Placing Yourself in the Action": how he lets the audience know, when necessary, where the action is taking place

"Making Lemonade (from Lemons)": how he compensates for the simplicity of the Elizabethan/Jacobean stage

"Taking Advantage": how he turns that same simplicity to his benefit

(continued)

"Threading the Needle": how he interconnects the various plots so the audience can follow the story

"Varying the Tempo": how he mixes long and short scenes for variety

"Easing up on the Rack": how he mixes comedy with tragedy to make the latter more intense

"Painting in Chiaroscuro": how he mixes mundane stage business with profound philosophical speculation to keep the audience guessing

"Internalizing the Playwright": metadrama as a commentary on the link between the stage and life

Internalizing the Playwright

Thus far, in ten sections I've highlighted the major devices Shakespeare uses in his stagecraft: what each device is, and why each device matters to an understanding of Shakespeare's work. To that list, I've added one more to be discussed in this section: **metadrama**.

I've left the discussion of metadrama (a useful piece of jargon which roughly translates as "the ways in which the plays comment upon the nature of drama itself") to the last for a couple of reasons. I think it shows Shakespeare at his most clever; and it encompasses every other aspect of his stagecraft. More than that, Shakespeare's use of metadrama emphasizes one simple fact: what happens on the stage constitutes a commentary on real life because human beings are always playing roles.

"All the World's a Stage"

The first and most important point to note about Shakespeare as playwright is that for him the line between stage action and real life was next to nonexistent. This is not to suggest that he couldn't tell the difference. It simply means that—as Shakespeare sees it—all human beings act throughout their lives by assuming roles according to circumstances. They do so both consciously and unconsciously. For him, then, what happens on stage is synecdochic (a *part* representing the *whole*) for life itself. It is, if you like, one example of a universal rule.

Even the briefest study of a Shakespeare concordance shows how frequently Shakespeare saw life itself as taking place on a stage, for you can see how many times he uses the words *stage*, *play*, and *player* (i.e. actor). The most famous speeches about this connection between life and acting occur in *As You Like It*, *The Merchant of Venice*, *King Lear*, and *Macbeth*.

◇ JAQUES: All the world's a stage,
              And all the men and women merely players.

	They have their exits and their entrances,
	And one man in his time plays many parts (2.7.138–41).
◇ ANTONIO:	I hold the world but as the world, Gratiano—
	A stage where every man must play a part,
	And mine a sad one (1.1.77–78).
◇ LEAR:	When we are born, we cry that we are come
	To this great stage of fools (4.6.182–83).
◇ MACBETH:	Life's but a walking shadow, a poor player
	That struts and frets his hour upon the stage
	And then is heard no more (5.5.24–26).

However, these are only the most famous among an extraordinary number of such references in the plays. There are about 500 references in the Shakespeare canon to those key words with which I began: *stage, play,* and *player,* as well as associated terms such as *playhouse.* By no means all of these references are metadramatic, of course, for each of these three words does have meanings that are not associated with acting. However, the number is still remarkable.

The majority of references fall in the comedies, but there are many from every genre:

◇ From the history plays, there is the Porter in *Henry VIII,* who makes fun of the riotous behavior of those commoners celebrating the christening of the infant Elizabeth: "These are the youths that thunder at a play-/house and fight for bitten apples" (5.4.59–60).

◇ From the tragedies, there's Iago's effort to convince the audience that he advises Cassio well in his efforts to get back into Othello's favor: "And what's he then that says I play the villain . . . ?" (2.3.330).

◇ From the romances, there's Posthumus's brutal treatment of Imogen when she asserts her innocence: "Shall's have a play of this? Thou scornful page,/There lies thy part" (5.5.230–31).

"The Play's the Thing"

The second point to make about Shakespeare's use of metadrama is that it serves a crucial purpose in the development of several of his plays because it allows him to internalize the real flesh-and-blood audience for his plays within the on-stage drama itself. In such a way, he draws the actual audience into the drama and, so, makes the experience of watching (or reading) the play a more compelling experience. We are asked, as readers or watchers, to imagine ourselves as that on-stage audience observing a play-within-the-play. For that *on-stage* audience bears the same relation to the action in the play-within-the-play as the *theatre* audience does to the larger drama of Shakespeare's play. And the device does allow Shakespeare to show us how good his plays truly are. The play-within-the-play (whether "The Mousetrap" in *Hamlet* or "'A tedious brief scene of young Pyramus/ And his love Thisbe'" in *A Midsummer Night's Dream* [5.1.56–57]) never gets remotely close to achieving transcendence. By contrast, Shakespeare's plays when well directed and performed routinely make us willingly suspend our disbelief so that for the time the play is performed it is reality for us.

Such a device also, of course, puts front and center the whole issue of what value the presentation of fiction has and what relation fiction may have to the reality of our everyday lives. At its simplest, Shakespeare's use of metadrama makes us ask whether, on the one hand, our personalities mirror those of Hamlet, Claudius, Gertrude, or even Rosencrantz and Guildenstern, and, on the other, whether we are more spectators than actors. When we knowingly act in real life are we as wooden and unconvincing as Flute, Bottom, Quince, Snout, Snug, and Starveling? Their rendition in *A Midsummer Night's Dream* of a scene from the tragedy of Pyramus and Thisbe is painfully bad. Is our audience in real life as cruel as Theseus, Hippolyta, Demetrius, and Lysander are when they watch that tragedy? We can never know, but Shakespeare's metadrama gives that question some urgency with any audience. At its most sophisticated, Shakespeare's use of metadrama boldly erases the distinction between fiction and reality. For example, when Hamlet is dying, he talks directly to "You that look pale and tremble at this chance,/That are but mutes or audience to this act" (5.2.336–37). And who are the members of this pale, trembling, and hushed audience? Both the dramatic characters in the play who are still alive, *and* the audience in the theatre.

The play-within-the-play strategy is rightly famous, yet the value Shakespeare saw in such a strategy is perhaps greater than might initially be thought because in several of his plays he adopts a stripped-down version of this same strategy. In *Hamlet*, for example, Claudius and Polonius create a "playlet" involving Ophelia and Hamlet (3.1). Their intent is to try to discover whether Hamlet's madness is the result of his love for Ophelia. They are the playwrights *and* hidden audience; Ophelia and Hamlet, the actors; and Hamlet, an unwitting spectator. The play is not a success, however, for Hamlet seems to sense the trap. He is, in a way, rather like a resistant audience that doesn't like actors toying with its feelings. This playlet is, nevertheless, markedly more successful than Polonius's later version with essentially the same plot (3.4). Now he is the sole playwright and hidden audience; Gertrude, Hamlet, and the Ghost are the actors; and Hamlet once again an unwitting spectator at a scene devised especially for him. Despite Polonius's coaching of Gertrude ("Look you lay home to him" [3.4.1]), Hamlet cares so little for the plot that when Polonius foolishly reveals his presence behind a tapestry, Hamlet runs him through with his sword. Perhaps the only consolation from Polonius's point of view is that

Hamlet killed him because he thought he was a different playwright and a different audience: Claudius himself.

Not all of Shakespeare's "playlets" end so disastrously. In *Richard III*, the King and Buckingham devise a short scene of only about 70 lines in which they pretend that they are being pursued by forces intent on murdering them. Their motive is to justify their earlier killing of Lord Hastings. Their internal audience is the Lord Mayor of London, and Buckingham promises he can do a great acting job. He can, he says:

> counterfeit the deep tragedian,
> Speak and look back, and pry on every side,
> Tremble and start at wagging of a straw;
> Intending deep suspicion, ghastly looks
> Are at my service, like enforcèd smiles;
> And both are ready in their offices,
> At any time, to grace my stratagems (3.5.5–11).

He is true to his word. It helps, too, that he and the King are dressed in clothes that show the terrible effects of having to run from pursuit: "*rotten armor, marvelous ill-favored,*" the stage direction reads at the beginning of the scene.

In *Twelfth Night*, Maria, Sir Toby Belch, and Sir Andrew Aguecheek devise a short scene by means of which to humiliate Malvolio, Olivia's steward (2.5). Their complaint—beyond the fact that he is an officious fool—centers on Malvolio's having overstepped his authority in trying to put a stop to their late-night revelry. Their solution (thanks to Maria's agile mind): to have Malvolio think Olivia is in love with him, with the "evidence" consisting of a note to Malvolio from his admirer, forged by Maria. This note is dropped on a garden path along which Malvolio is walking. He picks up the note, reads it, and falls for the device hook, line, sinker, and fishing rod. So here, Maria is the playwright; Sir Toby and Sir Andrew are the audience (hidden in a boxtree); and Malvolio is the gullible actor, who plays his part beautifully. The result—in part because of the humorous comments from the hidden audience—is one of the funniest scenes in all of Shakespeare. It is also a scene which makes the *real* spectators at *Twelfth Night* assess and reassess their interpretation of the play's meaning in light of Shakespeare's stagecraft. Are they being taken in by the action of the play? Should they resist Shakespeare's efforts to make them respond to the action in a certain fashion?

The Playwright Front and Center

If Shakespeare doesn't let his audience off easily, but rather makes it work, mentally, for its entertainment, the same could be said for the playwright himself. In his plays, Shakespeare enjoys examining with a critical eye the nature and value of the playwright's art. The most famous example of this self-reflexive gaze at work is the character of Prospero in *The Tempest*. Critics have frequently seen in him a portrait of Shakespeare himself, and, indeed, *The Tempest* may well be read as Shakespeare's farewell to the stage. If Prospero is Shakespeare in another guise, then for the playwright the art of drama is explicitly based on magic, for it is by magic that Prospero controls the action from the very beginning of the play. If Prospero is Shakespeare, then the portrait is not an entirely flattering one, for his treatment of some of the characters in the play is not beyond reproach. One thinks most obviously of the humiliation accorded Caliban, Stephano, and Trinculo as well as the way in which Prospero manipulates Ferdinand and Miranda. Is Shakespeare asking us to critique the power of the playwright to move us and to make us believe that "this insubstantial pageant" of the play has substance (4.1.155)? Certainly Prospero himself rejects his "rough magic" in the end, for he says:

> I'll break my staff,
> Bury it certain fathoms in the earth,
> And deeper than did ever plummet sound
> I'll drown my book (5.1.54–57).

Nor is this the only unflattering portrait of the power of the artist-at-work. In *A Midsummer Night's Dream*, both Oberon, who orchestrates the action in the wood, and Theseus, who manages the action in the city, handle their tasks poorly. The first "playwright" (Oberon) botches so badly the job of enchanting the lovers that it takes until 4.1 for the situation to be unraveled. The second (Theseus) manages only a mediocre performance. At the beginning, for example, he seems intent on enforcing marriage between the pairs of lovers in a way similar to how he married Hippolyta: by patriarchal conquest. The result is that two of his "actors" (Hermia and Lysander) flee to the Athenian wood. At the end, he cannot help making some hurtful comments about the rude mechanicals' play-within-the-play, and making them loudly enough to be overheard: Of the Prologue's speech, for instance, he remarks, "His speech was like a tangled chain" (5.1.124). About the performance of the Moon, he comments: "This is the greatest error of all the rest" (5.1.242). These comments come despite his insistence that he will be complimentary to the actors: "The kinder we, to give them thanks for nothing" (5.1.89).

Finally, there's the remarkable case of Duke Vincentio in *Measure for Measure*. He appoints Angelo to run Vienna and then—disguised as Friar Lodowick—watches to see if he will fail. He orchestrates everything so that the play ends happily, but not without some twists and turns and hard bumps along the way. The Duke tempts Isabella to maintain her virtue by getting another woman, Mariana, to have sex with Angelo. The Duke forces Angelo to marry Mariana at the end of the play even though he shows no desire whatsoever to do so. The Duke forces Lucio, a dissolute gentleman, to marry the woman he got pregnant, and threatens him with being whipped and hanged afterwards. The Duke proposes marriage to Isabella, but she says not a word—even though he explicitly entreats her, "Give me your hand and say you will be mine" (5.1.503). For the remainder of the play (no less than another 47 lines), she is silent—perhaps so annoyed with the way in which he has manipulated the action and toyed with the emotions of all concerned in the drama that she doesn't wish to marry him.

Some critics have seen the Duke only as a necessary device and appear untroubled by his methods. Others have seen him as manipulative and hypocritical, someone intent upon re-achieving harmony at the end of the play through marrying off the principals regardless of their wishes. Many have seen him as Shakespeare's critique of his own profession: playwright. He clearly sees the value of drama as entertainment; he seems less sure about the price paid to maintain the illusion. In the end, he wants us as readers and spectators to see the spectacle created by his stagecraft from three perspectives:

◇ As entertainment. In this way, we are taken in by the illusion, enjoy it, and are moved by it.

◇ As metadrama. In this way, we are asked to think about how effective plays succeed in moving us so much that we believe them, for the time of the stage action, to be real.

◇ As personal commentary. In this way, we cannot help but apply what we see on stage to our own lives and to the lives of those we know.

Writing and Discussion Assignments

1. Choose two opening scenes (one from a comedy and one from a history play). Which is more successful and why as far as exposition is concerned? *Much Ado about Nothing* and *1 Henry IV* would work well for this assignment.

2. Choose an opening scene from one of the plays. How do the characters identify each other? How successful do you think Shakespeare is in his handling of this "naming" process"? *Cymbeline* would work well for this assignment.

3. Construct a schematic diagram for the way in which one of the plays handles exits and entrances. How well does Shakespeare perform the task? Give examples. *The Merchant of Venice* would work well for this assignment.

4. Analyze the interweaving of scenes in one of the plays. What can you say, based on how the scenes are interwoven, about which scenes and which plots seem important? *Macbeth* or *Romeo and Juliet* would work well for this assignment.

5. Choose one entire Act in one of the plays and track how the playwright handles its pacing. How effective are the changes in pace that you find? Act Three of *All's Well That's Ends Well* would work well for this assignment.

6. Examine the comedy in one of Shakespeare's plays. Describe what the comedy consists of, and how it makes the audience reconsider the play's tragic elements. *King Lear* would work well for this assignment.

7. Imagine you're a director for a production of one of Shakespeare's plays. Focus on just one scene, and describe what you see as the major difficulties in staging that particular scene. Why do such difficulties arise? *Hamlet* would work well for this assignment.

Further Reading

Barton, John. *Playing Shakespeare*. London: Methuen, 1984.

Bevington, David. *Action Is Eloquence*. Cambridge: Harvard UP, 1984.

Jones, Emrys. *Scenic Form in Shakespeare*. Oxford: Clarendon P, 1985.

McGuire, Philip C., and David A. Samuelson. *Shakespeare: The Theatrical Dimension*. New York: AMS P, 1979.

Styan, J.L. *Shakespeare's Stagecraft*. Cambridge: Cambridge UP, 1967.

Worthen, William B. *Shakespeare and the Authority of Performance*. Cambridge: Cambridge UP, 1997.

Chapter 7

This huge stage presenteth naught but shows

Sonnets *15.3*

Shakespeare in Performance: Stage and Screen

<u>Chapter Overview</u>

◇ Appreciating the differences among stage, film, and TV as media.
◇ Analyzing and appreciating the creative options available to actors and directors of stage productions of Shakespearean drama.
   Focus: theatrical reviews.
◇ Analyzing and appreciating the creative options available to actors and directors in film and TV versions of Shakespearean drama.
   Focus: five film versions of Hamlet.

In this final chapter, we return to the core concern of this book: to understand and appreciate Shakespeare through the active engagement of the imagination. As Frank Kermode has argued in "Shakespeare in the Movies," Shakespeare's plays "have to be reborn in the imagination of another" (quoted in Davies 4). That *other* is anyone who reads or sees a Shakespeare play. Without that effort at rebirth in the minds of audience or readers, Shakespeare's magnificent words and ideas fail to live. To that end of making Shakespeare live in the imagination, we'll look in the next few pages at how his plays have been interpreted by others on stage, on film, and on TV. The value of such a discussion is that you'll see how wide a range of interpretation of Shakespeare's plays there can be, and you'll get used to (even revel in) the idea that there is no one right performance of Shakespeare. As Jack Jorgens notes in his classic work *Shakespeare on Film:*

"the script is not the work, but the *score* for the work" (3). Whether you are reading or watching a Shakespeare play, that play needs to be orchestrated by audience, actors, and director alike.

Stage, Film, and Television: Some Preliminary Definitions

Before we look at how others have interpreted Shakespeare's work, it's crucial to distinguish among the three media under discussion, for each necessarily brings with it inherent and unalterable characteristics. In *Filming Shakespeare's Plays*, Anthony Davies lays out the distinctions between stage and film very neatly in terms of how they treat "the complex field of spatial relationships" (5). In his *Watching Shakespeare on Television*, H. R. Coursen describes the unique qualities of televised versions of Shakespeare. The generalizations that follow depend heavily on Davies' and Coursen's insights. These generalizations are meant as a provocative opening for further discussion about the nature of the three media: stage, film, and television.

Theatre, Film, and TV
Some Important Distinctions

The stage is three dimensional; film and TV are two dimensional.

The stage is live, immediate, ephemeral, and unique; film and TV are recorded, mediated, distanced, permanent, and reproducible.

The stage because of its continuity emphasizes the complexities of language; film and TV because of their choppiness simplify that complexity.

The stage lives and dies by the word, film and TV by the image.

The stage has a fixed relation between audience and actors; film and TV use various devices (zooming, tracking, tilting, craning, and so on) that disrupt the relation between audience and actors.

The stage contract between actors and audience is complex; the contract between film or TV and its audience is essentially fixed.

The stage is centripetal (with the action moving inwards from the setting and towards the actors); film and TV are centrifugal (with the movement being away from the actors towards the "real" world).

The stage moves from text to performance; film and TV move from performance to celluloid or to digital recording.

The stage and film are communal experiences shared by an audience largely of strangers; TV is often watched alone or in small, domestic groups.

The stage is life-sized; film is much larger than life; TV reduces and distorts the human scale.

Nonetheless, despite such differences, discussion of how the stage, film, and TV re-present Shakespeare frequently centers on the same key terms and work with the same set of generalizations.

Theatre, Film, and TV

Some Important Continuities

The traditional labels used in the analysis of literature—character, gesture, language, setting, structure, subtext, theme, and so on—can be applied equally well to stage, film, and TV.

The tension in drama (whether on stage, film, or TV) comes from the way in which action and character development fight against imagery and language. The first pairing is sometimes referred to as the **horizontal axis** because both action and character development take place over time. The second pairing is sometimes called the **vertical axis** because of the depth that imagery and language give to drama.

The three "treatments" any Shakespeare play can undergo at the hands of directors and actors—in Jack Jorgens' phrasing, **presentation, interpretation,** and **adaptation**—can be applied equally well to stage, film, and TV. Presentation tries to reproduce the Shakespeare that Elizabethans and Jacobeans would have known. Interpretation shapes the play according to a particular view of its overall meaning. Adaptation creates a new work of art, sometimes in a different literary subgenre or artistic genre. Jane Smiley's novel *A Thousand Acres* is, for example, a modern adaptation of *King Lear.*

Shakespeare on Stage: Antony and Cleopatra

Drama is, by its very nature, so ephemeral that it's impossible to present an analysis in print of a theatrical performance of a Shakespeare play that most (or even a few) readers of this book will have watched. Millions, for example, will have seen the Mel Gibson or Kenneth Branagh film versions of *Hamlet*, but how few thousands Ralph Fiennes' lead role in *Richard II* at the Gainsborough Studios in London in the spring of 2000? With that ephemeral quality of theatrical drama in mind, I offer not an analysis of film clips known to most if not to all, but instead a discussion of a review of a recent staging of *Antony and Cleopatra* at the recreated Globe in south London (with Giles Block as director).[1]

My purpose is to show how my imagination was sparked by the director's and the actors' interpretation of the play. Even just the description of what happened on stage forces me—as a reader of and spectator at Shakespeare's plays—to visualize the words Shakespeare wrote so long ago, to see before me in new ways the extraordinarily profound ideas he presents. The review was written by the well-known drama critic Michael Billington, and appeared in the *Guardian Weekly* (London) in August 1999.

"Comedy Becomes Cleopatra"

Is *Antony and Cleopatra* really a tragedy? Harold Bloom recently argued that it is "funnier than any of the great Shakespearean comedies." And that is the line taken by Giles Block's refreshingly swift, airy production at the Globe in south London: for once, some genuinely funny things happen on the way to the monument.

The tone is set by Mark Rylance's exuberant Egyptian queen: the chief gain of having a man play the role is not any spurious "authenticity" but the way it highlights the character's histrionic excess. Cleopatra is a born performer who likes to theatricalise the state of love: not since Judi Dench have I seen anyone bring out so clearly Cleopatra's humour or capacity for self-dramatisation.

Rylance is first seen in a low-cut, lime-green gown, tumbling auburn wig and military headgear: a reminder that Cleo and Antony get a good deal of erotic fun out of cross-dressing. But Rylance's key quality is an itchy restlessness: in Antony's absence he is forever hurling himself at cushions or hopscotching around the stage in a self-conscious demonstration of sexual fever.

He is at his funniest, however, in the two scenes with the messenger who brings news of Antony's marriage. Rylance pulls a knife from his knickers and hauls the chap round the stage by his hair before scoring a huge laugh by promising, "I will not hurt him." In order to quiz him about Octavia's height and demeanour, Rylance even dons cothurni [platform shoes] to add cubits to his stature and lend himself the appropriate majesty. [See Fig. 7.1.]

But does the stress on comic role-playing prepare us for the long adagio of Cleopatra's end? In fact, Block's production implies that even the business of pulleying Antony up to the monument was meant to raise laughs as well as a body. [See Fig. 7.2.]

But Rylance shows a remarkable ability to switch moods, turning "The crown o' th' earth doth melt" into a sky-rending cry of despair and treating Cleopatra's death as a solemn ritual in which robes and headgear disguise human frailty and a tufty, balding scalp. It is a fine performance suggesting Cleopatra remained a consummate actress to the last.

I suspect, however, that Antony is a much harder part to play: few actors have conquered it. Paul Shelley here gives a perfectly decent performance, bringing out the character's sexual obsessiveness and self-conscious decline: he makes something touching out of Antony's indictment of Caesar for "harping on what I am, Not

Figure 7.1
Mark Rylance as Cleopatra in the New Globe's production of *Antony and Cleopatra* (1999). Note the platform shoes (*cothurni*) that the actor is wearing.

what he knew I was." But it is just that hint of past grandeur that I miss in his performance. The ideal Antony should be, as a critic once said of the aged John Philip Kemble, "the ruin of a magnificent temple in which the divinity still resides."

For the rest, it is an evening of ups and downs. On the credit side, the pace is fast, the Jacobean costumes unobtrusive and Mark Lewis Jones as Pompey and Benedict Wong as Menas offer well-spoken support. On the debit side, John McEnery seems ill-at-ease as Enobarbus. Ben Walden is an overly neurotic Octavius and certain staging ideas need to be re-examined: the off-stage battle behind the closed walls of an inner recess suggests kids fighting in a broom cupboard.

But although I still find Shakespeare's Globe a difficult place to watch a play—seated in the lower gallery you become unduly aware of the chatting, chaffing and canoodling going on in the yard in front of you—on this occasion the show overcomes the sundry distractions. Lightness and laughter are the keynotes, suggesting that *Antony and Cleopatra* should be placed on the Shakespeare transfer-list and moved from the tragedies to the comedies.

Figure 7.2
Paul Shelley as Antony in the New Globe's production of *Antony and Cleopatra* (1999). He is being raised by block and tackle into Cleopatra's monument.

Analysis

The first thing I notice in the review is, of course, Billington's direct question: Is *Antony and Cleopatra* a comedy rather than—as it has traditionally been viewed—a tragedy? My knee-jerk response is "no," in large measure because the re-creation of the play in my imagination clearly labels the play a tragedy. I've always thought of *Antony and Cleopatra* as being about two noble people who risk all for love and—according to their own charmed logic—win. On the other hand, Giles Block's emphasis on comedy does make me think differently about some of the scenes in the play. Cleopatra's dragging the messenger up and down the stage (in 2.5) because he comes to announce Antony's marriage to Octavia is—on reflection—funnier than I used to think it was. Similarly, the Clown's dialogue with Cleopatra (in 5.2) as he enters carrying the deadly asps is humorous even though (or, perhaps, because) Cleopatra dies so soon afterwards.

Then comes the production's major break with tradition: Cleopatra is played by a man (Mark Rylance) in drag. My initial reaction to such an idea is disdain and puzzlement: do we have here a case of what Richard David terms "the purely parasitic director" (229), someone who tries to make a reputation for himself or herself on the back of someone else's work? I vividly remember Janet Suzman doing a wonderful job with the exotic and erotic role of Cleopatra more than 30 years ago at Stratford, and indeed the role itself surely needs to be played by a woman. So, the text and theatrical tradition are against the director. Then I remember that on the Shakespearean stage the role of Cleopatra would have been played by a young boy anyway. So, tradition are actually in favor of Block's selection of gender if not of age. Then I remember, too, that Othello has sometimes been played by a white actor even though the role "requires" that he be black (none other than Laurence Olivier himself springs to mind in this connection). And I remember, finally, Cleopatra's nightmarish (and ironic) conviction at the end of the play that if she surrenders to Octavius Caesar she will be taken to Rome and there she will made to watch some "squeaking Cleopatra boy my greatness/I' the posture of a whore" (5.2.220–21).

My disdain and puzzlement are replaced by a far more useful response: What does the play gain from such a radical piece of casting? How does it help the audience to understand the play better? Billington, in part, suggests an answer. It emphasizes Cleopatra's self-conscious theatricality. It also stresses the element of play—almost of juvenile play—in the courtship of Antony and Cleopatra. My concern is that such a casting choice loses more than it gains, for a modern audience is bound to be unsettled by what it would consider a gender switch. It would be hard not to be distracted by Rylance dressed as a queen in both senses of the word: as Billington describes it, he enters "in a low-cut, lime-green gown, tumbling auburn wig and military headgear." It's hard to appreciate the subtle effect of

Shakespeare's language and stagecraft when faced with so radical an undercutting of expectation.

Moreover, the Cleopatra that Rylance projects, with her "itchy restlessness" and "sexual fever," makes more sense for a modern audience when played by a woman rather than by a man. It makes it easier for most people willingly to suspend their disbelief. In essence, the director (Block) distracts the audience more than he illuminates the text by deciding to have a man play Cleopatra. He made a particularly contemporary mistake, I think, in the staging of Shakespeare: the pursuit of novelty for its own sake. The proof for such a claim lies in Block's slapstick reading of the scene (3.3) in which Cleopatra asks the messenger about Octavius's appearance. It's wonderfully funny how Cleopatra manages to distort the messenger's description of Antony's new wife, Octavia, into her being "Dull of tongue, and dwarfish" (17). It hardly needs Cleopatra wearing *cothurni* (platform shoes) to make the point. To my mind, such a costuming decision simply unbalances the tension between the horizontal and the vertical movements in drama, although it does at the same time, it's true, emphasize yet again Cleopatra's self-conscious theatricality.

Billington dwells on two other issues in *Antony and Cleopatra*, both of which show that, to his credit, Giles Block did intend to spark the audience's imagination by making Shakespeare's words and stagecraft live as an artistic creation. The first issue is casting; the second, staging.

Paul Shelley may not have been the best choice for Antony (I've only once seen the role played well—by Richard Johnson), but Block is right to see the character as sexually obsessive and self-consciously in decline. For his part, Billington is surely right to be looking for "past grandeur" in Antony's affect. Block and Ben Walden's reading of Octavius as "neurotic" is illuminating since throughout the play Antony's rival seems so much in control of himself and of others. Presumably, the director and the actor offer an interpretation that picks up on (among other cues) the speed with which Octavius can move so quickly from goal-driven leader at the beginning of 5.1 to the elegiac poet of Antony's decline at lines 40 to 48 of the same scene.

The staging, too, helps any reader see the interpretive choices. The "unobtrusive" Jacobean costumes show Block to be a traditionalist in that regard if not in the matter of Cleopatra's casting. The decision to go for a fast pace is wise since *Antony and Cleopatra* is distinguished by the fluidity of action in its numerous scenes. Billington seems troubled by the "offstage battle" that sounds like little "kids fighting in a broom cupboard." For me, however, Block is simply dwelling on the way in which Shakespeare in his plays treats armed conflict metonymically. He had few other choices, after all, given that staging a *real* battle on the Globe stage was not an option. Indeed, the battles of Actium and Alexandria only work if Scarus, one of Antony's soldiers, by himself represents legions.

The most difficult piece of staging is to lift the dying Antony up into Cleopatra's monument in 4.15. I've *never* seen this piece of stage business done well (however that might be done), but at least Block's decision to play it for laughs avoids the problem of unintended laughter at the ludicrous in the midst of high tragedy. I don't think the scene was meant to be played for laughs (although Cleopatra's "Here's sport indeed!" [33] is lighthearted), but whatever tricks Shakespeare used to avoid bathos are lost to us now. Perhaps the problem of staging this particular scene is that Shakespeare's sensibility is not entirely ours, that he was an Elizabethan and Jacobean first and an immortal only by accident of genius.

Billington concludes his review of the production in this way: "Lightness and laughter are the keynotes, suggesting that *Antony and Cleopatra* should be placed on the Shakespeare transfer-list and moved from the tragedies to the comedies." I don't agree, but I do feel that Giles Block's interpretation of the play has made me see it in a different light. I had forgotten—or never saw—Antony and Cleopatra as quite so self-consciously theatrical. Perhaps what I used to take for the true expression of profound love in the play is actually only middle-aged erotic dalliance. Perhaps. At any event, the play and the issues it raises are renewed for me—even by just carefully reading the review of a stage production.

Before I began the analysis of Billington's review, I emphasized the value of seeing Shakespeare's plays performed as a spur to the imagination. There really is no substitute, for as Edward Partridge argues in his "Re-Presenting Shakespeare": "to *read* a play is a contradiction in terms, except as one speaks of reading a score in preparation for playing or listening to music. Plays are to be seen and heard and responded to as one responds to a rite or spectacle. They cannot be simply read as one reads a novel" (3). Yet, the reality is that only a lucky few can see with any frequency Shakespeare performed. In the absence of such exposure to live theatre, Partridge offers this advice, which I heartily second: "we must try to re-create by explication, analysis, and interpretation the play we cannot actually or often see and hear" (5). Videotape and DVD have helped alleviate this problem to some degree, but neither is the equal of a live performance.

Shakespeare on Stage: King Lear

In the effort to have Shakespeare on the page transform itself into living, imaginatively re-created drama, let's look at one further review. It's again written by Michael Billington, and it's of a production of *King Lear* by the Royal Shakespeare Company at the Barbican theatre in London in the fall of 1999. The director was Yukio Ninagawa, and King Lear was played by Nigel Hawthorne (best known for his lead role in the film *The Madness of King George*). This time, rather than analyze the review's content for what

Figure 7.3
Robin Weaver as Cordelia and Nigel Hawthorne as Lear in the RSC's production of
King Lear (1999). Is Hawthorne a "miniaturist" or a "megawatt actor"?

it reveals of the performance and its interpretation of Shakespeare, I'll follow it with some questions designed to spark discussion by focusing your
attention on ways in which the performance of the play gives new meaning to one of Shakespeare's greatest tragedies. The review appeared in the
Guardian Weekly (London) in November 1999.

"King Nigel's Shakespearean Tragedy"

King Lear is the Everest of world theatre. But the critical consensus
is that neither Nigel Hawthorne nor his Japanese director, Yukio
Ninagawa, has got beyond the foothills in the Royal Shakespeare
Company production at London's Barbican.

"More like Wurzel Gummidge [a scarecrow in a cult TV series]
than a mighty monarch," says the *Daily Mail* of Hawthorne's performance. "Little more than pique in his rages," claims the *Times*.
So have we got a famous disaster, worthy to be ranked alongside
Peter O'Toole's Macbeth? Absolutely not.

Hawthorne is miscast rather than actively bad: anyone who
has followed his work over the years would know that his forte is
not the big bow-wow effect but moral decency flecked with irony.
He is a miniaturist rather than a megawatt actor. [See Fig. 7.3.]

Where I dissent from my colleagues is their verdict on Ninagawa's production: it has an elegiac oriental beauty that I warmed to. As in his famous Samurai *Macbeth*, Ninagawa shows that tragedy is not incompatible with aesthetic grace.

Hawthorne's failure to measure up to Lear seems entirely predictable. The part requires a huge tonal range, a Blakeian ability to move in a moment from the domestic to the cosmic, and a quality of ecstasy in which, to quote the critic James Agate, "the soul stands beside the body."

Pathos, irony, and moral goodness are Hawthorne's gifts. Even when cast beyond his natural range, Hawthorne has his moments. He is good in the opening scene where he enters at a gallop, pre-emptively places Cordelia on his throne, and exits, unable to believe France would marry his discarded daughter. He picks up laughs through bathetic irony: viewing the bedraggled Poor Tom, he wanly inquires, "have his daughters brought him to this pass?"

But his well modulated, dry-sherry voice is unable to encompass Lear's titanic rages, and there is no sense of Lear progressing through madness to a tormented self-knowledge. Hawthorne substitutes the minutiae of pathos for the grandeur of tragedy.

In a more domestic production he might have been more effective, but Ninagawa's concept cries out for large-scale gestural acting. The stage is dominated by wooden doors, encrusted with pine-leaves, that open on to a vast cosmic emptiness.

Visually the production is stunning. Ninagawa's use of descending rocks and boulders conjures a world in which Nature's moulds are cracked. The image of the enchained Lear and Cordelia dragged across the vast length of the Barbican stage is also memorable. And Lily Komine's costumes harmoniously blend dazzling kimonos with rough hessian. [See Fig. 7.4.]

Ninagawa, in short, has created an impressive framework. What his production fatally lacks is a Lear whose heart and mind crack under his own folly. But the cruelty of theatre is that the actor has to carry the can. The mistake was to assume an actor of wry irony had the vocal iron for an assault on this play's treacherous summit.

Discussion Questions on Character

Billington's review prompts a number of questions for me about how the central role of Lear should be played:

1. The critical consensus is that Hawthorne is miscast as Lear because, as Billington puts it, he's "a miniaturist rather than a megawatt actor." However, does the role indeed require a megawatt actor? Are there scenes

Figure 7.4
Anna Chancellor as Regan and Sian Thomas as Goneril in the RSC's production of *King Lear* (1999). Note the kimono costumes.

in the play where a quieter performance by Lear is required? Are there scenes where physical presence and power are essential?

2. Billington sees the role of Lear as requiring a "huge tonal range": from the domestic to the cosmic to the ecstatic. Do you agree? Can you give an example of each? Are there parts of the "tonal range" that Billington hasn't mentioned? The regal, for example, or the dynastic? Describe them.

3. What do you think of Billington's chart of Lear's psychological state: from "madness" to "a tormented self-knowledge"? How does Lear begin the play? How does he end the play? From my perspective, Billington needs to define Lear's mental state at the beginning of the play, and he also needs to account for his harrowing sorrow at the end over Cordelia's death. Isn't Lear once more insane at that latter point?

4. Billington focuses on the subtext of one line in particular. It's spoken by Lear about Edgar as Poor Tom: "Ha[ve] his daughters brought him to this pass?" (3.4.62). Billington says the line is spoken "wanly" and with "bathetic irony." Do you agree that it should be? Are there other ways in which the line might be spoken?

5. According to Billington, Lear's "heart and mind crack under his own folly." Are there other ways of explaining Lear's fall from kingship to death?

Discussion Questions on Staging

Much time in the review is spent on Ninagawa's staging. Billington's discussion prompts a range of questions.

1. The staging has "an elegiac oriental beauty" and "aesthetic grace." Where in the play, do you think, Ninagawa got the idea for staging the play in such a way? What do you think Ninagawa was trying to gain from doing so?

2. The review specifically describes the scenery used in the play. It's clear from the description that Ninagawa wasn't opting for a traditional rendering of the play, for in Shakespeare's time the scenery would have been minimal indeed. Instead, Ninagawa uses "descending rocks and boulders" to depict "a world in which Nature's moulds are cracked." In addition, he chooses to have the stage dominated by "wooden doors, encrusted with pine-leaves, that open on to a vast cosmic emptiness." What do you think of Ninagawa's choice of scenery? What thematic point in the play is he trying to reinforce? What scenery would *you* use to stage the play?

3. The review also mentions how the actors are costumed: "dazzling kimonos" blend with "rough hessian." What point is the costumer, Lily Komine, trying to make with such a choice? What is the purpose of the contrast between silk and hessian? How do *you* envisage the actors' clothing?

Discussion Questions on Acting

Billington also glances at the issue of acting style. And that glance prompts
yet more questions.

1. In general terms, Billington talks of the need in the play for "large-scale
   gestural acting." Do you agree? What specifically is there about the play
   which might require that sort of acting? Are there parts of the play where
   another sort of acting style would work better?
2. Billington specifically calls the reader's attention to the way in which
   Lear places Cordelia on his throne at the beginning of the play and
   peremptorily exits. What do you think of such an interpretation? How
   do you see Lear showing on stage his attitude to his favorite daughter?
   Do the stage directions offer any help?
3. Billington specifically mentions, too, the way in which Lear and Cordelia
   are removed to prison in 5.3. The stage direction at line 26 simply reads:
   "*Exit [with Cordelia guarded]*." From such a minimal hint, Ninagawa
   decides to have the two characters "dragged across the vast length of the
   Barbican stage." Billington understandably finds such a movement "memorable," but is Ninagawa after more than just a powerful piece of stage
   business? How would *you* stage the exit at 5.3.26?

Shakespeare on Film: Hamlet

Despite the fact that Shakespeare's plays were written to be produced in
the theatre, most people nowadays see them at the movies or on TV.
Increasingly, videotape and DVD are the media of choice. One can bemoan
these facts, but to do so doesn't change anything and, moreover, it ignores
the very real educational strengths that film and TV versions of
Shakespeare's plays possess. Movies and TV allow the restricted Shakespearean stage to be opened up; videotape and DVD allow for a scene to be
studied and re-studied in depth.

In this part of the chapter, we will take advantage of modern technol-
ogy's rewind button by looking in depth at five versions of one scene from
Shakespeare's most famous play, *Hamlet*. As always, our concern is with
the imaginative re-creation of Shakespeare. What can an audience or
reader learn about the possibilities of interpretation from seeing words
variously enacted? The details of the discussion are these:

◇ The scene is 3.1. The action consists of Polonius using Ophelia to try to
   understand why Hamlet is so distracted in his behavior. The scene also
   includes Hamlet's famous "To be, or not to be" soliloquy.
◇ The five versions are, in chronological order: the 1948 J. Arthur Rank
   Enterprise/Two Cities Film production directed by and starring Laurence
   Olivier; the 1969 Columbia Pictures/Filmway production (directed by

Tony Richardson and starring Nicol Williamson); the 1980 BBC/Time Life production (directed by Rodney Bennett and starring Derek Jacobi); the 1990 Warner Bros./Nelson Entertainment/Icon production (directed by Franco Zeffirelli and starring Mel Gibson); and the 1996 Columbia/Castle Rock Entertainment production (directed by and starring Kenneth Branagh).[2] All are readily available on videotape or DVD.

The analysis is organized around a few key terms: *editing, staging, cinematography, language, characterization,* and *theme*. It concludes with an overall assessment of where the five versions fall along two continua. The first continuum runs from *presentation*, to *interpretation*, to *adaptation*. The second applies directly to cinematic treatments of drama, a continuum that runs (in Jorgens' terms) from *theatrical*, to *realistic*, to *filmic*.

Key Terms Used in the Discussion of Hamlet

Adaptation describes a film that creates a whole new work of art, sometimes in a different literary or artistic genre from the original.

Aspect ratio describes the ratio of the horizontal to the vertical dimensions of the screen.

Cinematography includes every aspect of the camera work in a film.

Editing includes *textual accuracy* and *structure*.

Filmic refers to a film that draws attention to the techniques of filmmaking.

Interpretation describes a film that emphasizes the director's particular view of the play's meaning.

Language includes concepts of *delivery* and *subtext*.

Montage describes a sequence of rapidly changing shots in a film.

Presentation describes a film that tries to reproduce the Shakespeare play that Elizabethans and Jacobeans knew.

Realistic describes a film that broadens out the play by making it more lifelike.

Staging includes *costumes, gestures, music, props,* and *setting*.

Theatrical describes a film that tries to reproduce a play as it would have been acted on the stage.

The Olivier Version (1948)

Editing. Olivier changes Shakespeare's original a great deal. He alters the structure of the scene by moving the soliloquy from lines 57–89 to the end. In addition, he cuts lines 1–42, 45–55, 106–15, 118–21, 137–42, 144–45, 153–64, 173, 177–78, and 188–90. Finally, the action involving the traveling players, which in the original brackets 3.1, is all moved to a position immediately after the scene. So, the beginning of Olivier's version of 3.1

(Polonius's instruction, "Ophelia, walk you here" [43]) now comes immediately after Hamlet's "except my life, except/ my life, except/my life" (2.2.216–17). There are also some changes in wording (*despised* for *disprized* [73], for example), inversions, and rephrasing.

The effect of such editing? We only get the highlights of the scene: no Rosencrantz and Guildenstern (1–28), no speech by the queen (37–42), no lengthy aside from Claudius (51–55), no major statement by Ophelia bemoaning the change in Hamlet (153–164). We also get the sense that Hamlet's soliloquy is *caused* by his conversation with Ophelia since it now comes after it; in fact, the play indicates no such relation.

Staging. The costumes are Elizabethan/Jacobean; the setting is a fake Norman castle with wall hangings and friezes; the scene begins as an interior and then moves out, for the soliloquy, to an exterior. The props and gestures are not unexpected: Ophelia reads a book; Hamlet enters reading a book, but tosses it away before talking with Ophelia; the "remembrances" which Ophelia wants to return to Hamlet (94–96) consist of a necklace; Polonius and Claudius hide behind a curtain; Hamlet is physically violent towards Ophelia and throws her down on the castle steps (at line 148).

The staging does, however, rise above the ordinary and contribute to a deeper understanding of the scene in three places. The dagger which Hamlet draws for the "bodkin" line in the soliloquy (60) is dropped into the sea at line 82 as if to test what it would be like for him to jump onto the rocks below. The music, which begins as a quiet combination of oboe and violin, becomes intensely romantic and expressive as the scene shifts to the soliloquy. It's as if the music is intended to reinforce the emotional state of the speakers in the scene. (This version of *Hamlet* is one of only two that I'm analyzing—the other is the 1996 Branagh—which uses music. The remaining three use language unassisted by orchestral accompaniment.) Finally, Olivier makes clear that by the time Hamlet asks Ophelia, "Where's your father?" he knows that Polonius (and probably Claudius, too) are hiding behind a curtain. He knows the scene is a trap. So, he delivers his condemnation of marriage ("Those that are married already—all but/one—shall live" [150–51]) directly to the on-stage listeners hidden behind the curtain. (See Fig. 7.5.)

Cinematography. By contemporary standards, the cinematography is straightforward and largely theatrical. Nevertheless, Olivier makes some interesting choices. The play is filmed in black and white (his earlier *Henry V* had been in color) presumably to reinforce the somber mood. The camera pulls away from Ophelia crying on the castle steps (foreground) after Hamlet's exit and pans to Claudius and Polonius discussing the results of their stratagem (background). The effect is to emphasize Ophelia's status as a pawn in a nasty dynastic game. The camera then pans up flight after flight of a spiral staircase as if following Hamlet's route to the top of the

Figure 7.5
Laurence Olivier as Hamlet in the 1948 film version of the play. Here he points at the tapestry behind which Claudius and Polonius are hiding as he delivers part of his speech.

tower. Once there, the film presents a *montage* (or sequence of rapidly changing shots) which includes some experimental out-of-focus photography of the sea in turmoil. The montage is intended presumably to mimic Hamlet's anguished state. (See Fig. 7.6.)

Language. By contemporary standards, Olivier's delivery is theatrical and Ophelia's grief artificial. Her crying seems more symbolic than realistic. Nothing in the subtext is foregrounded although Jean Simmons (as Ophelia) does introduce one fascinating change, perhaps at Olivier's direction. Her line, "O, help him, you sweet heavens!" becomes "O, help *me*, you sweet heavens!" (135; emphasis added). Such a change is brilliant because it makes her so human, but it isn't pursued in the scene by giving her all her lines. On the contrary, her role is significantly reduced. She becomes little more than a foil for Hamlet, and a virginal foil at that since she and Hamlet, rather chastely, never kiss in the scene.

Characterization. Hamlet comes across as melancholy, and only becomes active once he knows he's walked into a trap. Ophelia genuinely loves Hamlet and is intensely emotional and markedly passive. Polonius loves

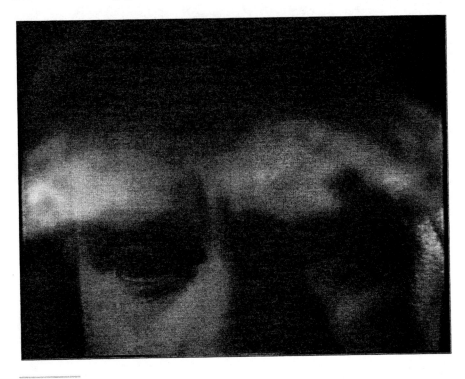

Figure 7.6
A montage effect in the Olivier film of *Hamlet* (1948). His face dissolves to be replaced by an ominous cloudscape.

Ophelia, and seems foolish but loyal to the king. Claudius appears very much in control but not particularly devious.

Theme. What Olivier's interpretation of 3.1 conveyed was hatred of entrapment.

The Richardson/Williamson Version (1969)

Editing. In keeping with the Olivier version more than twenty years before, Richardson radically alters the text of 3.1. He does not, however, move the soliloquy to the end of the scene as Olivier did in 1948 and Zeffirelli would do in his 1990 version. It stays firmly where it is in Shakespeare's play: lines 57–89. The scene runs the shortest of the five under discussion at only 8 mins. 6 secs. in a film of just 104 mins. When one considers that the full-length version of the play lasts more than four hours, the extent of the cuts is obvious. Just as did Olivier, Richardson takes out almost all of the opening part of the scene (1–55) featuring Rosencrantz and Guildenstern, Gertrude, and Claudius's crucial aside. Rather clumsily, however, he splices the new beginning of the scene ("Read on this book") to an *even earlier* part of 2.2 than Olivier chose: "At such a time I'll loose my daughter to him" (162). There are substantial cuts elsewhere (lines 162–64 and 174–78) as well as a confusing rewrite of line 184 whereby Polonius now says to Claudius: "I will myself go try him [Hamlet]. Let me alone to sound the depth of him." The overall effect of such cuts is unexpected and innovative: a much greater focus on the relationship between Hamlet and Ophelia. It is for this reason, presumably, that Richardson keeps in Ophelia's crucial "noble mind" speech (153–63) even if he does cut the last two lines from it.

Staging. The setting, like the setting in much of the Olivier version, looks like a stage set, and the costumes are, as in the earlier scene, Elizabethan/Jacobean. (By unintended contrast, the make up—Ophelia wearing more than her fair share of mascara—is vintage '60's, and looks terribly dated.) This film departs from the 1948 version, however, by daringly staging most of the scene on beds as if to suggest the passion between Hamlet and Ophelia. Williamson, as Hamlet, delivers the first 27 lines of the soliloquy while lying on his bed, only getting up for the transition to "Thus conscience does make cowards of us all" (84). Ophelia (played by Marianne Faithfull) and Hamlet converse while both lie on a tapestried hammock. The effect is to make their relationship noticeably more intimate than it was in 1948, even at the cost of Richardson creating an illogical transition between the end of Hamlet's soliloquy and the beginning of dialogue between the lovers. "Soft you now,/The fair Ophelia" (89) works as a transition only if one of the two characters is moving towards the other, but Richardson simply cheat-cuts from Hamlet at his bedside to Ophelia on her hammock.

The props are also a little unexpected: Hamlet has neither book nor dagger for his soliloquy (Olivier had both at different times); the curtain behind which Polonius and Claudius hide is more implied by shadow than substantial; Ophelia's "remembrances" are not a necklace as they were in the Olivier version and would later be in Zeffirelli's 1990 interpretation but, instead, a ring on the ring finger of her left hand. The gestures, by contrast, are as one might expect after the Olivier version although Hamlet's violence towards Ophelia now takes the form of his pinning her firmly to the hammock when she struggles to break free rather than casting her down on the castle steps.

The staging also offers a new interpretation of just how suspicious Hamlet is that the scene is a trap laid by Polonius and Claudius. In all the other versions, Hamlet is either suspicious right from the beginning or knows for sure that some plan is being executed. In Williamson's reading of the part, however, Hamlet suspects nothing until he catches sight of Polonius spying on him from the shadows. That sudden recognition is what directly provokes his question to Ophelia, "Where's your father?" (131), and utterly changes his mood.

Cinematography. Much of the scene is done in tightly framed close-up, and the camera work is proficient but uninteresting. It's meant to imitate the fixed position of an audience. At one point, however, the cinematography is more than routine. The discovery scene (where Hamlet sees Polonius) is accomplished by a simple pull back from the kissing couple on the hammock to Ophelia's father listening and watching. It's an elegant device.

Language. Williamson offers one odd reading and several insightful ones in the scene. At line 149, he seems to read "mad" in the American sense of "angry" rather than the English sense of "insane." In his soliloquy, he neatly emphasizes the dangers of dreaming by stressing certain words and by awaking from a reverie at "perchance to dream" (66). He also does a good job of turning "Thus conscience does make cowards of us all" into self-mockery (84). Overall, he changes pace several times, but generally reads his lines too fast so that the scene is over almost before it has started. Williamson is notorious for this trait, and he displays it here to the detriment of understanding the scene's full range of meaning. Faithfull, as Ophelia, does her best with her major speech, but (like Lalla Ward in the 1980 BBC/Time Life production) is unconvincing and adds nothing to the subtext.

Characterization. Hamlet comes across as disgusted with himself and the world. Ophelia begins calm and then too suddenly becomes distraught. Claudius is very much in control and rather more sinister than he was in the 1948 film. Polonius isn't laughable this time, but competent and reasonably affectionate toward his daughter.

Theme. From the Richardson/Williamson 1969 film comes a very different sense of what the point of the scene is. Now, the emphasis seems to be more on betrayal than (as it was for Olivier) on hatred of entrapment.

The Bennett/Jacobi Version (1980)

Editing. For the first time, 3.1 is presented *in its entirety.* In this regard, the Bennett/Jacobi and the 1996 Branagh versions stand out sharply from the other three we're looking at. Both are faithful to the text, with the Bennett/Jacobi film making only four very minor alterations to the original and the Branagh only five. This 1980 version of the scene runs to 13 mins. 27 secs.; the 1996 Branagh film to 13 mins. 55 secs. So, the 1980 and 1996 productions are alike in their textual fidelity and completeness, but there the similarities end. For, the Bennett/Jacobi version differs from the Branagh film in its intent: to reproduce as far as possible a *theatrical* rather than a *filmic* production. It differs from all the other productions under discussion, too, because it was shot for television. The rest were designed for the cinema and suffer in various ways from usually being reduced to the *aspect ratio* of the TV (1.33:1) rather than of the big screen (1.85:1). Even the 1948 Olivier film (with an original aspect ratio of only 1.37:1) looks slightly cramped or foreshortened on TV.

Staging. In keeping with its traditional intent, this film uses a wooden stage and a minimalist set. It doesn't have the bareness of a Globe production, but it's nonetheless very simply done. The costumes are Elizabethan/ Jacobean. The props are something borrowed and something new. Jacobi, as Hamlet, uses a dagger extensively during his soliloquy (as did Olivier), but Ophelia's "remembrances" are neither the necklace of the 1948 and 1990 films, nor the ring of 1969, nor the love letters of the 1996 version. Here, they are symbolized by a handkerchief (although it is given by Ophelia to Hamlet so long after the lines to which it refers that the relation between word and object is not as clear as it might be). Similarly, Jacobi injects a sense of the new into his soliloquy by delivering it neither from a cliff top (à la Olivier) nor from his bed (à la Williamson) but from a chair. However, the tour de force in staging as far as props are concerned is the director's decision to have Ophelia hold *wrong way up* the book she is pretending to read and to have Hamlet take note of the fact and right it for her. With one simple gesture, Hamlet shows that he must now suspect a trap.

In its use of gestures, too, the Bennett/Jacobi production forces the viewer to think hard about the scene and its meaning. So, Hamlet shakes Ophelia rather than throwing her on the ground or holding her down on a hammock. It's as if he's trying to say: "Can't you see reason?" So, he shrugs his shoulders in response to Ophelia's "I was the more deceived" (121) as if to say "What do you want me to do about it?" And so, most daringly, he grabs for Ophelia's genitalia when he says, "Why wouldst thou be a/breeder of sinners?" (122–23). In this way, the action reinforces the sense of the words.

Cinematography. Again in keeping with the production's concern with authenticity and the theatrical experience, the Bennett/Jacobi production's camera work is very simple, for it uses mainly close ups and fixed camera positions. The most interesting directorial decision as far as camera work is concerned is Hamlet's looking directly at the lens as he delivers his soliloquy. Indeed, he goes further by catching sight of it for the first time *just before* he launches into "To be, or not to be." It's as if he is establishing a relation to the camera (and, so, to us as TV viewers) analogous to that which should exist between an actor alone on stage and the audience.

Language. The intent of the BBC/Time Life productions of Shakespeare's plays is to make accurate interpretations of Shakespearean drama available to anyone with a TV and a VCR. With that in mind, the actors focus on vividly enacting Shakespeare's words. So, their delivery charts a middle way between Olivier's self-conscious theatricality and the intimate, sotto voce presentation in the 1969 Richardson/Williamson production.

However, Jacobi, in particular, among the cast in the 1980 version of *Hamlet* goes far beyond playing it safe, for he does some remarkable work with the subtext of the lines he speaks. When he delivers his soliloquy, it is as if he's learning for the first time about the horribly syllogistic relation that exists between death, sleep, and dream. When, in the soliloquy, he describes his fear of "the undiscovered country" (80), he looks at a medallion on his chest (presumably stamped with his father's image). So, his fear becomes also sorrow for his dead father, who will never return to be among the living again.

There are some other fine readings by Jacobi, too. At the end of his soliloquy, when he sees Ophelia and remarks: "Soft you, now," he seems genuinely surprised to see her. Later, when he tries to persuade Ophelia to enter a nunnery by showing how sinful he is—"I am very proud,/revengeful, ambitious" (125–26)—he shouts the words at the screen behind which Polonius and Claudius are hiding. It's as if he is chastising them, his hidden listeners, as much as criticizing himself. His best work, however, is his interpretation of the simple statement: "it hath made me mad" (149). For the first and only time among these five versions of *Hamlet*, the lead character realizes that he is no longer merely acting the part of someone who is insane. He realizes that he has in fact gone mad. His moment of self-realization is one that's shared with the audience, and Jacobi's reading of the line suddenly makes sense out of his erratic behavior in the scene. Everything comes into focus through the subtext.

Characterization.   Hamlet is very emotional right from the beginning of the scene, with a complex mixture of anger, depression, self-loathing, and bitterness as well as genuine affection for Ophelia. Ophelia is also very emotional right from the beginning, but never gets beyond that opening expression of her overwrought state of mind. Polonius is cold and calculating, a perfect foil for Claudius. He seems uninterested in Ophelia except as a pawn in court intrigue. Claudius is calculating and clever, a good actor in the role of a king. Gertrude is restrainedly lustful. And Rosencrantz and Guildenstern (whom we see for the first time, since Olivier and Richardson both cut the duo out of their versions of the play)? They come across as flunkies—albeit flunkies who are more astute than foolish.

Theme.   This production presents a theme different from the two earlier versions. If Olivier emphasized entrapment and Richardson/Williamson betrayal, Bennett/Jacobi see the destructiveness of love as central to the meaning of 3.1.

The Zeffirelli/Gibson Version (1990)

Editing.   Although this rendering of *Hamlet* 3.1 lasts 26 seconds longer than the Richardson/Williamson 1969 production (8 mins. 32 secs. versus 8 mins.

6 secs.), it cuts significantly more of Shakespeare's text. In addition, it plays around with the structure of the scene in very much the same way that Olivier did: by moving the soliloquy to the end of the scene. The result? The most radically altered iteration of Shakespeare's original. To me, it looks more like edited highlights. Just as did Olivier's, it jumps from 2.2.216–17 ("except my life, except/my life, except my life") to 3.1. However, it picks up the story at 3.1.38 (Gertrude's speech to Ophelia: "And for your part . . .") rather than at Olivier's choice of 3.1.44 (Polonius's instruction to Ophelia: "Read on this book"). It cuts whole speeches and parts of speeches. The litany by lines is 1–37, 44–55, 89–90, 102–03, 112–16, 118–31, 135, 138–39, 141–42, 152–70, 177–90. So great are the cuts in fact that Zeffirelli has to invent a bridging line for Polonius ("We must watch him and that most carefully") in order to move the action from Hamlet's "The rest shall keep as they are" (151) to Claudius's "I have in quick determination" (171).

The effect of the cuts is seriously to alter the meaning of the scene. Gone entirely is Hamlet's repetitious concern with Ophelia's seeking safety in a nunnery. Gone is the universal quality of his soliloquy, for now it seems to arise directly from his dialogue with Ophelia. Gone is any significant role for Ophelia. She only has 30 lines in the original scene (out of 191), but that number is now cut in half. The interpretive effect is to draw attention even more to Hamlet as the central figure in the drama.

Staging. Some of what Zeffirelli does harkens back to Olivier: Hamlet's violence towards Ophelia is shown by his casting her away (onto the ground in Olivier's *Hamlet,* into a stone wall in Zeffirelli's); Hamlet suspects a trap right from the beginning; Ophelia's "remembrances" are once again symbolized—as they were in 1948—by a necklace. Some of Zeffirelli's choices, however, are innovative and allow the audience to see something new in the scene. The setting for much of what takes place in 3.1 is the courtyard of a real medieval castle; the costumes are likewise medieval. So, gone is the faux Elizabethan/Jacobean look of all the earlier productions. The movement of the actors around the setting is likewise new. Hamlet walks right past Ophelia intending apparently to ignore her. He only stops and returns when she addresses him: "Good my lord,/How does your honor for this many a day?" (91–92). Similarly, the soliloquy is delivered in a new but appropriate spot given its content: the castle's family crypt.

Cinematography. This rendering of *Hamlet* is by far the most filmic of the four we've thus far discussed. Hamlet's speech that begins at line 136 is accompanied by some effective work behind the camera: a 360-degree pan following Hamlet as he circles Ophelia. The camera movement suggests both aggression and disorientation. In addition, Hamlet's soliloquy is broken up with frequent, brief jump-cuts to the sarcophagi in the niches of the walls of the crypt in which he delivers the speech. Indeed, part of what he says is directed at an effigy as audience—possibly that of his father. The effect is to reinforce the theme of mortality central to the meaning of the words.

Language. Much of what the production does with Shakespeare's language is routine: competent rather than inspired. Nevertheless, the production does rise to the occasion a few times to offer some new interpretations of what Shakespeare meant. Helena Bonham Carter (as Ophelia) is a more disputatious Ophelia than we have seen before. She pointedly contradicts Hamlet's version of their past history when she responds to his assertion that he never gave her any tokens of love with the bald statement: "My honored lord, you know right well you did" (98). Mel Gibson as Hamlet offers a couple of interesting readings in his soliloquy by stressing the "'tis" of "whether 'tis nobler" (58) and "calamity" in "calamity of so long life" (70). The first choice focuses on the genuine uncertainty of the question; the second (as a four-syllable word) draws out the sorrow of the natural human lifespan.

Characterization. Hamlet seems upset, but more than anything else by Ophelia's betrayal of him, for she is Polonius and Claudius's stooge in the scene. Ophelia appears both extraordinarily passive (she says very few words) and unexpectedly assertive when she talks with Hamlet. Claudius seems both hasty and nasty. Polonius appears abrupt and devious. Gertrude on the basis of her only reaction shot in the scene comes across as sinister—the closest in all the five versions to a queen who may be complicit in Claudius's actions.

Theme. This production provides a very different sense of what the scene conveys. For me this time, it's about the corrosiveness of suspicion and doubt.

The Branagh Version (1996)

Editing. As with the Bennett/Jacobi production, Branagh gives the audience an uncut rendering of the scene. He makes five very minor changes in individual words, but definitely intends to let the text stand on its own merits.

Staging. Branagh is obviously searching for novelty in his staging of the play. Rather than Elizabethan/Jacobean costumes and setting (as with Olivier, Richardson/Williamson, and Bennett/Jacobi) or the medieval equivalent (with Zeffirelli/Gibson), he moves the chronology forward to what looks like Prussia in the nineteenth century. His intent is, presumably, to focus on the long neglected military aspects of the plot. (He includes the character of the militaristic Fortinbras, which is a rarity in cinematic productions, and even accompanies the last half of Hamlet's soliloquy with the muffled sound of drums.)

As far as props and gestures are concerned, the focus remains on innovation. Hamlet delivers his soliloquy with the requisite dagger (or "bodkin"), but he does so to a mirror in a hall of mirrors. The meaning is clear: Hamlet is losing touch with himself in a world in which everyone watches everyone else. Hamlet is much more violent physically with Ophelia than in the earlier versions. He drags her around the ballroom, pushes her face up against the one-way mirror behind which Claudius and Polonius are hiding, and throws her down on the ground. Ophelia's "remembrances" (which had included, in previous productions, a necklace, a ring, and a handkerchief) consist in this version of love letters tied in a bundle with a ribbon. Branagh's choice here is masterful but so obvious it's astonishing that the earlier productions had not thought of it.

Not everything about the staging is masterful, however. Polonius delivers his entire final speech in the scene (179–90) while embracing his daughter, Ophelia. The purpose, I assume, is to show the audience his love for her, but the effect is to make nonsense out of his comforting statement: "How now, Ophelia?/You need not tell us what Lord Hamlet said;/We heard it all" (181–83). The statement comes naturally from a father crossing the stage to comfort a suddenly distressed daughter; it doesn't work if they are embracing throughout the speech. It frankly looks odd.

Cinematography. Branagh's rendering of the scene is far and away the most filmic. The scene (based on the different camera techniques used) breaks into five sections: the first (1–56) uses a repeated and rather disorienting 360-degree tracking movement focusing on the characters' backs. The soliloquy (57–89) uses a static camera focused on Hamlet's reflection in a full-length mirror. The first part of the dialogue between Hamlet and Ophelia (91–132) consists of a static two-head close-up. The second part (133–52) involves rapid movement as the camera follows Hamlet dragging Ophelia around the ballroom in search of Polonius (and Claudius) behind the mirrored doors. In the final section (153–91), we return to something like stasis (or an absence of motion) as Ophelia, Claudius, and Polonius deliver their judgments on what they have witnessed.

At times, the attention to technique is distracting (especially the rather fussy 360-degree tracking), but the interpretive value greatly outweighs any unintended annoyance. The camera work begins by emphasizing the omnipresence of suspicion and confusion in the court. It moves on in the soliloquy to suggest that Hamlet is being pulled apart by his role as his father's reluctant avenger. Then, it suggests that Hamlet and Ophelia's love is like the stillness of a hurricane's eye. And that hurricane hits the innocent Ophelia as soon as Hamlet knows that Polonius (and Claudius) are watching. He hears a noise behind the mirrored walls and asks Ophelia, "Where's your father?" (131). But he suspects already. Finally, we return to a sort of exhausted stasis. Polonius's stratagem has solved nothing.

Language. Branagh, in my judgment, is the best modern actor at bringing out the meaning of Shakespeare's lines without making them sound stilted or rehearsed. His interpretation of the soliloquy is wonderfully fresh: he takes the audience through a series of logical propositions (from the initial question to the triad of death—sleep—dream to a sad conclusion ["Thus"] about why human beings cannot act even when everything calls on them to do so). Kate Winslet, as Ophelia, does a much more convincing job with the subtext of her major speech (153–64) than does either Marianne Faithfull in the 1969 film or Lalla Ward in the 1980 BBC/Time Life version. It is, however, Derek Jacobi as Claudius (he had played Hamlet sixteen years before in the 1980 version) who wrings the most out of his lines. By simply stressing the word "lawful" as he tries to explain to Gertrude what he and Polonius intend, he reveals the depths of his uncertainty and doubt. He has killed his brother, married his dead brother's wife, and stolen the throne from his nephew. It matters to him *terribly* that Gertrude should think that he and Polonius are "lawful espials" (32) as they snoop on her son, Hamlet, and Ophelia in conversation.

Characterization. Hamlet comes across as disturbed, self-critical, and angry at Ophelia's betrayal. Ophelia seems puzzled about, even distraught at, Hamlet's behavior, but she clearly loves him. Claudius is angry, dangerous, and scared. Gertrude is enigmatic: acquiescent to her new husband and affectionate to Ophelia. Polonius is officious (as usual), but loves his daughter more deeply than in any other version we've examined. That love even leads him to show some unexpected annoyance towards Claudius and himself for jeopardizing his daughter by their stratagem. "My lord, do as you please" (183), he snaps at the king. And Rosencrantz and Guildenstern? In the 1980 production, they were more astute than foolish. Here they are obsequious nonentities.

Theme. Once again, this production chooses to emphasize something new in this well-known scene. We've had entrapment, betrayal, the destructiveness of love, the corrosiveness of suspicion and doubt. Here, Branagh does seem to touch on all of these, but he adds one more to the mix: anger as fundamental motivation.

Hamlet on Film: Some Final Thoughts

So, where do these five versions of *Hamlet* 3.1 fall on the continua from *presentation* to *interpretation* to *adaptation* on the one hand, and from *theatrical* to *realistic* to *filmic* on the other? The answer is clear cut. The Olivier (1948), Richardson/Williamson (1969), and Bennett/Jacobi (1980) productions mix presentation with interpretation. Each presents the audience with simple, pseudo-Shakespearean staging, but does so in order to foreground its particular view of what Shakespeare intended in the scene.

Similarly, all three are more theatrical than realistic. The viewer is aware that what is being depicted is artificial, a stage on which actors are portraying a playwright's characters. There may be moments of transcendence for an audience, but these occur because of the play's strengths not because of sophisticated film technique.

The Zeffirelli/Gibson (1990) and the Branagh (1996) are markedly different. They move *Hamlet* from the stage to the "real" world (or at least, to a powerful illusion of that world). They are not content simply to present Shakespeare. Rather, they interpret and, to a limited degree, adapt Shakespeare's fictive world to the expectations of a late-twentieth-century audience. To accomplish such a goal, they adopt two strategies. First, they produce movie versions of *Hamlet* that are markedly more filmic. Technique dominates, and if the audience is moved by the spectacle it is as much due to film technique as to the brilliance of Shakespeare's play. Second, they cast actors who are well known and liked. The 1990 Zeffirelli version is a standout in this regard. To cast Mel Gibson as Hamlet was a coup. Ever since *Mad Max* in 1979, he has been regarded as a heartthrob. It helps, too—as *Hamlet* shows—that he can act very capably as well.

So, what can one learn from using film as an adjunct to studying Shakespeare on the page? Simply this: that film provides the viewer of Shakespearean drama with an extraordinary number of interpretive insights. Again and again, film helps the reader to visualize a scene or to consider how particular actions could be performed or certain lines spoken. The power of the human imagination is boundless, and film can energize that power if the words on the page are not enough.

Writing and Discussion Assignments

1. Go to a performance of a Shakespeare play. What did the performance reveal about the meaning of the play that you were not aware of from simply reading it? If there were parts of the performance where you found yourself disagreeing with the interpretation, how do you explain such disagreements?

2. Go to a performance of a Shakespeare play, and write a review of it. How does that review compare with the one(s) that appeared in the local press or the college newspaper? Where there are significant differences, how do you explain their existence?

3. In 2000, a new cinematic version of *Hamlet* was released starring Ethan Hawke as the melancholy Dane. Compare its treatment of 3.1 to the other five renderings discussed in this chapter. What new insights does it offer?

4. Compare and contrast any one scene in several versions of any Shakespeare play other than *Hamlet*. The opening scene in *King Lear* or the final scene in *Romeo and Juliet* (5.3) would be a good choice. Organize your analysis chronologically so you can consider whether there are trends in the way Shakespeare has been interpreted on film.

5. None of the versions of *Hamlet* that we looked at in this chapter is an adaptation. Each sticks broadly to the original as it tries to illuminate what the director and actors see as Shakespeare's meaning. By contrast, adaptations take Shakespeare's original only as a starting point in the creation of new art. Consider one of those adaptations, for example, the film *10 Things I Hate about You*, which rewrites *The Taming of the Shrew* for a modern audience, or the film version of Jane Smiley's novel *A Thousand Acres* (an adaptation of *King Lear*). How radical are the changes? What is lost and gained by such an adaptation?

6. Imagine that you've been hired to direct a Shakespeare play, either for the stage or the screen. Analyze a small section of your chosen play with a particular concern in mind, and discuss in detail the choices you would make. For example, you could choose to direct a production of *Twelfth Night* for the screen. How would you stage the meeting between Malvolio and Feste (as Sir Topas the curate) in 4.2? Explain your choices in detail, and remember that staging includes costumes, props, gestures, music, and movement around the stage (known as "blocking"). Spend some time, too, on describing stagecraft ideas that you think would not work in addition to those that you finally chose.

Further Reading

Brown, John Russell. *Shakespeare's Plays in Performance*. New and rev. ed. New York: Applause Books, 1993.

Buchman, Lorne. *Still in Movement: Shakespeare on Screen*. Oxford: Oxford UP, 1991.

Crowl, Samuel. *Shakespeare Observed: Studies in Performance on Stage and Screen*. Athens: U of Ohio P, 1992.

Jackson, Russell. *The Cambridge Companion to Shakespeare on Film*. Cambridge: Cambridge UP, 2000.

Kennedy, Dennis. *Looking at Shakespeare: A Visual History of Twentieth-Century Performance*. Cambridge: Cambridge UP, 1993.

Rothwell, Kenneth S. *A History of Shakespeare on Screen: A Century of Film and Television*. Cambridge: Cambridge UP, 1999.

Notes

1. For useful background information on the New Globe's performance of *Antony and Cleopatra*, go to the University of Reading's website at < http://www.rdg.ac.uk/globe/research/1999/1999ac.htm >. It includes an extensive analysis of the performance by Dr. Jaq Bessell. For additional photographs of the performance, go to another part of the same website: < http://www.rdg.ac.uk/globe/research/1999/acpictures.htm >. This link provides 35 very useful photographs—taken from the balcony—of the performance.

2. For useful background information on the 1996 Branagh *Hamlet*, go to < http://www.cinema1.com/movies97/hamlet/us.html >.

Appendix

Shakespeare Resources: Websites, Books, and Journals

This section is deliberately intended to be both short and useful. It covers a dozen of the best websites; and it lists the books and journals that I have found most helpful in my own studies. I've added occasional brief annotations where I thought they might aid the student or general reader.

Websites

The last time I did a "William Shakespeare" search using Google, it showed a total of 231,000 results. So, my list of the best Shakespeare sites is both personal and highly selective. They are the sites that I have found most useful and trouble-free. There are a great many weak sites on the Web when it comes to Shakespeare, and too much repetition of content. With this list, I've tried to sift the gold from the dross.

A Compendium of Common Knowledge: 1558–1603
> < http://www.renaissance.dm.net/compendium/ >

> A cornucopia of information about everyday living in the Elizabethan Age in England.

Concordances—Shakespeare: Works
> < http://www.concordance.com/shakespe.htm >

> The best concordance to Shakespeare's works on the Web. There is another (at tech-two.mit.edu/Shakespeare/), but I don't find that site as

user-friendly. The concordance.com site allows for double-word searches, and provides the context for quotations and word usage. I don't like the way the quotations are formatted, but that's a minor gripe. It's a very reliable site.

Educating Shakespeare. School Life in Elizabethan England
< http://homepages.nationwideisp.net/ ~ gsa/welcomeeduc.htm >

An explanation of what Shakespeare's school life would have been like. This site, run by the Guild School Association in Stratford-upon-Avon, England, is a little text heavy, but it does have a good further-reading list.

Mr. William Shakespeare and the Internet
< http://daphne.palomar.edu/shakespeare/ >

Eight sections (works, life and times, criticism, sources, and so on). It also lists other sites, and has a very good "Best Sites" page. This site uses frames, but is nicely laid out. I think it's the best place to start any internet search on Shakespeare.

The Shakespeare Birthplace Trust, Stratford-upon-Avon, UK
< http://www.shakespeare.org.uk/ >

Several sections, among them: records (plain text versions of parish records, and so on), Shakespeare's authorship, and library holdings. This site includes a useful site search box.

Shakespeare Bookshelf: The Internet Public Library
< http://www.ipl.org/reading/shakespeare/shakespeare.html >

Excellent e-texts of Shakespeare's works as well as links to other Shakespeare sites.

Shakespeare Illustrated
< http://www.cc.emory.edu/ENGLISH/classes/Shakespeare_Illustrated/ Shakespeare.html >

Detailed, fascinating connections among "nineteenth century paintings, criticism and productions of Shakespeare's plays and their influence on one another." Set up by Harry Rusche of the English Department at Emory University.

The Shakespeare Mystery
< http://www.pbs.org/wgbh/pages/frontline/shakespeare/index.html >

An impressive, entertaining, and interactive ancillary to the Frontline program of the same name devoted to the question of who Shakespeare was.

The Shakespeare Resource Center
< http://www.bardweb.net >

The usual sections devoted to the man and his work. It includes a transcription of Shakespeare's will complete with strikeouts and interlineations. It's a very simple site to navigate.

Shakespeare's Globe Research Database
< http://www.rdg.ac.uk/globe >

A wealth of information about the original Globe theatre, the new Globe, and Shakespeare in performance. This site is at the University of Reading in England.

Soundings
< http://www.theatlantic.com/unbound/poetry/soundings/shakespeare.htm >

RealAudio readings of Sonnet 116 by four well-known poets: Linda Gregerson; Mark Doty; W.S. Merwin; and Lloyd Schwartz. The opportunity to hear varied versions of the same sonnet shows how important the sound of poetry is to its meaning.

"Surfing with the Bard: Your Shakespeare Classroom on the Internet!"
< http://www.ulen.com/Shakespeare/ >

A good varied collection of links to other sites more than makes up for the silly title.

The Wars of the Roses
< http://www.northcoast.com/ ~ ming/roses/roses.html >

Some good information about the Wars of the Roses. It's a work in progress. It's not a scholarly site, and has a terribly fussy design.

Books

For the sake of clarity and ease of reference, I've divided this list of books into the following subheadings: Editions of Shakespeare; Reference Books; and Background Reading. *These books are in addition to those listed at the end of each chapter.*

Editions of Shakespeare

Allen, Michael J. B., and Kenneth Muir. *Shakespeare's Plays in Quarto*. A Facsimile ed. Berkeley: U of California P, 1981.

It's useful to compare plays in this edition with their printing in the First Folio. It includes an appendix listing the conventional act and scene divisions in the plays.

Bevington, David. *The Complete Works of Shakespeare*. Updated 4th ed. New York: Longman, 1997.

Particularly good on life in Shakespearean England. The textual notes are a model of clarity.

Evans, G. Blakemore, and J. J. M. Tobin, eds. *The Riverside Shakespeare*. 2nd ed. Boston: Houghton Mifflin, 1997.

Introductory material in this volume is particularly well laid out and helpful.

Greenblatt, Stephen, et al., eds. *The Norton Shakespeare.* New York: W.W. Norton, 1997.

> Excellent introductory material with a good range of illustrations, but a horrid book as far as its format is concerned.

Hinman, Charlton, prep. *The First Folio of Shakespeare.* The Norton Facsimile Edition. 2nd ed. New York: W.W. Norton, 1996.

> Includes an introduction discussing the history of the printing of the First Folio. It's useful to compare this text with the quarto printings and with modern editions.

Reference Books

Bergeron, David M., and Geraldo U. de Sousa. *Shakespeare: A Study and Research Guide.* Lawrence: UP of Kansas, 1995.

Bock, Philip K. *Shakespeare & Elizabethan Culture.* New York: Schocken Books, 1984.

Boyce, Charles. *Shakespeare A to Z.* New York: Delta, 1990.

> Not the latest alphabetical guide, but still the best.

Champion, Larry S. *The Essential Shakespeare: An Annotated Bibliography of Major Modern Studies.* New York: G. K. Hall, 1993.

Evans, Gareth, and Barbara Lloyd. *The Shakespeare Companion.* New York: Charles Scribner's Sons, 1978.

> Includes a section dealing with terminology used in discussing the characteristics of the printed texts of Shakespeare's plays.

Harner, James L., ed. *The World Shakespeare Bibliography on CD-ROM 1980–1996.* Cambridge: Cambridge UP, 1999.

Kay, Dennis. *Shakespeare: His Life, Work, and Era.* New York: William Morrow, 1992.

Kolin, Philip C. *Shakespeare and Feminist Criticism: An Annotated Bibliography and Commentary.* New York: Garland, 1991.

McConnell, Louise, ed. *Dictionary of Shakespeare.* Chicago: Fitzroy Dearborn, 2000.

McLean, Andrew M. *Shakespeare: Annotated Bibliographies and Media Guide for Teachers.* Urbana, IL: NCTE, 1980.

McManaway, James G., and Jeanne Addison Roberts. *A Selective Bibliography of Shakespeare.* Washington, DC: Folger Shakespeare Library, 1979.

McMurtry, Jo. *Understanding Shakespeare's England. A Companion for the American Reader.* Hamden, CT: Archon Books, 1989.

Partridge, Eric. *Shakespeare's Bawdy.* London: Routledge, 1996.

> The classic in the field.

Pritchard, R.E., ed. *Shakespeare's England: Life in Elizabethan and Jacobean Times.* Stroud: Sutton, 1999.

Rosenblum, Joseph, comp. *Shakespeare: An Annotated Bibliography.* Pasadena, CA: Salem, 1992.

Rothwell, Kenneth S., and A. Henkin Melzer. *Shakespeare on Screen: An International Filmography and Videography.* London: Mansell, 1990.

Rubinstein, Frankie. *A Dictionary of Shakespeare's Sexual Puns and Their Significance.* New York: St. Martin's P, 1995.

I prefer Rubinstein's analysis of language to Partridge's, but some of her claims are misguided.

Schoenbaum, S. *Shakespeare. The Globe & The World.* New York: Folger Shakespeare Library, 1979.

Spevack, Marvin. *The Harvard Concordance to Shakespeare.* Cambridge: Belknap-Harvard UP, 1973.

Trussler, Simon. *Shakespearean Concepts.* London: Methuen, 1989.

Wagner, John A. *Historical Dictionary of the Elizabethan World: Britain, Ireland, Europe, and America.* Phoenix: The Oryx P, 1999.

The best recent compendium of all things Elizabethan.

Wells, Stanley, ed. *Shakespeare: A Bibliographical Guide.* New ed. Oxford: Clarendon P, 1990.

Williams, Gordon. *A Glossary of Shakespeare's Sexual Language.* London: Athlone, 1997.

Background Reading

Film Studies

Brode, Douglas. *Shakespeare in the Movies: From the Silent Era to* Shakespeare in Love. Oxford: Oxford UP, 2000.

Burt, Richard, and Lynda Boose, eds. *Shakespeare, the Movie: Popularizing the Plays on Film, TV, and Video.* London: Routledge, 1997.

Davies, E.A., and Stanley Wells, ed. *Shakespeare and the Moving Image.* Cambridge: Cambridge UP, 1994.

Howlett, Kathy M. *Framing Shakespeare on Film.* Athens: Ohio UP, 2000.

Pilkington, Ace G. *Screening Shakespeare from* Richard II *to* Henry V. Newark: U of Delaware P, 1991.

Rothwell, Kenneth S. *A History of Shakespeare on Screen: A Century of Film and Television.* Cambridge: Cambridge UP, 1999.

Gender Studies

Barker, Deborah, and Ivo Kamps, ed. *Shakespeare and Gender: A History*. London: Verso, 1995.

Burt, Richard. *Unspeakable ShaXXXspeares: Queer Theory and American Kiddie Culture*. New York: St. Martin's P, 1998.

Callaghan, Dympna, ed. *A Feminist Companion to Shakespeare*. Malden, MA: Blackwell, 2000.

Chedgzoy, Kate. *Shakespeare's Queer Children: Sexual Politics and Contemporary Culture*. Manchester, Eng.: Manchester UP, 1995.

Dusinberre, Juliet. *Shakespeare and the Nature of Women*. New York: St. Martin's P, 1996.

Garner, Shirley Nelson, and Madelon Sprengnether, ed. *Shakespearean Tragedy and Gender*. Bloomington: Indiana UP, 1996.

Jardine, Lisa. *Still Harping on Daughters: Women and Drama in the Age of Shakespeare*. New York: Harvester Wheatsheaf, 1989.

Levine, Nina S. *Women's Matters: Politics, Gender, and Nation in Shakespeare's Early History Plays*. Newark: U of Delaware P, 1998.

Orgel, Stephen. *Impersonations: The Performance of Gender in Shakespeare's England*. Cambridge: Cambridge UP, 1996.

Roberts, Jeanne Addison. *The Shakespearean Wild: Geography, Genus, and Gender*. Lincoln: U of Nebraska P, 1991.

Shapiro, Michael. *Gender in Play on the Shakespearean Stage: Boy Heroines and Female Pages*. Ann Arbor: U of Michigan P, 1994.

Ziegler, Georgianna, Frances E. Dolan, and Jeanne Addison Roberts. *Shakespeare's Unruly Women*. Washington, DC: Folger Shakespeare Library, 1997.

Genre Studies

Howard, Jean E., and Phyllis Rackin. *Engendering a Nation: A Feminist Account of Shakespeare's English Histories*. London: Routledge, 1997.

Hart, Jonathan. *Theater and the World: The Problematics of Shakespeare's History*. Boston: Northeastern UP, 1992.

Hawkins, Harriett. *Classics and Trash: Traditions and Taboos in High Literature and Popular Modern Genres*. Toronto: U of Toronto P, 1990.

Sterling, Eric. *The Movement towards Subversion: The English History Play from Skelton to Shakespeare*. Lanham, MD: UP of America, 1996.

History

Carpenter, Christine. *The Wars of the Roses*. Cambridge: Cambridge UP, 1997.

Orgel, Stephen, and Sean Keilen, eds. *Shakespeare and History*. New York: Garland, 1999.

Saccio, Peter. *Shakespeare's English Kings: History, Chronicle, and Drama.* 2nd ed. Oxford: Oxford UP, 2000.

Tillyard, E. M. W. *The Elizabethan World Picture.* 1943. New York: Random House, 1959.

>Dated and too schematic, but still an informative read.

Tricomi, Albert H. *Contextualizing the Renaissance: Returns to History.* Binghamton, NY: Center for Medieval and Early Modern Studies, 1999.

Language

Blake, N.F. *Essays on Shakespeare's Language, First Series.* Misterton, UK: The Language P, 1996.

Desmet, Christy. *Reading Shakespeare's Characters: Rhetoric, Ethics, and Identity.* Amherst: U of Massachusetts P, 1992.

Gilbert, Antony J. *Shakespeare's Dramatic Speech.* Lewiston, NJ: The Edwin Mellen P, 1997.

Magnusson, Lynne. *Shakespeare and Social Dialogue: Dramatic Language and Elizabethan Letters.* Cambridge: Cambridge UP, 1999.

Thorne, Alison. *Vision and Rhetoric in Shakespeare: Looking through Language.* New York: St. Martin's P, 2000.

Wells, Stanley, ed. "Shakespeare and Language." *Shakespeare Survey* 50 (1997).

Willbern, David. *Poetic Will: Shakespeare and the Play of Language.* Philadelphia: U of Pennsylvania P, 1997.

New Historicism

Bradshaw, Graham. *Misrepresentations: Shakespeare and the Materialists.* Ithaca, NY: Cornell UP, 1993.

Briggs, Julia. *This Stage-Play World: Texts and Contexts, 1580–1625.* Oxford: Oxford UP, 1997.

Dubrow, Heather. *Shakespeare and Domestic Loss: Forms of Deprivation, Mourning and Recuperation.* Cambridge: Cambridge UP, 1999.

Jardine, Lisa. *Reading Shakespeare Historically.* London: Routledge, 1996.

Mallin, Eric Scott. *Inscribing the Time: Shakespeare and the End of Elizabethan England.* Berkeley: U of California P, 1995.

Pechter, Edward. *What Was Shakespeare? Renaissance Plays and Changing Critical Practice.* Ithaca, NY: Cornell UP, 1995.

Wilson, Jean. *The Archaeology of Shakespeare: The Material Legacy of Shakespeare's Theatre.* Far Thrupp, Gloucs., Eng: Alan Sutton, 1995.

Performance Studies

Bate, Jonathan, and Russell Jackson, ed. *Shakespeare: An Illustrated Stage History.* Oxford: Oxford UP, 1996.

Buzacott, Martin. *The Death of the Actor: Shakespeare on Page and Stage.* London: Routledge, 1991.

Coursen, H. R. *Shakespearean Performance as Interpretation.* Newark: U of Delaware P, 1992.

Fischlin, Daniel, and Mark Fortier, ed. *Adaptations of Shakespeare: A Critical Anthology of Plays from the Seventeenth Century to the Present.* London: Routledge, 2000.

Holland, Peter. *English Shakespeares: Shakespeare on the English Stage in the 1990s.* Cambridge: Cambridge UP, 1997.

Kennedy, Dennis. *Looking at Shakespeare: A Visual History of Twentieth-Century Performance.* Cambridge: Cambridge UP, 1993.

Marsden, Jean I. *The Re-Imagined Text: Shakespeare, Adaptation, & Eighteenth-Century Literary Theory.* Lexington: UP of Kentucky, 1995.

Parsons, Keith, and Pamela Mason, ed. *Shakespeare in Performance.* London: Salamander Books, 1995.

Schafer, Elizabeth. *Ms-Directing Shakespeare: Women Direct Shakespeare.* New York: St. Martin's P, 2000.

Wells, Stanley, ed. *Shakespeare in the Theatre: An Anthology of Criticism.* Oxford: Clarendon P, 1997.

Worthen, W. B. *Shakespeare and the Authority of Performance.* Cambridge: Cambridge UP, 1997.

Psychological Criticism

Armstrong, Philip. *Shakespeare's Visual Regime: Tragedy, Psychoanalysis, and the Gaze.* New York: St. Martin's P, 2000.

Bloom, Allan. *Shakespeare on Love and Friendship.* Chicago: U of Chicago P, 2000.

Bloom, Harold. *Shakespeare: The Invention of the Human.* New York: Riverhead Books, 1999.

Charnes, Linda. *Notorious Identity: Materializing the Subject in Shakespeare.* Cambridge: Harvard UP, 1993.

Charney, Maurice. *Shakespeare on Love and Lust.* New York: Columbia UP, 2000.

Freedman, Barbara. *Staging the Gaze: Postmodernism, Psychoanalysis, and Shakespearean Comedy.* Ithaca, NY: Cornell UP, 1991.

Lupton, Julia Reinhard, and Kenneth Reinhard. *After Oedipus: Shakespeare in Psychoanalysis.* Ithaca, NY: Cornell UP, 1993.

Murray, Peter B. *Shakespeare's Imagined Persons: The Psychology of Role-Playing and Acting.* Lanham, MD: Barnes & Noble, 1996.

Sources

Bate, Jonathan. *Shakespeare and Ovid.* Oxford: Oxford UP, 1993.

> An excellent discussion of a critical source issue in Shakespeare studies.

Brown, Richard Danson, and David Johnson, eds. *A Shakespeare Reader: Sources and Criticism.* New York: St. Martin's P, 2000.

Lynch, Stephen J. *Shakespearean Intertextuality: Studies in Selected Sources and Plays.* Westport, CT: Greenwood, 1998.

Miola, Robert S. *Shakespeare's Reading.* Oxford: Oxford UP, 2000.

Theatres and Staging

Bentley, Gerald Eades. *The Professions of Player and Dramatist in Shakespeare's Time, 1590–1642.* Princeton: Princeton UP, 1993.

Chambers, E.K. *The Elizabethan Stage.* 4 vols. 1923; rpt. Oxford: Clarendon P, 1961.

> Still authoritative even after more than 75 years.

Gurr, Andrew. *The Shakespearean Playing Companies.* Oxford: Oxford UP, 1996.

———. *The Shakespearean Stage, 1574–1642.* 3rd ed. Cambridge: Cambridge UP, 1992.

———, and Mariko Ichikawa. *Staging in Shakespeare's Theatres.* Oxford: Oxford UP, 2000.

Hodges, C. Walter. *Enter the Whole Army: A Pictorial Study of Shakespearean Staging 1576–1616.* Cambridge: Cambridge UP, 1999.

Marra, Giulio. *Shakespeare and This 'Imperfect' World: Dramatic Form and the Nature of Knowing.* New York: Peter Lang, 1997.

Montrose, Louis. *The Purpose of Playing: Shakespeare and the Cultural Politics of the Elizabethan Theatre.* Chicago: U of Chicago P, 1996.

Orrell, John. *The Human Stage: English Theatre Design, 1567–1640.* Cambridge: Cambridge UP, 1988.

Wiggins, Martin. *Shakespeare and the Drama of His Time.* Oxford: Oxford UP, 2000.

Journals

Shakespeare Bulletin. Lafayette College, Easton, PA

Shakespeare Magazine. Georgetown University, Washington, DC

Shakespeare Newsletter. Iona College, New Rochelle, NY

Shakespeare Quarterly. Folger Shakespeare Library, Washington, DC

Shakespeare Survey. The Shakespeare Institute, Stratford-upon-Avon, England

Works Cited

Allen, Michael J. B., and Kenneth Muir, eds. *Shakespeare's Plays in Quarto. A Facsimile Edition of Copies Primarily from the Henry E. Huntington Library.* Berkeley: U of California P, 1981.

Aristotle. *Poetics.* 330 B.C.? Trans. Malcolm Heath. London: Penguin Books, 1996.

Bale, John. *King John.* 1539. *John Bale's King Johan.* Ed. Barry Banfield Adams. San Marino, CA: Huntington Library, 1969.

Barnet, Sylvan, ed. *The Complete Signet Classic Shakespeare.* New York: Harcourt Brace Jovanovich, 1972.

Beckett, Samuel. *Waiting for Godot: A Tragicomedy in 2 Acts.* London: Faber, 1956.

Bevington, David. *The Complete Works of Shakespeare.* Updated 4th ed. New York: Longman, 1997.

Billington, Michael. "Comedy Becomes Cleopatra." *Guardian Weekly* (London) Aug. 12–18, 1999: 24.

———. "King Nigel's Shakespearean Tragedy." *Guardian Weekly* (London) Nov. 11–17, 1999: 19.

Blundeville, Thomas. *True Order and Methode of Wryting and Reading Hystories.* London: Willyam Seres, 1574. Ed. Hans Peter Heinrich. Frankfurt am Main, Ger.: Peter Lang, 1986.

Boas, Frederick S. *Shakespeare and His Predecessors.* 1896. Rpt. New York: Gordian P, 1968.

Boccaccio, Giovanni. *De Casibus Illustrium Virorum.* 1520. Ed. Louis Brewer Hall. Gainesville, FL: Scholars' Facsimiles & Reprints, 1962.

———. *The Decameron.* 1349–1351. Eds. Guido Waldman and Jonathan Usher. Oxford: Oxford UP, 1998.

Boswell, James. *The Life of Samuel Johnson, LL.D.* 2 vols. London: Printed by Henry Baldwin for Charles Dilly, 1791. 3 vols. New York: The Heritage P, 1963.

Campbell, Oscar James, and Edward G. Quinn, eds. *The Reader's Encyclopedia of Shakespeare.* New York: Thomas Y. Crowell, 1966.

Cawdrey, Robert. *A Table Alphabeticall.* London: Printed by I.R. for Edmund Weaver, 1604.

Chaucer, Geoffrey. "The Monk's Tale." 1374? *The Works of Geoffrey Chaucer.* Ed. F. N. Robinson. 2nd ed. Boston: The Riverside P Cambridge-Houghton Mifflin, 1957. 188–98.

Coursen, H.R. *Watching Shakespeare on Television*. Rutherford: Fairleigh Dickinson UP, 1993.

Danson, Lawrence. *Shakespeare's Dramatic Genres*. Oxford: Oxford UP, 2000.

David, Richard. *Shakespeare in the Theatre*. Cambridge: Cambridge UP, 1978.

Davies, Anthony. *Filming Shakespeare's Plays*. Cambridge: Cambridge UP, 1988.

Dessen, Alan C. "Shakespeare and the Theatrical Conventions of His Time." *The Cambridge Companion to Shakespeare Studies*. Ed. Stanley Wells. Cambridge: Cambridge UP, 1986. 85–99.

Donatus, Aelius. *Terentius, P.A. Comoedia c[um] Duobus Commentis Ael. Donati et J. Calpurnii*. Venetiis: per Alberti num Vercellensem, 1500. See "The Comments on the Content and Form of the Comic Plot in the *Commentum Terenti* Ascribed to Donatus," by Paul Grady Moorehead. Diss. U of Chicago, 1923.

Euripides. *Hecuba*. Ed. Janet Lembke and Kenneth J. Reckford. New York: Oxford UP, 1991.

Evans, G. Blakemore, ed. *The Riverside Shakespeare*. Boston: Houghton Mifflin, 1974.

Everyman. 1500? *Everyman, and Medieval Miracle Plays*. New ed. Ed. A.C. Cawley. London: J.M. Dent, 1999.

Greene, Robert. *Friar Bacon and Friar Bungay*. 1589–1592. Lincoln: U of Nebraska P, 1963.

———. *Grenes Groatsworth of Wit: Bought with a Million of Repentance*. London: Printed for William Wright, 1592. Binghamton, NY: Center for Medieval and Early Renaissance Studies, SUNY at Binghamton, 1994.

———. *Pandosto: The Triumph of Time*. 1588. *Pereymedes the Blacksmith; and, Pandosto*. Ed. Stanley W. Wells. New York: Garland, 1988.

———. *The Scottish History of James the Fourth*. 1590. Ed. Norman Sanders. London: Methuen, 1970.

Hall, Edward. *Union of the Two Noble and Illustre Families of York and Lancaster*. London: Imprinted by Richard Grafton, 1548. Second ed. 1550. Menston, Eng.: Scolar P, 1970.

Hartwig, Joan. *Shakespeare's Tragicomic Vision*. Baton Rouge: Louisiana State UP, 1972.

Hobbes, Thomas. *Leviathan*. London: Printed for Andrew Crooke, at the Green Dragon in St. Pauls Church-yard, 1651. Ed. Richard Tuck. Cambridge: Cambridge UP, 1991.

Holinshed, Raphael. *Chronicles of England, Scotland, and Ireland*. London: Imprinted for Lucas Harrison, 1577. 2nd ed. 1587. New York: AMS P, 1976. 6 vols.

Horner, Winifred Bryan. *Rhetoric in the Classical Tradition*. New York: St. Martin's P, 1988.

Hussey, S. S. *The Literary Language of Shakespeare.* London: Longman, 1982.

Ibsen, Henrik. *A Doll's House.* 1879. Trans Frank McGuinness and Charlotte Barslund. London: Faber, 1996.

Ingram, William. "The Economics of Playing." *A Companion to Shakespeare.* Ed. David Scott Kastan. Oxford: Blackwell, 1999. 313–27.

Jorgens, Jack J. *Shakespeare on Film.* Bloomington: Indiana UP, 1977.

Kyd, Thomas. *The Spanish Tragedy.* 1587. Ed. Emma Smith. London: Penguin, 1998.

Lydgate, John. *The Fall of Princes.* London: Imprinted for John Wayland, 1554. *Lydgate's Fall of Princes.* London: Published for the Early English Text Society by Oxford UP, 1967. 4 vols.

Lyly, John. *Endymion.* 1588. Ed. David M. Bevington. New York: Manchester UP, 1996.

———. *Gallathea.* London: Printed by John Charlwoode for the widow Broome, 1592. Oxford: Published for the Malone Society by Oxford UP, 1998.

Mankind. 1470? *Three Late Medieval Morality Plays: Mankind, Everyman, Mundus et Infans.* Ed. G.A. Lester. New York: W.W. Norton, 1997.

Marlowe, Christopher. *Edward II.* 1591–1593. London: William Jones, 1594. Ed. Martin Wiggins and Robert Lindsey. Second ed. New York: W.W. Norton, 1994.

———. *Tamburlaine.* 1587. *Tamburlaine the Great.* Ed. J.S. Cunningham. Manchester, Eng.: Manchester UP, 1996.

Meres, Francis. *Palladis Tamia.* London: Printed by P. Short for Cuthbert Burbie, 1598. New York: Scholars' Facsimiles & Reprints, 1978.

Miller, Arthur. *Death of a Salesman: Certain Private Conversations in Two Acts, and a Requiem.* 1949. London: Penguin Books, 2000.

The Mirror for Magistrates. London: William Baldwin, 1559. Ed. Lily Bess Campbell. New York: Barnes & Noble, 1970.

Onions, C. T. *A Shakespeare Glossary.* 2nd ed., rev. Oxford: Clarendon P. 1972.

Partridge, Edward. "Re-Presenting Shakespeare." *Shakespeare: The Theatrical Dimension.* Eds. Philip C. McGuire and David A. Samuelson. New York: AMS P, 1979. 1–10.

Peacham, Henry. *The Garden of Eloquence.* London: H. Jackson, 1577. Gainesville, FL: Scholars' Facsimiles & Reprints, 1954.

Pickering, John. *A Newe Enterlude of Vice, Conteyninge the Histoyre of Horestes.* London: n.p., 1567.

Plato. "The Allegory of the Cave." 373 B.C.? *The Republic of Plato.* Trans. with Introd. and Notes by Francis MacDonald Cornford. Oxford: Oxford UP, 1941. 227–35

Plautus, Titius Maccius. *Captivi*. Ed. W.M. Lindsay. Rev. ed. Oxford: Oxford UP, 1966.

———. *Menaechmi*. Trans. William Warner. London, 1595. Ed. W.H.D. Rouse. London: Chatto & Windus, 1983.

Plutarch. *The Lives of the Noble Grecians and Romaines*. London: Richard Field, 1579. *Shakespeare's Plutarch*. London: Penguin, 1968.

Preston, Thomas. *A Lamentable Tragedy Mixed Ful of Pleasant Mirth, Conteyning the Life of Cambises, King of Percia*. 1561? London: John Allde, 1570.

Sackville, Thomas, and Thomas Norton. *The Tragedie of Gorboduc*. 1562. London: Imprinted by W. Griffith, 1565. Ed. Irby B. Cauthen. Lincoln: U of Nebraska P, 1970.

Schanzer, Ernest. *The Problem Plays of Shakespeare*. London: Routledge & Kegan Paul, 1963.

Sheridan, Richard. *The Rivals*. 2nd ed. London: Printed for John Wilkie, 1775. Ed. Michael Cordner. Oxford: Oxford UP, 1998.

Sidney, Philip. *A Defence of Poetry*. 1595. Ed. with an Introd. and Notes Jan Van Dorsten. London: Oxford UP, 1973.

Spurgeon, Caroline. *Shakespeare's Imagery and What It Tells Us*. Cambridge: Cambridge UP, 1935.

Stevenson, William. *A Ryght Pithy, Pleasaunt and Merie Comedie Intytuled Gammer Gurtons Needle*. 1552–1563. London: Imprinted by Thomas Colwell, 1575. New York: AMS P, 1970.

Terence. *The Second Comedy of Pub. Terentius, Called Eunuchus*. Menston, Eng.: Scolar P, 1972.

Tillyard, E. M. W. *Shakespeare's History Plays*. London: Chatto & Windus, 1944.

———. *Shakespeare's Problem Plays*. London: Chatto & Windus, 1950.

Udall, Nicholas. *Ralph Roister Doister*. 1550–1553. Ed. Clarence Griffin Child. Boston: Houghton Mifflin, 1972.

Wells, Stanley. *A Dictionary of Shakespeare*. Oxford: Oxford UP, 1998.

Credits

Page 107 Folger Shakespeare Library. Reprinted with permission.

Page 116 Folger Shakespeare Library. Reprinted with permission.

Page 161 Jon Greenfield for Pentagram. Reprinted with permission.

Page 166 Toby Widdicombe. Reprinted with permission.

Page 169 Toby Widdicombe. Reprinted with permission.

Page 189 Chantal Schütz (Globe Research and ENSAE, Paris). Reprinted with permission.

Page 190 Chantal Schütz (Globe Research and ENSAE, Paris). Reprinted with permission.

Page 194 RSC/Photography by Donald Cooper. Reprinted with permission.

Page 196 RSC/Photography by Donald Cooper. Reprinted with permission.

Page 201 Universal Studios. Reprinted with permission.

Page 202 Universal Studios. Reprinted with permission.

Index

Y

A Simplified Family Tree for the Wars of the Roses (1455–85)[1]

Edward III (1312–77; 1322–77)[2]

- Edward, The Black Prince (1330–76)
  - (1) Richard II (1367–1400, 1377–99)
- Lionel, D of Clarence (1338–68)
  - Philippa m. Edmund Mortimer[3] (1355–81) (1352–81)
    - Roger Mortimer (1373–98)
      - Anne Mortimer (1390–1411)
- John of Gaunt, D of Lancaster (1340–99) [The House of Lancaster & the red rose]
  - (2) Henry IV (1367–1413; 1399–1413)
    - (3) Henry V (1387–1422; 1413–22)
      - (4) Henry VI (1421–71; 1422–61)
        - Edward, P of Wales (1453–71)
- Edmund Langley, 1st D of York (1341–1402) [The House of York & the white rose]
  - Richard, E of Cambridge m. Anne Mortimer (1375–1415) (1390–1411)
    - Richard Plantagenet, D of York (1411–60)

- (5) Edward IV (1442–83; 1461–83)
  - Elizabeth (b. 1465) m. Henry Tudor, E of Richmond,[4]
    - (8) Henry VII (1457–1509; 1485–1509)[5]
  - (6) Edward V (1470–83; 1483) (one of the two Princes in the Tower)
- Edmund, E of Rutland (1442–60)
- George, D of Clarence (1449–78)
- (7) Richard III (1452–85; 1483–85)
  - Richard, D of York (d. 1483) (one of the two Princes in the Tower)

Notes

1. With claims to the throne, inheritance is by male primogeniture. An alternative viewpoint—Salic Law—denies right of inheritance to the female.

2. Dates: where two sets are given, the first is the length of the life, the second is the length of the reign.

3. The Mortimers' claim to the throne was considered weak by some because although it descended from Lionel, Duke of Clarence, John of Gaunt's *older* brother, it did so down the female line from Philippa, the Duke of Clarence's daughter and only child. The Duke of Clarence's line was joined to that of the House of York by the marriage of Anne Mortimer (Philippa's granddaughter) to Richard, Earl of Cambridge (the second son of Edmund Langley, the first Duke of York).

4. The Tudor claim to the throne (asserted by **Henry VII**, the grandfather of Elizabeth I) was weak. The name "Tudor" derives from Owen Tudor (1400–61), the second husband of Katherine of Valois, whose first husband was **Henry V**. The Tudors also claimed a connection to **Richard II's** uncle, John of Gaunt, through Gaunt's marriage to Katherine Swynford, his *third* wife. Gaunt and Swynford's first son was John Beaufort, Duke of Somerset (ca. 1371–1410). Beaufort's second son was John, the 3rd Duke of Somerset (1404–44). And *his* only child was Margaret Beaufort (1443–1509), who married Edmund Tudor (ca. 1430–56), the Earl of Richmond and **Henry VII's** father.

5. The warring Houses of Lancaster and York were finally united by the marriage of **Henry VII** (a Lancastrian) to Elizabeth of York, the daughter of **Edward IV** and the great-great-granddaughter of Edmund Langley, first Duke of York.

D = Duke   E = Earl   P = Prince

✠ = died in battle   ☠ = murdered   ⚔ = executed